The Declined Soul
and
the New Economy

The Declined Soul
and
the New Economy

Z E Graphics, Inc.
P.O. Box 1961
White Plains, New York 10602

The Declined Soul and the New Economy

Published by Z E Graphics, Inc.
P.O. Box 1961, White Plains, NY 10602

ISBN: 979-8-218-53423-3

Editing & Design:
Cover Design by Zeph Ernest
Interior Formatting by Zeph Ernest

This book is a work of nonfiction. While every effort has been made to
ensure accuracy, the author and publisher assume no responsibility for
errors or omissions. Any opinions expressed are those of the author and do
not necessarily reflect those of the publisher.

Printed in The United States of America
First Edition

For permissions, inquiries, and bulk purchases, contact:
zegraphicsinc@gmail.com

Table of Contents

Introduction

The Declined Soul and The New Economy covers a wide range of historical, philosophical, and economic topics, focusing on the moral decline and societal degregation associated with the Atlantic Slave Trade, colonialism, and the development of Western capitalism. Above all, it touches on the fatal flaw in the human psyche embedded in modern societies that drives economic expansions. The idea of what is appropriate behavior is ancient and often phrased in terms of vice and virtue. The distinction between the two is established thousands of years ago according to the earliest funereal works from ancient Kemet. We learn that the soul is immortal because it belongs to the Divine Unity or Universal Consciousness that we ignore at our own peril. According to Kemetic wisdom, humans have to uphold good or risk the destruction of the heart and the Earth.

The Degradation of Morals

The degradation of ethics in our recent history occurred rapidly, driven by a persistent societal chasm between spiritual forces seeking vindication in an unseen universe and the secular forces bent solely on acquiring wealth and power exclusively in the material world. The battle between vice and virtue has likely been waged, perhaps since the earliest emergence of the homo Sapiens. Over millennia, either spiritual or secular forces have predominated, depending on the tenor of the times, especially during periods of wealth accumulation. When secular forces triumph over the good, humanity descends into ethical degeneration, as we see during the Roman Empire and the rise of the Western paradigm from the early modern era to the contemporary period. It is the relentless thirst for unlimited wealth and power—the embrace of avarice as the ancients warned—that drives these destructive forces.

In contemporary times, society moves forward with an economic system based on unsecured fiat currency and usury that ironically helped to drive the Atlantic Slave Trade that slaughtered approximately 180 million Africans over 400 years, based on abolitionists Thomas F. Buxton and Thomas Cooper's work[1]. The events that Africans refer to as the Great Maafa dwell on a peculiar mechanism based on ideology that established a new paradigm of perception of a people so maligned that they remained at the receiving end of society's ill will for the last 500 years. To say that any person with black skin has a remarkable history and led the world in innovation is to utter a sacrilege worthy of extreme rebuke from professional archaeologists or laypersons alike.

At the beginning of the modern era, changes in ethics driven by the unscrupulous men who succumbed to greed contrary to the law helped launch a new era of unjustifiable wars and racial injustice. The unprovoked attacks displaced and enslaved unwary Africans and appropriated their land and gold while discarding traditional ethics and the Christian canon, which advocated for brotherhood and equity. These powerful commercial interests from the recent past left a legacy of atrocities in their pursuit of wealth as they demolished the long-standing ethical standards of civilization. *The Declined Soul and the New Economy* recognizes hundreds of millions who were sacrificed in the criminal enterprise of Oligarchs of Arab and Western civilizations that diverted from the ethics of the Mediterranean cultures of Kemet and Greece that once paid homage to the universal soul. The book elevates this ancient mechanism of the universal soul or the *anima mundi* (Latin), which encompasses the joint obligation to the Creation that binds all things as one according to the Shabaka Stone. The Divine Unity is the most profound concept of ancient Africans that strongly supports the rationale for natural law and individual rights.

Ancient Egyptian Beliefs on the Soul and Morality

Ancient Egyptian culture held a profound belief in the soul's immortality, which was thought to consist of multiple components, including the ka (life force) and the ba (personality). These elements would journey to the afterlife, where the deceased would face judgment. In the Hall of Ma'at, the

---

1   Buxton, *The African Slave Trade and Its Remedy* (London, 1967; orig. pub. 1839, 1840), 73.

individual's heart was weighed against the feather of Ma'at, symbolizing truth and justice. A heart lighter than the feather allowed passage to the afterlife, while a heavier heart resulted in the heart-soul being devoured by Ammit, leading to permanent destruction.

This belief system emphasized the importance of living a virtuous life, as moral conduct directly influenced one's fate in the afterlife. The concept of the soul's immortality and moral obligations were central to ancient Egyptian religion and daily life.

Historical Instances of Moral Decline and Economic Systems

Throughout history, periods of economic expansion are often accompanied by severe ethical challenges. For instance, the Atlantic Slave Trade, driven by the relentless pursuit of wealth, led to the forced displacement and suffering of millions of Africans. This era highlights how economic ambitions can override ethical considerations, resulting in widespread human rights violations.

Similarly, the decline of the Roman Empire has been attributed to various factors, including moral decay and economic instability. As the empire expanded, internal corruption and prioritizing wealth accumulation over civic virtue contributed to its eventual downfall.

Economic Growth and Ethical Standards

The relationship between economic growth and morality is complex. Benjamin Friedman's work, "The Moral Consequences of Economic Growth," argues that rising living standards can lead to social progress, including greater tolerance and fairness. Conversely, economic stagnation or decline can result in social regression and increased intolerance.[2]

However, pursuing of economic growth without ethical considerations can lead to adverse outcomes. The entrepreneurial work ethic, discussed in Historian Erik Baker's "Make Your Own Job," emphasizes personal success

---

2   Friedman, Benjamin M. *The Moral Consequences of Economic Growth.* Available at: https://www.carnegiecouncil.org/media/series/39/20051027-the-moral-consequences-of-economic-growth

and self-promotion, that often ignores the greater good. The mindset of rugged individualism can allow economic inequality as it builds the focus on self-centered goals without attention to ethical standards.

The interplay between economic systems and moral values has been a recurring theme throughout history. Ancient beliefs, historical events, and modern analyses underscore the importance of aligning economic pursuits with ethical considerations to ensure societal well-being.

The Obscured Perceptual Paradigm

As the ancient Africans observed and tracked the evidence of the universal consciousness in the material world, they left their megaliths, temples, and texts as silent sentries tracing paths that foretold the cycles. These ideas from the venerable traditions created from ancient beliefs and handed down through time contrast sharply with the ongoing deviation from the arduous search for truth. The philosophical expressions of the modern era almost exclusively speak of a spiritually vacuous world where logic and reason prevail. The adherence to the new philosophy as irrefutable would appear to be a fallacy if the widespread instances of its foibles were examined. The idea that morals are born of human sentiments disavows the reality of the unseen world of a universal consciousness that operates on the minutest and the largest scales.

Forty-thousand years before the contemporary Western tradition started in the 20th century, the ancients who had traversed the length and breadth of the African continent for more than a hundred thousand years believed the universe was a divine consciousness. In the Kemetic creation story, these ancients saw the creator as indispensable to life—creating it in the only possible way, from nothing, and sustaining it through consciousness. They concluded that humanity is obligated to uphold this natural order of Creation. They understood that failing to maintain that natural order would bring destruction. They believed that the Earth's destruction could be averted by following the laws of Ma'at.

After the fall of Kemet and ancient Greece, the Roman Empire eventually rose to prominence. Over centuries, it played a significant role in shaping religious and philosophical views. The Nicene Creed, established in 325 CE, enforced the Christian doctrine of the Trinity, which redefined the understanding of universal consciousness in a religious context. As the Roman Empire was being destroyed by the Visigoths, and its citizens blamed the new Christian religion for their downfall, Saint Augustine, in *The City of God*, admonished them to ignore the evils of the earthly city and instead turn their gaze to the City of God.

In many ways, *The Declined Soul and the New Economy* is the persistent, unethical foundation that condones widespread immorality. The myriad genocidal and exploitative policies that have occurred since the discovery of the New World redefined truth testifies to the nature of society's destructive path. The most brutal of these was chattel slavery, which was quickly followed by the labor exploitation of the Industrial Revolution. Institutional racism and wars of opportunity with casualties in the hundreds of millions occurred as debts soared and bankers profited. Typically, avarice is at the core of these immoral policies that often target those with the dark-brown skin. Social mores with no meaningful purpose except to satisfy a primal urge for wealth play a part in defining the current social strata.

Over several thousand years, the tendency to remain faithful to divine and natural law has shifted to a determined effort to rescind fundamental social mores acknowledging good as the basis for ethical standards. The newly adopted social mores emerging in the modern era wontedly embrace a utilitarian philosophy, which asserts that wealth is the best way to bring happiness to most people. As the avaricious and unscrupulous servants of the oligarchy scoured the earth for gold and slaves, the remaining population followed a path of willful ignorance. The utility of these immoral policies is measured by profits that increasingly require more significant debts and inflation that impoverishes the poorer members of society.

The Legacy of Willful Ignorance

As civilization progressed from prehistory to antiquity, considerable effort was put into preserving the mores from the early civilizations. The many artifacts are evidence of the original beliefs that championed good and highlighted the ultimate test of virtue as the requirement for the greatest prize of all—eternal life. Glimpses of these are in ancient burial scripts from Kemet and creation stories from prehistory. Notably, the ancient belief system of Kemet, the source of Christianity and Islam, passed into obscurity. As history progressed, the most vibrant historical memory of the modern era is of the Eastern Roman Republic or the Byzantine Empire. The Western system of law and philosophy came from The Code of Justinian, elements of which date to ancient Greece and Egypt. The

Roman influence on Christianity, notably its redefinition of God, produced the most profound changes in society. Rome redefined how its subjects perceived God as a Trinity, with the Son as an equal to the Father. The shift in perception resulted in the brutal suppression of the old order by Emperor Constantine. While the early centuries before the birth of Christ are markedly different from our current era, there is a distinguishing factor of dedication and duty to the truth that these ancient civilizations possessed that had become distorted or obscured beginning with the fall of the Western Roman Empire when Saint Augustine urged Romans blaming Christianity for their demise, to ignore the carnage in their midst.

Saint Augustine urged Christians to look past the city of Rome, the earthly city, and instead look to the kingdom of heaven. However, the modern era mode of ignoring evil is far from the example written by Saint Augustine, and it more aptly represents a willful participation in immorality. An act that would have stunned the Greeks, whose respect for divine law showed their attitude towards life. A case in point is Socrates's condemnation to death, which was for the crime of killing a slave, an act that the modern era oligarchy scoffed at. Socrates's punishment is from an era when the sanctity of life had much more meaning than in the modern era where chattel slavery became the preferred means of achieving profit objectives of societies that had become thoroughly corrupted by avarice and usury. The status of the enslaved in the modern era quickly devolved from a past where they were a protected class in Greece and Rome, to one in the modern era where their utility could be measured only in terms of monetary gain. Their lives became meaningless and substantially shortened by the brutality of the plantation system.

The Modern Economy's Moral Dilemma

The narratives of the modern era are generated by 18th and 19th-century political and economic decisions from merchants in the commercial sector, professors at universities, and state and religious officials whose arrogance led them to proclaim that their victims were scientifically proven to be sub-human and could only benefit from exposure to a superior civilization. These Western Oligarchs believed that they alone possessed the ability to reason and the capability of expressing the truth based on science. Their economic decisions were often made disregarding ethical considerations, which were traditionally based on fairness and justice as in prior epochs. The Atlantic Slave Trade is a pivotal event that shaped economic thought and practice, highlighting the newly evolved tradition of ignoring moral responsibilities and generating fabricated counter-narratives that invert the truth. In the current society, which is based on the white supremacist racial theories of the 18th century, denying the common bond among all humans is the automatic reflex action to the dark brown and black skin color.

Black-skinned people are automatically relegated to a separate and unequal category, which is metaphysically impossible in the ancient worldview. Colloquialisms abound that systematically denigrate people of color. Since the slave trade, the consequences of these racist acts have been expressed in the narratives of the enslaved to the victims of the Black Codes and of institutional racism. A recent case from the Tulsa Oklahoma, race massacre of 1921 features survivors from these decades past, with evidence of their destroyed lives and property who cannot get justice as of 2024. However, similar cases abound and escalate as accumulated capital is dispensed according to status and race. The crimes of yesterday are dispensed with clerical efficiency as the victims struggle for survival.

At the core of the failures in modern society is a regime of willful ignorance where responsibility for wrongdoing remains irrelevant to the aims of the individual. We are all programmed to believe that the golden rule is a mirage—good deeds are no longer rewarded. It took approximately two thousand years from the beginning of the Hellenic Age when Greece conquered Kemet to the advent of Christianity during the Roman rule of the Mediterranean region to lay aside the human aspiration that sought freedom in universal consciousness to one that catered to a promise of everlasting life only in return for one's faith in the religion.

The Soul's Decline

The importance of the human link to one ultimate source of reality and truth has diminished substantially since the 18th and 19th centuries when Enlightenment philosophers embraced empiricism. The change in philosophy occurred at the height of the Slave Trade as commercial traders became horrified by the prospect of losing their livelihood if the slave trade were to end. Traditional views of morality as a shared tradition of all peoples under one God gave way to one which could differ drastically according to individual or personal whims based on the dictates of reason operating strictly in a material world. The excuses to keep human beings in bondage became the science of the new era as all efforts went towards justifying slavery. Nevertheless, although the rules-based system in the modern era had legalized chattel slavery and dehumanized African people, the true source of the morals remained perceptible to the enslaved. The glaring 400-year reign of injustice and anti-Black terror would still be called out by the many victims who fought and died for freedom.

The old saying, *to the victor belongs the spoils*, is one of many crutches that enable the deluge of organized campaigns designed by well-funded organizations seeking to re-institute an iron fist mentality wielded against unprotected populations. As the cycles of time complete, the real promise of the ancients is in salvation.

The Declined Soul
and
the New Economy

Chapter 1

The Declined Soul and
The New Economy

The evidence for belief in a creator god and the immortality of the human essence is conceivably as ancient as the archaeologically dated emergence of homo sapiens. The earliest known ritualistic non-modern human behavior suggests that the extinct species of archaic human, Homo naledi, might have deliberately buried their dead in Rising Star Cave, South Africa, 335–241 thousand years ago (kya).[1] Also, in South Africa, evidence of modern human burials in Blombos Cave occurred in the Middle Stone Age, 74–100 kya. More recently, in North East Africa, c. 3400–2686 B.C.E., Hieroglyphics and tomb paintings in the Old Kingdom that aided the soul in traversing the afterlife made direct references to the continued existence of the human soul. The burial script of Ani from "The Book of the Dead," c. 2686 B.C.E., shows Ani's soul as a bird with the deceased's likeness, flying to the eternal resting place in the northern sky. The ancient Africans who created Kemet's civilization revealed in their writing and illustrations that everlasting life is possible, but only after judgment, if the heart-soul weighs lighter than the feather of the goddess Ma'at.

The connection of ethics to the universal principles of truth, balance, order, harmony, law, morality, and justice personified by the goddess Ma'at had their beginning in early African civilizations long before Ma'at appears in the Pyramid texts around 2375–2345 B.C.E. These ideas existed in the oral traditions of predynastic Kemet, centuries before the start of written history in 3440–3100 B.C.E.[2] The profundity of Ma'at's laws could only become known during the judgment of the deceased individual's heart-soul, which records all transgressions. Without the effort to remain virtuous, the deceased's impure heart-soul could not achieve everlasting life. For the greater part of Egyptian

---

1   National Geographic. Available at: www.nationalgeographic.com/science/article/earliest-human-burial-homo-naledi-berger. Accessed 3/17/2024.
2   Timeline is according to Bernal, (1991, 27–9), and Mellaart, (1979, 6-19)

predynastic and written history, up to the Hellenic Age after the Greek conquest of Egypt, virtuous living was central to attaining the promise of eternal life.

When the Greeks conquered the Persian Empire in 332 B.C.E. they also freed Kemet from 132 years of occupation and started the Hellenic civilization that combined Greek and Egyptian cultures. The Hellenic civilization, with its capital city of Alexandria, adopted Egyptian culture, including burial rites. However, they gradually established new criteria for achieving eternal life based on Greek heroism. Among the early Greeks, Plato's philosophical viewpoint closely aligns with the Kemetic pantheist concept of God as consciousness permeating *all* aspects of the universe. Plato describes the cosmos as a living being with a soul, and in *Timaeus*, he suggests that the universe is a divine entity—a form of the Good that permeates reality. However, in Plato's lifetime, his student Aristotle developed a materialist philosophy where God is separate from his creation. His concept was a radical departure from pantheism as it promoted individualism and happiness as the overarching aim of life. The virtue of the Egyptians gave way to Herculean labors as the key to gaining eternal life in the Elysian Fields. Despite the divergence of Hellenic civilization's ethics from that of the ancient world, the historical timeline up to the end of the Roman Empire upheld a fundamental truth about Homo Sapiens that we are predisposed to labor for the reward of immortality.

Centuries after Rome's occupation of Greece and Egypt, Alexandria, the former Greek capital city, built in 331 B.C.E., had developed into a large cosmopolitan center. It was a melting pot of ideas from around the known world. The city was the source of religious ideas, particularly Judaism and its divergences that established the basis for Christianity. The old idea of a universal soul and Ma'at had lost its prominence in the melting pot. In its place were the Zoroastrian religions of Babylon, Persia, and Judaism. From these religions originated the concepts of heaven and Earth, where Earth was the devil's creation that imprisoned the suffering human race. These religions shared the belief in a messiah sent by God that would save humans from the devil and transform his Earthly possession into a place that mirrored God's place in heaven. Amid the persecution of the Jews during the Roman rule over Alexandria and Jerusalem, they anticipated their prophesied messiah and his transforming of the Earth into God's kingdom, where justice reigns. While Jews awaited the coming of the messiah, their differing beliefs on his nature as either spiritual or human created a split in Judaism. The Ebionite Jews believed in Christ as the Jewish Messiah and an ordinary man. Approximately 100 years after the birth of Christ, the Marcionites defined Jesus's nature as divine and Yhwh as an evil demiurge, and they differentiated Christianity from Judaism.

More than 100 years after the birth of Christ, during the Patristic Period (100 C.E. to 451 C.E.), Christian writers, including Saint Augustine, began to formally define Christianity. The test of virtue depicted in Kemet's Judgment of Ani's Soul still applies to some Christians. However, others believed in a novel concept of universal salvation by divine grace. The Christian concept of God's grace has its roots in the interpretation of Christ's teachings, which the Apostle Paul expounds on in his New Testament letters.[3] Grace was a gift from God that could not be earned or attained through human effort. The transition from Judaism to Christianity provided a means of salvation for believers who could not fulfill the strict requirements of Jewish Law. The doctrine of grace gained prominence in the fourth century with the works of Saint Augustine, whose teachings emphasized the idea of original sin and the need for God's grace to save humanity from eternal damnation. He was influential in shaping the theology of the Western Christian Church and making the concept of grace a fundamental aspect of Christian doctrine.

After Rome had adopted Christianity in 381 c.e., they redefined the Trinity and established the Nicene Creed that mandated how to perceive God. The Roman authoritarian style set the early theocratic foundations and hierarchical organization of the Roman Catholic Church. Under the yoke of Roman authoritarianism, Christianity became Emperor Constantine's tool to unify his empire through edicts. When Rome fell and its institutions disintegrated, the surviving Christian Church had no idea what it meant to be a Christian. Only then did Christianity turn to the teachings of Christ and adopt the humble lifestyles of the desert monks epitomized by Saint Anthony of Egypt, who lived near the end of the Roman Empire (251–356 C.E.). Saint Anthony's monastic conversion was inspired by the biblical passage Matthew 19:21:

> Jesus said to him, "If you want to be perfect, go, sell what you have and give to the poor, and you will have treasure in heaven; and come, follow Me."
> —Matthew 19:21

The passage reflects the early Christian teachings of Christ that prompted Saint Anthony to sell his possessions, donate the proceeds, and join the ascetic desert dwellers in Egypt. The Christian monastic tradition, which began with these early ascetics, particularly their penchant for living free of earthly possessions in the service of others, became the new model for the Christian Church. Evidence of the early Papal Bulls reflects the

---

3   Ephesians 2:8 "By this undeserved kindness, indeed, you have been saved through faith; and this not owing to works, in order that no man should have ground for boasting."

Church's history of compassion for the poor Christian and non-Christian alike. However, during Europe's medieval period (c. 13th century) and its descent into feudalism, the Church developed a hostile stance towards the heretic and non-Christians.

From Medieval Morality to Modern Morass

In the early modern era, the original meaning of God's grace became a point of contention between two religious reformers and the Roman Catholic Church during the Protestant Reformation. Martin Luther and John Calvin revived the doctrine of *sola gratia*, or salvation by grace alone. They challenged the Catholic Church's belief in the necessity of good works, sacraments for salvation, and adherence to Church authority. Luther and Calvin asserted that salvation was solely by God's grace, received through faith, and not dependent on human merit or works. The Catholic Church's reliance on good works proved to be a corruption of ethics emanating from the greed of its leaders, who practiced indulgences where sinners were allowed to pay the Church exorbitant sums of money for their salvation.

The Western historical dating paradigm obscures a seemingly endless extent of time, long before Kemet fell and pantheism that saw god as encompassing all, gave way to theism, where the universal consciousness appears as a person. In its comparatively brief existence, theism's perception of a personal God with an affinity for a chosen people has presided over growing ethical divergences where immoral forces anticipated salvation even amid the widespread avarice, cultural chauvinism, and the historically unparalleled 400-year genocide of the human family in Africa and the Americas that began in the early modern era. A significantly weakened moral stance that gave rise to the personal God of the chosen ones allowed the trampling of the pantheist ideas that had united all living things in nature.

From the Early Modern Era (c. 1400–1500) to the beginning of the Age of Revolutions (c. 1800), Christianity in the Western world succumbed to the growing lust for wealth and collaborated in exploiting the very people—the poor, meek, and generous—that the Church had vowed to emulate and protect. The Church diverted from its commitment to piety and collaborated with the commercial sectors to legitimize usury and jeopardize the vital link of law to God. Usury, which was synonymous with any form of greed to the medieval mind, made avarice acceptable to churchgoers and commercial traders alike, as it infiltrated the highest ranks of the moral order. The unbridled greed foreshadowed the corruption of the idea of *civilization* as a cooperative endeavor. Usury corrupted the concept of the immortal soul, which is linked to a divine spiritual source. It brought to life material corruption, which was revealed in the avaricious destruction of peoples and great civilizations. It enabled the creation of a pseudo-culture premised on money, unjustifiable war, chattel slavery, and species differentiation between humans.

A profound failure of humanity emerged from the chaos of chattel slavery, and it persists in the internecine warfare that continually seeks to eradicate the human family. The historically unparalleled genocide of the Atlantic and Arab Slave Trades, the wars of colonization, and World Wars I and II occurred in *our* modern era. During the current period, the apparent failure began when monarchs, oligarchs, and merchants took over the reins of civilization and transformed it into a pseudo-culture entrenched in greed, superficiality, manipulation, and perpetuated by usurious practices. Avarice, one of the vices that would deny eternal life, became a vital part of the social and economic fabric of the modern period. Social mores grew increasingly irrational, such that even the reasoning man of the Enlightenment succumbed to a profound racial bias concocted to ensure profits. The corruption of the moral order showed in scientific works disseminated to an ever-growing population of young scholars. These works maliciously attributed the broken societies created by centuries of racial indoctrination to the victims.

The nature of the evil that struck the human species, which originated in the practice of chattel slavery, appears irrepressible and focuses wherever there are people of color. The highly organized but senseless racial indoctrination, reinforced by random lynch mobs, remains a permanent feature in modern society. The increasing racism is a link to a tragic era when Western nations had defiantly built their economies on the genocide of millions of African people. The insatiable drive for racial domination and slavery flourished even during the intellectual awakening of the Enlightenment, which sought to gain freedom and happiness for humanity.

The atrocities of the Slave Trade occurred as the acclaimed intellectuals of the modern world pontificated about liberty and improving the human condition after rediscovering the natural law theories of the Classical period of ancient Rome. What stands out prominently amid the widely known ethical violations of the Slave Trade is the deliberately devised methodology to subjugate human beings through a racial, ideological indoctrination methodology, replete with arbitrary violence and obscuring of history. These methodologies ran contrary to reason and created and perpetuated the monstrous image of the subhuman African in media, science, and educational systems. The indoctrination process continues in myriad ways and serves a similar purpose as during the Slave Trade to inflict physical and psychic pain and suffering.

For centuries, without regret, the monarchs, oligarchs, plutocrats, philosophers, scientists, and educational institutions benefiting from the Slave Trade all claimed ownership of the noble idea of civilization. Yet, it was clear for all to see that humanity had lost its way chasing the mirage of unlimited wealth under every rock, in every cave, and, if need be, from every emaciated body in Africa. Injustice reigned supreme, and regrettably, the greater society embraced the unparalleled brutality of the morally bankrupt executioners of the African holocaust. Judging by the sheer size, duration, and casualties of the Slave Trade, society had discarded all obligations to the moral order. The world appeared mad, casting all reverence for a God concept and a universal soul aside. The centuries of brutality normalized the vice at the core of the corruption—the avarice the ancients had condemned, which fueled the commercialization of innocent human beings. The terms *commerce or trade* grossly understate the vast criminal enterprise measured in *hundreds of millions of deaths*, in millions of tons of human beings annually transported on thousands of ships for hundreds of years.

The Atlantic Slave Trade is the most disruptive era in human history, yet it remains obscured. The abolitionists and English Parliamentarians of the late 18th century calculated millions of casualties on the mainland, the slave ships, and in the New World.[4] Africa's population growth rate turned negative—a grievous crime perpetuated by a broad section of Western society, to obscure the truth until the Abolitionists movement gained attention. After abolition, the collective wisdom of the civilized society had learned nothing of the sanctity of life except a better way to generate profits. The grand society's breach of ethics thus remains unchecked. The hunger for wealth, power, and slaughter evident during the Slave Trade mushroomed into industrial capitalism, the precursor to World Wars I and II. Mass production became re-purposed to extinguish millions of lives with scientific efficiency on the seas, in the air, in cities large and small,

---

4   *William Wilberforce's 1789 Abolition Speech*. From 'Debate on Mr. Wilberforce's Resolutions respecting the Slave Trade' in William Cobbett, The Parliamentary History of England. From the Norman Conquest in 1066 to the year 1803, 36 vols (London: T. Curson Hansard, 1806-1820), 28 (1789-91), cols 42-68.
Buxton, *The African Slave Trade and Its Remedy* (London, 1967; orig. pub. 1839, 1840), 61–73.
Herbert S. Klein, Stanley L. Engerman, Robin Haines, and Ralph Shlomowitz. *Transoceanic Mortality: The Slave Trade in Comparative Perspective*, p. 19. Based on (Thomas Cooper, Supplement to Mr. Cooper's Letter on the Slave Trade (Manchester, 1788), 3, 4.)

and across the barren, frozen lands of the Northern hemisphere in Russia. Even in peacetime, greed gallops, unbridled by the captains of industry and political hacks who feign a lack of awareness as the land, oceans, and outer space become choked with the toxic garbage from a spiritually diminished existence punctuated by avarice.

A white supremacist ethos emerged from the ruins of slavery to nurture the vice that had motivated the slave traders of the 18th century. It focused on preserving wealth and power through racial indoctrination. It created an artificial scarcity and famine, increased warfare, concentrated wealth, and held hostage a subservient class stripped of their cultural heritage and natural resources. Vital human behaviors from the distant Neolithic, kept by traditional cultures, vanished. Civility, compassion, cooperation, and tolerance became the province of the superior race but were denied to black-skinned peoples worldwide. The immoral behaviors witnessed during 400 years of barbarism and its immediate aftermath of an irrepressible urge to annihilate the human species based on race had not happened before. The human species could not have survived in its infancy if this tendency had existed. Inevitably, the misguided belief in greed and selfishness promises only more injustice, and the *Isfet*, the priests of Kemet, predicted that results directly from injustice.

Although contemporary world civilizations claim it as their own, the Western concept of the *soul* is part of an ancient East African spiritual doctrine that transcends all world religions. The idea of a spiritual link to God dates back to the deepest historical epochs of African civilization. The laws of Ma'at were central to African cosmology. From the outset of the creation story in Kush, Ma'at was essential to the creation of the universe. The universe cannot work without its laws. On a personal level, a sinner whose heart-soul proved heavier than the feather of Ma'at at the judgment is doomed to destruction. Despite the gravity of the ancient ethics, the early civilizations in Northeast Africa, including Nubia, Kush, and Kemet, did not condemn the unfaithful to either slavery or death, like later patriarchal societies. These early civilizations maintained a reverence for the Great Mother in their matrilineal order that succumbed to the patriarchy and slavery.

The root culture that established the first civilization dates to the end of the Middle Stone Age, 20–15 thousand years ago (kya) in North East Africa. The pertinent facts from modern scholars are relatively recent revelations after centuries of a fabricated Westernized history of civilization. When Greeks such as Pythagoras began arriving to study in Kemet in the 5th century B.C.E., the golden age when Africans had built and maintained the most advanced civilizations had endured for thousands of years. Essential technologies and ideas, such as distinctly human symbolic behaviors, including personal ornaments, engraved and painted objects, and rituals, highlighted the emergence of group behavior and self-identification associated with all human beings. Specialized toolmaking, regular long-distance exchange over thousands of miles, complex cognition, images, agriculture, animal domestication, and permanent settlements with advanced architecture and medical advances occurred as humans rapidly advanced civilization in prehistory. These behaviors, ideas, technologies, and the science that enabled them are the foundation of modern societies. Yet, they exist only as vague abstractions in the present—divorced from their roots in Africa and their vital functions in ensuring the miracle of human survival and prosperity. As modern societies have adopted a linear view of history, these ancient peoples are seen as inferior because they are from the past but, more importantly, because of their black skin color and geographic locale in Africa.

The ancient science and messages of cooperation among the human family became obscured through faux science and racial ideology. The deceit has altered the course of human development as it changed Africa. As the continent's history and culture disappeared, so did the eons of evolved acculturation that ensured human survival through extraordinary tribulations. Though severely weakened today, the capacity to cooperate and innovate enabled humans to prosper and merge into the ancient world's first great civilizations. The primary concern of early man was neither war nor greed but technological innovation for food production and sustenance to contend with the pressing challenges, including cycles of hot and cold climate changes lasting thousands of years. While modern humans benefit from nature's benevolence, our reverence for the life-giver and nurturer—the Great Mother—has disappeared.

The archaeological evidence that ancient humans were aware of a direct link to God predates their cultural awakening during the transition from hunter-gatherer to settled life. Around halfway through the Middle Stone Age, or approximately 130 kya, ritualistic burial practices were standard during the transition from the archaic to the modern human. These burials and adornment of the dead show complex analytical or abstract thinking, demonstrating self-awareness and a link to God. However, contemporary humans have set aside adherence to the noblest idea of a spiritual connection to a creator god that remains active in the afterlife. Humans in the modern era are even more dismissive of the ancient cultures and achievements that occurred during the transition from a hunter-gatherer stage to settled farming communities in the Neolithic Era. These early African-originated technologies that humans depend on today do not feature prominently as miraculous and venerable achievements primarily because they originated in Africa. These achievements became the legacies of a new people—the infamous, non-African originators—because a virulent racial ideology habitually restricts the recognition of Africa and its original innovators. The continent, three times larger than the United States, remains the least researched region of Earth and the most neglected.

Modern theories of human development that exclude Africa occurred in the 17th–19th centuries—when slavery was most profitable. By then, life on the massive continent had become chaotic and destroyed by the slave trade. One hundred and fifty years after the Portuguese landed in Ceuta in 1415, the continent had succumbed to the greed of the slave trader. The vibrant inter-continent river trade ceased, and war, famine, disease, and genocide spread. African people were at war with demonic powers demanding unlimited wealth and suffered a catastrophic decline. Immorality and injustice reigned supreme, and profit at any cost became the governing principle. The mechanism Kemet had revered as the barometer of the divine self—the heart-soul that records all transgressions—remains broken through these hundreds of years of carnage.

The gatekeepers of Western culture in modern universities sowed division among the human species. The black-skinned African had his designated place, in an improbable, opposite extremity to God—without a soul. The idea of one God and one human family did not occur in Europe's plunge into the abyss of white supremacist ideology. The ethics of the Slave Trade found widespread support from scholars who fabricated the evidence for separate origins of the races. Propaganda, war, and the destruction of diverse cultures left the worldwide mono-culture of the profiteer practicing a racial ideology that severely limits the natural capacity of the species to innovate and overcome unforeseen and severe challenges. The extreme climatic challenges early humans had overcome in Africa now loom, destined to severely test the mettle of the new mono-culture trapped in selfishness and greed and without mutual respect and reverence.

The agnostic, who has neither faith nor disbelief and the atheist, with complete disbelief in God, were not the main enemies of The Good. Neither played a decisive role in the explosive growth of the commoditizing of human beings. Up to abolition in the late 19th century, the offenses against civilization emanated from God-fearing societies, institutions, and men and women who deliberately violated the ethics based on natural law, which is inherent. While these societies knew about the soul's link to God, their paradigm had shifted considerably from the original concept of reality emanating from God's consciousness. German Philosopher Georg Wilhelm Friedrich Hegel sums up the firm societal consensus in lectures to his students as he denied African people even the capacity as self-actualized human beings to know God and, in doing so, implied that despite their immense suffering, they were deserving of their fate.

The rampant normalization of a corrupted materialist worldview based on species differentiation among humans highlights the failure of a society that grows increasingly incapable of grasping the essence of reality as spirit. The reformed, modern man can calculate gravity by measuring the descent rate of a falling object but does not care to know the power that actively keeps the atmosphere clinging to Earth and makes the breath of life possible. The ancient Kemitu name for that force of nature that holds the sky aloft is *Shu.* There are things that the ancients did not fully understand but had the higher intelligence to acknowledge as profoundly essential aspects of the Creator. Contrary to our ancestors' messages, modern science recognizes only the material world seen through a hierarchical organization and linear time. The widely taught scientific conclusion about the creation's origin is supported by the science that concludes that no question can address a material world that never existed before the Big Bang. Many accept these limitations without thinking that belief must also extend beyond the limits of the material universe.

The broken trust in the unseen and unknowable creative power evokes significant opposition to the ancient Kemetic epistemology written on the *Shabaka Stone* that dates back to the Neolithic (7,000–1,700 B.C.E.). The metaphysics highlights the primal link between all life and the Father of Creation. The Mdw Ntchr (The sounds of the spirit), the oldest written language and precursor to the Semitic languages, states that all life is in the Creator Ptah's image. Other inscriptions of ancient Kemet elaborate further on the human connection to a Father of Creation through a nine-part construct of the soul. Humans can approach the good through moral integrity and obeying the laws of Ma'at. In the cosmology of Kemet, consciousness links all humans to the Father of Creation through the immortal soul.

Despite the proclamations of contemporary scholars based on science, new ideas about reality still begin with the subjective opinions that have evolved into social norms. Negative popular beliefs about race, supported by white supremacist ideology, control the negative perception of African people globally. Science, for example, has succumbed to speculation that the present is more advanced than the past based on a hierarchical worldview. The belief that the bible is world history has forced a narration that fits the chronology and has controlled theoretical derivations over several centuries. Science's bid to uphold the inferiority of African people begins with Aristotelian and modern biblical assertions about the slave and the black-skinned race that permeate scientific literature.[5] Theories supporting the inferiority of Africans also erroneously rely on Darwin's Theory of Evolution and the Bell Curve's statistical analysis. These theories have become re-purposed to support racial speculation that defies reason and the cognitive senses, conjuring an alternate reality that is plausible exclusively in the hierarchically organized universe with a personalized god.

The accumulated effects show up in the statistically skewed race-based measures taken in the United States, where African descendants in America have existed at the bottom of a hierarchical social order created during the Atlantic Slave Trade. These measures show a consistent 5-sigma deviation below the mean for people of color, whether in income, health, education, incarceration, or life expectancy. On the other hand, Caucasians show a 5-sigma deviation above the mean. Labeling these results as part of a deliberate genocidal policy would be fair, based on mortality rates in black communities. These consistent statistical anomalies do not occur in nature but have remained unchanged since the U.S. government began keeping records based on a separation of the races in the mid-20th century. The unnatural divergences in living standards between the races have never been a significant concern of the majority population in the United States and Europe. The divisions created by racism now appear as permanent fixtures in society. The entrenched opinions of scholars in the modern era to explain poverty, crime, or any other consequence of racism are the African people's and their descendants' supposed cultural and genetic deficiencies. Inequality has become acceptable and defended by a morally relativistic philosophy where the victim's culture becomes the reason for his social status. Education, law, religion, and nationalism are all deeply embedded in the ethics of the 18th century—consequently, they all contribute to the inversion of morality.

The inversion of morality is most insidious in the scientific works of the 18th – 20th centuries. Scientific ideas were not based on facts but emerged from racist popular opinion that insisted on a racial hierarchy. Unfortunate Africans like Dutty Boukman, whose prayer to God for victory against the cruel God of the whites shortly before the Haitian Revolution in 1804, exemplify the hopelessness generated by the abandonment of the sacred obligation to the unity of the divine creation. This attitude had scarcely changed at the beginning of the 19th century when England and the United States finally abolished slavery in 1833 and 1865. However, chattel slavery, as the most severe form of labor exploitation, evolved into a newer, more

---

5   *See*: William Jones, or Max Muller (1875)

palatable form of servitude, which shows that freedom for the enslaved Africans was not the objective of abolition. England, for example, did not pay reparations to the enslaved Africans but compensated enslavers in the West Indies and their financial backers in London. The paper money went to investors, who promptly invested it in the industrial revolution to begin a new round of labor exploitation. In the United States, those freed bore the responsibility for their fate, yet they immediately fell victim to the oppressive forces allied against them. The ethics of the slave societies evolved in ever more inventive ways. Its new forms showed in the exploitation of sharecroppers, Jim Crow segregation, the convict labor system, the prison industrial complex, colonialism, neo-colonialism, and institutional racism. The social mores of racism remain steeped in the ethics of the slave trade.

Underpinning the relentless drive for profit is *usury*. Aristotle described it as making money from money, equating it to thievery. The Catholic Church consequently maintained restrictions on the practice. However, after the mathematical technique for calculating minute interest rates was brought to Europe from the Near East, it became possible to calculate minuscule rates not considered by the Church's decree. Like a shot of adrenaline to the economy, usury immediately enriched the earliest Florentine bankers of the Medici family after Fibonacci first introduced *Liber Abaci* to Europe in the 13th century. Though Christendom had controlled usury for thousands of years, the legalization of the vice and its application in profiteering fueled the corresponding rise in deaths and enslavement of African people. The Africans had become items of trade in an equation, essential cogs in the wheel of Agrarian Capitalism, as the illustration of the Slave Ship Brookes shows. Nineteenth-century English abolitionists and Parliamentarians Wilberforce and Buxton revealed the mind-boggling causalities and depth of depravity in their groundbreaking work that led to the abolition of the Atlantic Slave Trade. The rapidly expanding economies and the fabulous wealth from centuries of slavery never quelled the blinding greed of the monarchies, oligarchic landowners, commercial traders, merchants, and individual investors. By the mid-nineteenth century, the demand for enslaved people increased by thousands of percentage points. It betrayed society's total disregard and contempt for the old idea of compassion and the sanctity of life.

In Africa, the transition from stability to chaos occurred rapidly. Within a hundred and fifty years after the Portuguese arrival in the fifteenth century, the King of Kongo revealed in a letter to the King of Portugal that slave traders had destroyed the cultural cohesion of his kingdom. Within two hundred years after the Jesuit priest de las Casas had written his devastating report on Spanish slavery in the New World in the late

Chapter 2

The Ancient Worldview Obscured

In the present and more than 190 years after England abolished slavery in 1833, racially biased views proliferate that dehumanize African people while obscuring their vital contributions to world history. The proliferation of racism, biased literature, and science play persistent roles in perpetuating the negative African stereotypes that once supported chattel slavery and genocide. The long list of transgressions, ranging from brutal acts of subjugation and human scientific experimentation to blatant lies in the literature, all fit into the dedicated effort to support Western culture's deeply embedded racialized ethics born out of the enslavement and deaths of African people.

The plethora of mindless racial outbursts occurring around the Western world owe their legitimacy to the recent past. The European aristocracy's need to perpetuate the white supremacist ethic began earnestly in the 19th century after the French archaeologist Volney Constantin learned that the creators of the revered culture of Kemet were the same black-skinned race of human beings Europeans had enslaved and detested. The world succumbed to a prolonged span of racial indoctrination and historical revisionism that evokes and sustains the perception of African inferiority.

The efforts of European intellectuals to obscure revelations about world history are significant enough to cause a paradigm shift in human perception, which is comparable to the realization that the Earth is not flat. The redefinition of history, based solely on racial determinants, is on the same level as the discovery of the New World or the rise of the nation-state with representative government. The discovery of the role of black-skinned Africans in creating the world's first civilization was so shocking to European sensibilities that it prompted the reconfiguration of reality into a racial hierarchy that sought to permanently deny Africans their natural rights, land and history.

Amid the flood of absurd racial hypotheses and fabricated evidence from pseudo-scientists devised to prove archaic racial speculation are countless acts of brutality against African people. The story of Sarah Baartman, from Southern Africa, is one of the many troubling occurrences that point to the deeply embedded effects of white supremacist indoctrination in European society. In 1810, at age 22, she was brought to Europe and exhibited at freak shows as the Huttontot Venus. That was the name given to her by her captors to sensationalize her large buttocks. The profiteers exposed her body to public scrutiny at large gatherings in theaters across Europe. Even after her death, she could not rest five years later as her remains were preserved and displayed at a Paris museum. Frederic Cuvier, a French naturalist, zoologist, and the founding father of paleontology, used her remains to perpetuate the myth of a Caucasian origin of Kemetic civilization. Cuvier compared Sarah Bartman's remains with the mummified remains taken from Egyptian tombs to differentiate her from an imaginary Hamitic species Europeans had hastily credited with creating the great civilization of Kemet. When she was alive, Curvier examined her and later performed an autopsy on her body after her death. His morally bankrupt motive was to substantiate the Aryan Model of Civilization crafted in 1790. The model sought to obscure the truth about Africa's influence in creating civilization. It presented a fabricated narrative supported by the newly devised investigative process of science that was devised to replace the word of God in the bible. Europeans placed high confidence in the new scientific process of interpreting history while falsifying the data upon which the new social reality rested. In *Black Athena,* author Martin Banel writes:

> . . . proponents of the Aryan Model base their claim to superiority less on the amount of information available to them than on the contention that they, unlike the 'credulous' Classical and Hellenistic writers, have a 'critical approach' and a scientific viewpoint which more than compensate for any lack of information.[1]

While some of the scholarly publications from the recent past are less heinous than the work of Curvier, they all aimed to achieve the same result of systematically fabricating an image of the monstrous African. They sought to substantiate the rampant speculation in European society that grew out of the ethics of the Atlantic Slave Trade. Across the spectrum of modern-day scientific works, a hierarchical worldview emerges from scientific efforts to validate

---

1 Bernal, Martin. *Black Athena. Volume II.* P. 9.

opinions that, more often than not, resulted in half-truths parading as infallible science. It includes Darwin's ideas on natural selection, defined in his 1860 publication of *Origin of Species."* However, while it does not intentionally debase the value of human life, it is conditioned by Aristotelean-hierarchical thinking that permeated the social consciousness of the 18th and 19th centuries. Pre-Darwinian ideas on evolution held by Jean-Baptiste Lamarck claimed that the evolution of life followed natural laws. Darwin's work was a more detailed analysis that proved natural selection as the driving force in evolution. From the 1758 10th edition of *Systema Naturae* by Carl Linnaeus to the 20th-century book by the English Ethnologist Charles Seligman *Races of Africa (1930),* these works launched the pseudo-scientific idea of a mythical Hamitic race that acquired widespread legitimacy as sound science despite their corrupted views on race.

Carl Linnaeus created modern taxonomy, the preferred Western system for classifying and communicating ideas about the natural world. Although he followed Aristotle's hierarchical classification method to a large extent, his work evolved to reflect the race-based superstition of his time. He used a *binomial naming system* that defines all life according to genus and species. However, it followed social norms and misrepresented Africans as a lesser species. Students studying modern taxonomy learn to reinforce latent ideas on racial hierarchy by referencing Linnaeus's hierarchical classification of the four races of humans. His rank of the Africanus at the bottom, depicted with the most inhuman features bordering on the monstrous, reflected the popular opinion and will of Christian society that had opposed his equating man and ape and African and European. Such firm but speculative opinions influenced Linnaeus and 18th-century Europeans to distinguish between humans and apes and superior and inferior humans. His taxonomy remains the modern learning method about the natural world, still adopted by children in their formative school years.

Disdain for Africans in European society had gradually emerged centuries before Linnaeus and Cuvier. The earliest reference to the Curse of Ham occurred in Annius of Viterbo's writing in the 15th century, around the beginning of the Atlantic Slave Trade. The discredited Italian Dominican friar referenced Genesis 9 as the reason for the ongoing Arab enslavement of African people. The Hamitic hypothesis which attributes all evidence of civilization in Africa to a Hamite-caucasian group only to substantiate the subhuman status of Africans and to perpetuate their burgeoning slave-trading and plantations enterprises built on African labor. When Charles G. Seligman published *The Races of Africa* in 1930, a century after England abolished slavery, these ideas on race were vibrant. His ethics remained unchanged and conditioned by the white supremacist ethos crafted in European universities bent on scientifically verifying a racialized worldview based on manufactured evidence. At the height of the Slave Trade in the 18th and 19th centuries, not a shred of the African's humanity remained. The deaths and suffering of African people had become as meaningless as that of life forms designated as lower by Linneaus' faux science. In the detail of *The Slave Ship* painted by Turner in 1840, shown below, the artist has depicted a crime committed by the captain and crew of the Zong ship, who threw sick and dead Africans overboard and filed an insurance claim to cover their financial losses. However, the Zong trial had more to do with the insurance company's avoidance of liability than with the murders of human beings. Such activity was typical in the 19th century when widespread racial indoctrination spurred genocide around the world.

Left: A detail of *The Slave Ship* by J.M.W. Turner, painted in 1840, is based on the story of the Zong, a British ship whose captain had thrown overboard the sick and dying kidnapped Africans in 1781 to collect insurance money.

As profits of the burgeoning European economies increased, racial propaganda simultaneously exacerbated and obscured the horrific genocide occurring in Africa, on the seas, and in the New World. Eyewitness reports of slave raids in Africa and analyses of the casualties of the Slave Trade by European Parliamentarian and abolitionist Sir William Wilberforce, with a conclusion by Thomas Cooper, stated that ten Africans died for every survivor from the continent.[2] However, the 19th-century European intellectuals and slave traders adhered to a 16th-century deterministic worldview, which held that God predetermines events. Additionally, amid the immense wealth generated from the Slave Trade, Calvinists were prone to believe that those blessed with wealth had received their just reward for their faith and those suffering from disastrous circumstances

---

2   Herbert S. Klein, Stanley L. Engerman, Robin Haines, and Ralph Shlomowitz. *Transoceanic Mortality: The Slave Trade in Comparative Perspective*, p. 19. Based on (Thomas Cooper, Supplement to Mr. Cooper's Letter on the Slave Trade (Manchester, 1788), 3, 4.)

were punished for their lack of faith. The increasing number of Protestants enriched by the Slave Trade were predisposed to believe that God had preplanned the punishment of the enslaved Africans. German sociologist Max Weber points out that although Protestants were forbidden from indulging in luxury goods, their savings were, instead, invested and consequently went directly into the lucrative Slave Trade. The beneficiaries viewed the mind-boggling profits—the product of unbridled greed and violence—simply as the just reward of the faithful, which was dissociated from genocide. As the wealth of Africa and the Americas began flowing into Europe, the process of secularization defined by Weber, where religion loses its social and cultural significance, had already occurred during the Protestant Reformation, around three hundred years before Turner completed his painting *The Slave Ship*. The Middle Ages' practice of selling indulgences is the foremost example of the breakdown of morality as the old ideas about religion and spiritual purification based on good works shifted towards paying for everlasting life. As wealthy Christians approached death after they participated in the genocide, many opted to donate their estates to the church in return for the promise of entering the kingdom of heaven.

A Glimmer of Hope

There is a glimmer of hope that the mass psychosis engendered by racial indoctrination over the centuries will end as truth resurfaces. The unwritten law that controls the unconscious psyche and holds that those with black skin are the inferior ones, the violent criminal types, or the politically dangerous ones is absurd as scholars rediscover Africa's true history. In the narrow sphere of contemporary anthropology and archeology, unbiased scientific inquiry has begun to verify Africa's oral traditions. For the first time in several hundred years, scientists have started to correct the biased narratives about Africans that have formed the basis of the fabricated racial hierarchy used in the psychological conditioning of Africans as hereditary slaves. A new breed of scientists is taking African traditions seriously by investigating and scientifically verifying its oral traditions, with a determined effort to correct modern archeology and anthropology. The new revelations have disproved the flawed racial theories and show that early Africans were the first innovators of vital technologies for thousands of years.

Archaeologists are discovering evidence of ancient African innovations that occurred first in Africa and then spread from the south to the north and beyond the continent's borders. Modern scholars could quickly dispel the myth of inferior Africans by expanding the educational curriculum to include the discoveries. However, disinformation persists despite an African history dating back to the beginning of the unique Homo *sapien sapiens* symbolic behaviors. Towards the end of the Middle Stone Age, 60–20 kya, archaeologists show that early man developed vital technologies such as agriculture and animal domestication and created drought-resistant grasses for cattle. They had mastered tracking the stars and used their knowledge to commemorate major conjunctions in the sky with large regional gatherings in East Africa.

In Central Africa, they used polished stone axes to begin clearing forests and domesticating yams for the first time. The invention of ceramic technology in the Eastern Sahara (the Nihlo Sahara tradition) ca. 8,500–8,000 B.C.E. occurred three millennia before it did in the Near East and four millennia before it spread to Europe and India. Cultivation of sorghum occurred around 7,000 B.C.E., and evidence of the earliest domestication of cotton and spindle whorls from Khartoum emerged about 5,000 B.C.E.[3] Steel production in the Great Lakes region of Africa began 2,000–1,500 B.C.E. that achieved the required high temperature approaching 3,500 degrees. Europeans could not accomplish these temperatures until the invention of the Electric Arc Furnace in the 19th century.[4] Nevertheless, the erroneous idea of iron originating in Anatolia (Asia Minor or Turkey) in the 2nd millennium B.C.E. before arriving in Africa, persists primarily because of the reams of pseudoscience permeating the literature.

The exclusion of Africa from world history perpetuates the bizarre idea that slavery was a blessing to Africans or that the greatest civilization in antiquity was the invention of a Hamitic race. The fabrication of Africa's history makes the isolated development of Greek culture from Egypt plausible and the Caucasian ethnicity of King Tut a popular notion. By neglecting Africa's history, the old Classical Western archeology perpetuates the outdated and racist idea that the most significant advances of Homo *sapien sapiens* began only after the great migrations out of Africa 40–60 kya. Their messages reassert that the black-skinned race has offered nothing to the world.

Scientific literature based on the countless volumes of incorrect or racialized propaganda has led to severe errors in the scientific record. English archaeologists tasked with uncovering past human activity in essential re-

---

3   Carney, A. Judith and Rosomoff, N. Hard. *In the Shadow of Slavery: Africa's Botanical Legacy in the Atlantic World.* pp. 1–16.
4   www.thoughtco.com/steel-history-2340172

gions in Southern Africa in 1902 discounted ample sedimentary evidence that did not conform to their preconceived worldview of Africans as inferiors. According to the self-appointed archaeologists investigating an area of Southern Africa where Great Zimbabwe once thrived, the massive walls, built without cement, were attributable to sun-worshiping Semitic people and Himyarite Arabs, or medieval Arabs—all from regions outside of Africa. The gold-diggers and self-proclaimed archaeologists parroting negative opinions about African people had one misguided mission—to find the source of Great Zimbabwe's gold. In the first European documentation of the site, the centuries and miles of human development achieved by African people deferred to the imagined biblical gold of Ophir, ancient Israel, and ancient Arabia.[5]

At its height, Great Zimbabwe controlled trade in territory stretching for 100,000 square miles between the Zambezi and the Limpopo rivers. They controlled trade between the East Coast of Africa, Asia, China, and India. The excavation of Great Zimbabwe in 1902 began when Cecil Rhodes, the English colonial agent in Rhodesia, ordered the exploration of the ruins. As they searched for evidence of the biblical Gold of Ophir, the Queen of Sheba, and King Solomon's gold mine, their expectations were conditioned by the myths of European folklore, discarded the excavated sedimentary layers as useless rubbish. The revised opinion of modern-day archeology cannot undo the destruction of Africa's history in the overlooked sedimentary layers and the confiscated gold treasures melted into ingots.

A systematic racial bias persists in the scientific literature that attributes the earliest innovations from Africa to Sumer, Mesopotamia, Babylon, the Levant, and places beyond its borders. Scientific terms embedded in scientific journals have magnified the overt racial bias for over two centuries. Sub-Saharan Africa, Near East, the Middle East, Semitic, Afroasiatic, or Cushitic are value-laden terms created in the early 19th century and used explicitly to separate the primitive Negro from North Africa's people, languages, and geography. These are typical examples of the old portrayal of Africa as an offshoot of Asian and Semitic sources of civilization. The racially biased terms and racial attitudes embedded in the literature are nearly impossible to revise because of their widespread use as the Western standard. The belief that culture spread to Africa from outside its borders has led to the corresponding classification of African languages

---

5   Richard Nicklin Hall. Great Zimbabwe, Mashonaland, Rhodesia: An account of Two Years' Examination work in 1902–4 on behalf of the Government of Rhodesia, pp. xix, 194.

as Semitic and a branch of the *Afroasiatic* language family originating in West Asia. Even among Africans in northeast Africa, the out-of-Africa attitude persists, and the non-Negro, Semitic origin circulates. Backward thinking defies logic as even the newly discovered fossil evidence of inventions that spread through migration patterns within Africa does not undo the hierarchical mode of thought that relays Linnaeus' taxonomy, showing Africans at the bottom.

Modern research reveals that the North African language, particularly that of Kemet, originated from Proto-Nilo-Saharan in the Horn of Africa and split into two daughter languages, Proto-Amharic and Proto-Erythraean. (Christopher Ehret) Modern archeology traces developments in the Horn of Africa and the Southern Red Sea hills region around 15,000 B.C.E. using these early languages to trace technological developments (Christopher Ehret). The confusion created by the out-of-Africa theories has irreparably obscured human origins, mainly as evidence becomes re-purposed, destroyed, or hidden in private collections and museums.

The early Africans—with the darkest shade of color—had based their solar calendar on their knowledge of Sopdet, the star that marks December 25th and is part of the Sothic cycle as renamed by Romans. Africans had firsthand knowledge of the star's cycle, which they demonstrated in astronomical megalithic constructions such as the astronomical clock in the Sahara Desert in Sudan. The African science accounted for leap years in the calendar and tracked the most challenging cycle—the Precession of the Vernal Equinoxes, which completes approximately every 25,920 years. Ancient Kemet relayed these facts to the Greeks and Romans, who transcribed the original names of stars and methods. Yet, these achievements by Africans remain inconclusive to the modern researchers stuck in the out-of-Africa myth. Presently, the needed focus on the ancient worldview is less critical than research verifying a theoretical hierarchically-devised split in evolution separating gorillas, chimpanzees, and other primates from humans 7 million years before the proposed emergence of Homo *sapiens sapiens*. An even more determined focus is on genetic research reinforcing an evolutionary connection between hominins from 2.6 million years ago that became extinct long before humans emerged. The efforts leapfrog the humans on the African continent and focus on the hunter-gatherer in the Paleolithic era, the human-Neanderthal, and human-Denisovan genetic links.

In the knowledge vacuum about African contributions to world civilization, a growing body of information evolves from an Ancient Alien hypothesis popularized by an ever-increasing cult-like following. The Ancient Alien speculation gives credence to the lie that the great works of ancient African civilization—its celestial observatories, incomprehensible engineering projects of pyramids and vast temple complexes, its global presence, and metaphysics—required the intervention of ancient aliens. Consequently, many in Western popular culture remain defiantly unaware that their moral philosophy, psychological conditioning, and self-concept originate from a unique wellspring of civilization in the African continent's interior.

In the 19th-century pseudoscience of racial hierarchy, the German historian George Wilhelm Hegel, the father of Western History, had brazenly compared an imaginary superior culture to a diminished African society. He defined Africans as being without a history and incapable of forming a concept of God. In universities across Europe, the conjecture of the godless African, defended with biblically-based propaganda, falsified craniology, and anthropology, became the overarching reality.

The Aryan Model vs. the Ancient Model

Efforts to distort the identity and role of African people in world history succeeded despite early Greek scholars' acceptance of Kemet's African roots and its profound influence on ancient Greece. Their conclusions about Egypt's importance and superiority in all facets of culture had been accepted as fact in the Mediterranean region for thousands of years. However, The Aryan Model, which promoted a racialized worldview espousing species differentiation and separation in European society, succeeded despite its scientific claims that ignored the volumes of facts highlighted by author Martin Bernal. In *Black Athena, Volume II*, the author writes:

> In general, then, it is clear that, as well as having a 'feel' for the topic from their common culture, the writers working in the Ancient Model had more information about the Bronze Age than do the supporters of the Aryan one. However, proponents of the Aryan Model base their claim to superiority less on the amount of information available to them than on the contention that they, unlike the 'credulous' Classical and Hellenistic writers, have a 'critical approach' and a scientific viewpoint which more than compensate for any lack of information.[6]

The white supremacist speculation rose to the level of science because of the work of European intellectuals and scientists with a history of relying

---

6   Bernal Martin. *Black Athena, Volume II*, p. 9.

on empiricism as a source of knowledge. The pseudoscience promoted by Linnaeus and others began to crumble when they discovered that the very object of their scorn, the black-skinned Africans, were the creators of the tremendous civilization they had uncovered in the desert sands. The need to scientifically separate Africa from Europe began immediately with Europe's Antiquities project, which sought to redefine the race of the creators of Kemet's culture with the introduction of the Hamite hypothesis that insisted on a superior, non-African people as originators of all civilization and particularly Kemetic civilization in Africa. The blatant speculation from biblical sources once again, as during the Slave Trade, provided the basis for scientific theories seeking to discredit native Africans.

In 1820–40, German universities proposed The Aryan Model of Civilization, which based scientific conclusions on cultural norms that emerged during the Slave Trade. Author Martin Bernal discusses the model's assertions in the mid-19th century (1840s) that Aryan culture originated and developed in the Aegean, isolated from African influence during the Bronze Age (3,300–1,100 B.C.E.).[7] Since the efforts to validate the Aryan Model began, the theory gained traction in Western educational systems and media, and there has been a consensus of sympathetic classical anthropologists up to the present day. The 19th-century cultural mores espoused by the theory reinforce the implausible idea that the most critical developments in world civilization—art, ethics, agriculture, writing, astronomy, architecture, and natural philosophy—originated in a unique Aryan culture outside Africa. Since it discounts the role of dark-skinned people in human development in Greece, The Aryan Model fits the Polygenic Theory of Human Origins, postulating that human beings arose from different racial groups. The false claims of species differentiation between Caucasians and Africans are essential to maintaining the white supremacist racial hierarchy.

Problematic scientific claims of species differentiation among humans could advance as empirically verifiable only if differences between humans are proven to occur because of separate origins. As the difference in genetic material between races is barely discernible at 0.3%, one option used by supporters of racial science for claiming a statistically viable difference exists is often based on variations in intelligence statistics. However, critics of the intelligence tests claim that variations in intelligence are influenced more by socio-economic factors—the centuries of racial discrimination—than by

---

7   Bernal, Martin. *Black Athena*, pps. 1–12.

genetics. The pseudo-scientific premise of a racial hierarchy, which is often displayed in contemporary media, plays a prominent role in maintaining racial misconceptions in popular culture and scientific circles. Images of an imagined superior race with cultural and aesthetic motifs are represented as the typical and highest level of human evolution. The falsification of world history began as a scientific effort to discredit Africans to support existing racial speculation. At the inception of Egyptology in Europe, scholars such as Carl Richard Lepsius, Constantine-François Volney,[8] and Jean-François Champollion discovered that their revered Egyptian builders of Kemetic civilization were the same as the enslaved black Africans. Rather than reforming the existing racial bias, 19th-century scientists opted to discredit those whose heads they stood on. The obscuring of the distant epochs they undertook is not trivial. It includes four significant periods of history that define modern man's social and psychological evolution—the Paleolithic era or Old Stone Age (3.3 million years ago to 11,650 years ago), The Neolithic era or New Stone Age, Antiquity, and the Middle Ages.

The distortion of history is less evident in the Paleolithic or Old Stone Age fossils that mark modern humans' earliest appearance, as early as 315,000 years ago in Africa. However, modern scientists have nothing to say about the incredible megalithic constructions around the world. They prefer to focus on genetics to substantiate a linear human development theory that dwells on pre-human evolutionary developments from at least 2.6 million years ago. It discounts all the fundamental technical advances of inhabitants on the African continent before the great migrations out of Africa that populated the rest of the Earth 60 kya. Clearly, human development and innovation during the Neolithic or New Stone Age, ranging from the end of the Ice Age 12,000 B.C.E. up to 4,500 B.C.E. is generally repurposed as Hamitic-Caucasian, Near Eastern, Semitic, Sumerian, and Babylonian. The focus on world history then gravitates to Late Antiquity with the history of Greece and Rome. After Rome's collapse, humanity in Europe entered The Middle Ages, followed by the modern era.

Nevertheless, when Greeks began to travel and study in Kemet from 500-50 B.C.E., they routinely revealed that their religion, philosophy, and mathematics came from Egypt. These Greek sources for the obscured Ancient Model did not originate from the opinions of a controlling

---

8   Constantine-François Volney. *Travels through Syria and Egypt, in the Years 1783, 1784*, and 1785, p. 83)

class, like those of the modern era slave societies that fabricated the Out of Africa school of thought. It came from a long list of active participants in history—the people who had traveled and studied in Kemet. Mediterranean civilizations believed in The Ancient Model for more than two thousand years, From Classical Antiquity to the early 19th century, until the Aryan Model displaced it.

The incorrect assessment of modern humans increases with the volumes of fabricated information written solely to suppress links between African people and Europeans. In 1912, evidence of European efforts at supporting the assertions of white supremacists occurred in the use of the fabricated Piltdown Man skull fragment created by joining human and animal bones. The British Science Academy received the bones presented as the widely sought scientific proof of an extinct white ancestor. It was a crude attempt that betrays the level of desperation to substantiate the white supremacist thesis of a unique origin of the Caucasian race originating in Sussex, England. Despite the failure of the Piltdown Man hoax, pseudo-scientific proclamations, media manipulation, and misplaced emphasis on Greece and Asia proliferated and obscured the facts of Kemet's black African ancestry.

The ongoing degradation of the Homo *sapiens sapiens* self-identity has consequences that have yet to manifest. Suppressing the vital human behaviors that arose from African origins erases critical survival instincts and invites unforeseen disadvantages and fruitless evolutionary paths. Long-established vital, naturally developed social mores from hundreds of thousands of years of observing nature no longer guide the species or are lost entirely. Inevitably, nature, the revered mother and teacher, protected and emulated by early man in all facets of life—agriculture, alchemy, architecture, art, dance, and language—has receded.

Nature's vital links to the species have become more and more irrelevant. Reasserting the truth of our origins achieves nothing substantive except to harden the resolve of obscurantists who, for example, deleted the black Egyptian type from The Table of Nations relief from the 20th Dynasty, which shows Egyptians depicting themselves as black-skinned people in African garb. Surviving photographs of the original artifact preserve the knowledge that the Egyptians illustrated themselves identically to the second black-skinned African in the relief. Even in the remotest desert region near the Sudan border, historical revisionists actively threaten the truth by partly destroying the megalith at Nabta Playa. This regional-ceremonial gathering place functioned as an astronomical clock that measures precession cycles. Herodotus wrote that the mystery teachers of the heavens told him that Egyptians tracked three precession cycles.[9] The combined years of observation would predate the beginning of the last migrations of humans out of Africa to populate the world approximately 60,000 years ago.

The most significant argument for the inclusion of Africa in world history began at the 1964 UNESCO conference on the General History of Africa (GHA), where two renowned African scientists sought to remedy the racial bias in Africa's history and its lack of an African perspective. The Senegalese, Cheikh Anta Diop, an anthropologist, historian, physicist, and author of *The African Origin of Civilization* and the Congolese Théophile Obenga, a philosopher, historian, educator, and author of *African Philosophy: The Pharaonic Period, 2780-330 B.C.*, both insisted on Africa's contributions to world history in the *UNESCO History of Africa, Volume II*.[10] In his lectures, Diop notes that modern man is the only one of six species of Homo sapiens that survived in equatorial Africa. The first three species had a limited range, became extinct, and never left Africa. Three others left the continent, but the fourth and the fifth disappeared. Only the sixth human species remains, with remarkable adaptability and a global range nurtured in Africa.[11]

Nature gave her melanin generously to blacken the skin to protect life. Without these miraculous genes, the species would not have survived the burning tropical sun. The oldest fossils reveal that the new man emerged around 200 to 315 thousand years ago,[12] close to the beginning of the Middle Stone Age. That period marks the hunter-gatherer phase of archaic human types and modern humans who produced crude stone blades, spear points, and grindstones for pigment processing. The transition from the hunter-gatherer phase to a settled lifestyle occurred around 160–20 kya. Humans began widely practicing ritual burials and producing various tools for fishing and mining, barbed points for sawing, a wide variety of images, beads for personal identification, and long-distance exchanges of ideas.

In fact, many of the components of the "human revolution" claimed to appear at 40–50 ka are found in the African Middle Stone Age tens of thousands of

9   Massey, Gerald. *Ancient Egypt, Light of the World*, pp. 581–582.
10   General History of Africa. Available at: (https://en.unesco.org/general-history-africa)
11   *Conférence télévisée de CHEIKH ANTA DIOP à l'émission "FOR THE PEOPLE."* Accessed 10/10/2020. Available at: https://www.youtube.com/watch?v=lz3O--TGQ9g
12   Callaway, Ewen (7 June 2017). "Oldest Homo sapiens fossil claim rewrites our species' history". "Nature: Internatinal Weekly Journal of Science." Accessed 10/10/2020. Available at: www.nature.com/news/oldest-homo-sapiens-fossil-claim-rewrites-our-species-history-1.22114

years earlier. These features include blade and microlithic technology, bone tools, increased geographic range, specialized hunting, the use of aquatic resources, long distance trade, systematic processing and use of pigment, and art and decoration. These items do not occur suddenly together as predicted by the "human revolution" model, but at sites that are widely separated in space and time. This suggests a gradual assembling of the package of modern human behaviors in Africa, and its later export to other regions of the Old World.[13]

The archaeological evidence shows that the new man was bipedal and had an enlarged braincase, exceptional toolmaking, and analytical and creative abilities. More importantly, humans learned to sustain large and complex cultures and devised ways of sharing knowledge and cooperating over vast distances. Evidence of settlements and construction sites in Southern Africa from approximately 200,000 years ago and symbols from 73,000 years[14] ago reveal a characteristic sophistication of early humans. However, the more meaningful achievement is the development of symbolic communication that allows the transmission and preservation of abstract concepts. The earliest known symbol discovered in the Blombos cave in South Africa represents a permanent record of an idea transmitted from the invisible realm to the material world. The recording of ideas, particularly about the universal consciousness, preserved and conveyed the earliest ethical ideas that evolved into the foundation of the first known civilization of Kemet. Ancient symbols and rituals have consistently communicated the abstract notion of self as a duality of body and spirit with a soul, that define who we are as modern humans.

The early spiritual awakening of humans appears first in ceremonial burial rites. Approximately 75,000 years ago in Southern Africa, humans began burying the dead in prepared graves with their heads adorned in red ochre soil and facing the sky.[15] The body was committed to the Earth, and the head, the thinking part, belonged to the sky. Author Ivan Van Sertima notes that these ceremonial burials were pervasive enough that modern archaeologists have used them as markers to map the migrations of modern man out of Africa. Ritualistic burials infer that humans had an early understanding of

---

13 McBrearty, S. and Brooks, A.S. (2000) The Revolution That Wasn't: A New Interpretation of the Origin of Modern Human Behavior. Journal of Human Evolution, 39, 453-563.

14 www.nationalgeographic.com/science/2018/09/news-ancient-humans-art-hashtag-ochre-south-africa-archaeology/#close (Accessed 5/12/2020)

15 Ehret, Christopher. The Civilizations of Africa: A History to 1800, p. 73, 91.

the self encompassing reverence for a universal consciousness. Burial rituals, fertility rites, and personalized adornment for self-identification all point to a predominant belief system shaping social values that delineated modern man's perception of a dual world of spirit and matter. While these early rituals are insufficient evidence to prove an entire doctrine of spiritual science during the Middle Stone Age, the evidence becomes indisputable during the Neolithic or the New Stone Age (12,000–6,500 B.C.E.).

The unique capacity for more advanced abstract thought developed because of the miraculous birth without a fused brain case that allowed the head of the first modern humans to grow substantially larger outside the womb.[16] The larger brain that endowed humans with exceptional analytical abilities also permitted the development of ethically based civilizations. Wherever human settlements occurred in a bountiful nature, early humans revered the Great Mother, the life-giver, nurturer, and provider. Africa's early matrilineal societies maintained a social structure where lineage, title to possessions, and territory were passed from mother to daughter for thousands of years before the patriarchy destroyed the kingship and communal social system.

In Southern and Northeast Africa, humans built megalithic structures to track the constellation scores of thousands of years ago. In the northeast, they named constellations of the original zodiac using familiar animal names. The early twentieth-century English Egyptologist Gerald Massey writes of the ancient African abstract thinking expressed first in zoomorphic forms of animals, birds, and reptiles. Massey reiterates that:

> "On every line of research, we discover that the representation of nature was pre-anthropomorphic at first, as we see on going back far enough, and on every line of descent, the zoomorphic passes ultimately into the human representation."[17]

Modern man had spent about 140,000 years traversing the continent's length and breadth before the first migrations out of Africa began around 60,000 years ago. A profound cosmology evolved that remains viable up to the present from these thousands of years of experience in nature. In early matrilineal societies, the most sacred symbol of the dot inscribed

---

16   The Homo *sapien sapien* brain grew 4-5 times larger than the nearest hominid brain which averaged 300kg.
17   Massey, Gerald. *Ancient Egypt: The Light of the World*, p.3.

within a circle evolved to represent the womb of life and the vital power that sustains life or the sun. The scarab beetle, which moves the ball of dung behind it, suggests the self-begotten, invisible force that moves the sun and moon. The lion's strength humans observed in nature developed to symbolize power and royalty. With the sun symbol above his head, the falcon-headed Ra evolved to represent creative energy.

Many epochs had passed before the unified civilization emerged in northeast Africa when populations converged along the Nile River as the Sahara gradually turned to desert. In Kemet's capital city of Meneffer (Memphis in Greek), centuries before the Pharaoh Narmer or Menes had unified his southern kingdom with the northern one in 3,100 B.C.E., the earliest evidence of a theory of knowledge of the self-begotten one had existed. Memphis is the source of the world's first epistemology written on papyrus and later transferred to stone after rediscovery by Pharaoh Shabaka of the 25th Dynasty (719–703 B.C.E.). Based on his written account regarding its antiquity, the papyrus dates to the founding of Meneffer, 3,400–3,100 B.C.E.[18] When Shabaka discovered it, the theology was already several thousand years old. The origin of the ancient knowledge appeared remote to the King in the same way he now seems distant to those in the modern world.

Egyptian priests told Herodotus about the antiquity of Egyptian civilization. They told him their priestly lineage, represented by statues of fathers and their succeeding sons, is 345 generations.[19] Herodotus calculated that the ancient line of priests extended back 11,340 years. The years of father and son succession date to the Neolithic Era before the Ice Age. Herodotus also referenced the Cycle of Precession, stating that the people of Kemet experienced three of these cycles. Conceivably, Zep Tepi, translated as *the first time* when the Divine ruled over Kemet, began for the ancient Africans 77,000 years ago in the Neolithic era, which links directly to the mode of thought and expression before the first migration out of Africa began during the Ice Age, 60,000 years ago. In the late Neolithic, ancient Africans had already built megalithic structures to track celestial objects that became the basis of the calendar. They had mapped the precession of the vernal equinox that delineated the ages and the psychological profile of the human species. They had designated the northern region of the sky as the most stable and fitting destination for the soul. An exceptional surviving example of the early African self-concept

---

18   Bernal, Martin. *Black Athena, Vol. 2*, p. 28. (Bernal places the founding of Memphis at 3400 B.C.E.)
19   Herodotus. *An Account of Egypt*, Section ix.

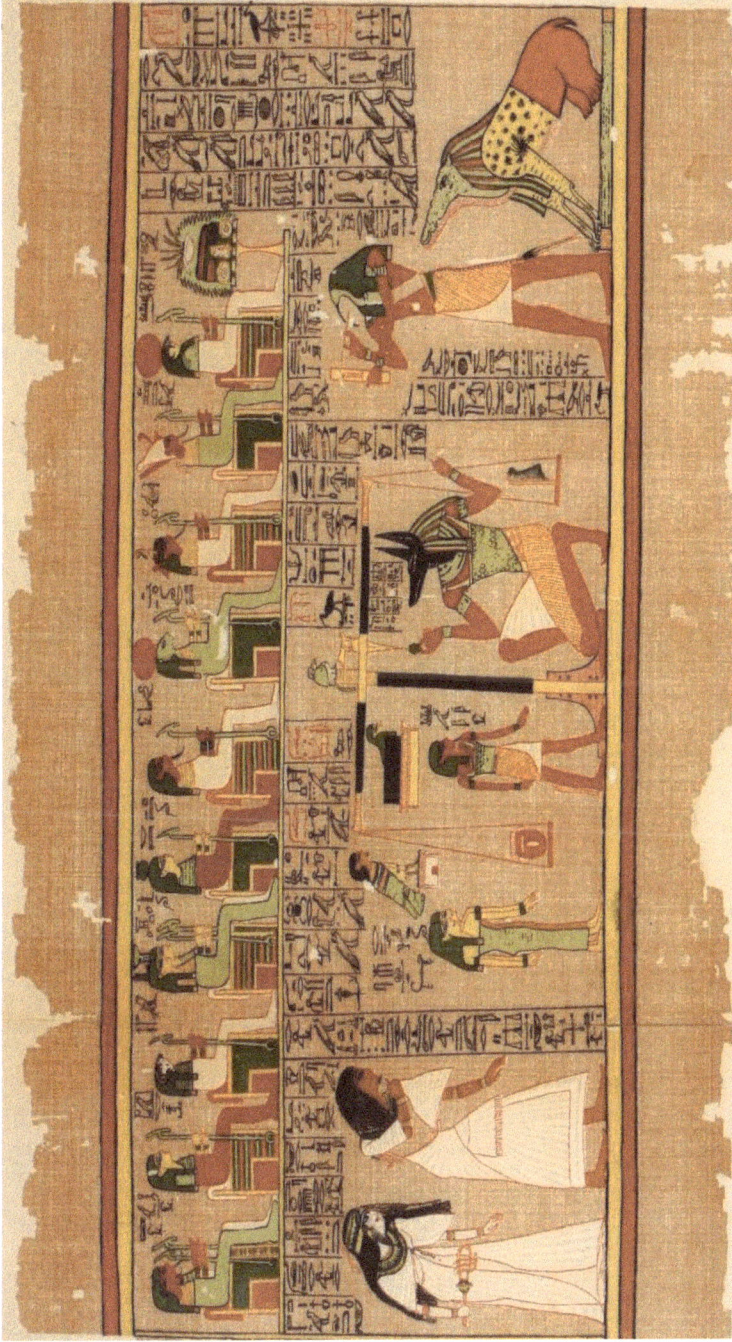

In a scene equal to the Last Judgement, the Jackal-headed Anpu (Anubis), the god of mummification and the afterlife, weighs Ani's heart against the feather of Ma'at.

as physical and spiritual is evident in The Papyrus of Ani (1,250 B.C.E.). In the burial script, Ani's soul is a bird with his likeness in the detailed image below. In other illustrations, the soul appears hovering over an interred body or flying towards an exit to illustrate a spirit free from the body.[20] The depiction of the soul in the papyrus as independent of the body transmits the ageless wisdom that the deceased is reborn.

Spiritual rebirth features prominently in the story of Ausar (Osiris), Auset (Isis), and her son Heru the younger (Horus), who form the first known trinity that links Heru to the human race. Heru, born of an immaculate conception, is like the sun that saves humanity from the darkness and is the original symbol of salvation. Two symbols depict Heru; one is Heru the Elder, and the other is Heru the Younger, child of Auset and the conquerer of the evil Set. Nile Valley civilizations represented Heru the Elder as a falcon with its wings shaped into a solar disk and Heru the Younger as the child with a braid and a finger in his mouth. While they are different symbols, both represent the solar principle or idea conveyed by the sun as the force that saves humanity from eternal darkness.

Detail: Ani's soul at the Judgement is represented as the likeness of Ani with wings to signify that it is spirit. Below, to the right, is his heart on the scale, balanced against the feather of Ma'at on the opposite side of the scale, which is not shown.

---

20   Budge, E.A. Wallis. The Book of The Dead: The Hieroglyphic Transcript of the Papyrus of ANI, p. 8 of front panels.

The ancient Kemetic knowledge and ethics taught at the Temple of Waset (Luxor, or Thebes) sought to cultivate the Divine Man balanced in body and spirit and capable of surviving The Last Judgment. French Egyptologist Schwaller de Lubicz elaborates on Kemetic metaphysics that Luxor's builders encoded in the temple's architecture to symbolize the human form and psychic centers.[21] In the last section of the temple complex, statues depict the evolved, divine man confidently striding out. The people of Kemet built the temple during the 12th Dynasty (1,991 B.C.E.), where they taught the spiritual alchemy that honed the uninitiated person into The Divine Man capable of completing the cycle of life, death, and rebirth. The philosophy is perhaps one of Kemet's most understated and unappreciated developments in elevating human consciousness.

Among the early Mediterranean scholars with direct experience of Kemet's greatness, Pythagoras (582–496 B.C.E.) was the first Pre-Socratic philosopher to receive instruction in the Mysteries that he later taught to his students in Croton, Italy. His education in Kemet was indispensable to developing virtue ethics and the educational system in Athens. Long after Greece became an empire, Kemet's Mystery Schools remained the foundation of moral philosophy and education in the Mediterranean region under the guidance of Luxor Temple. Late in Kemet's history, students from around the Mediterranean continued studying there.

These ancient Africans codified the concept of sidereal time as they measured the Earth's movements against a series of fixed stars. Consequently, they created the world's first calendar, which developed into a 24-hour day and 365.25 days per year. The Egyptians depicted the 24 hours of the day using the coils of Apep, the coiled snake that the Greeks called Apophis. Using the heliacal rise of the star Sophis that begins the 1,460-year Sothic cycle, [22] they calculated the year's length for their solar calendar. They created the lunar calendar of 12 months of 30 days each and a civil calendar of 360 days with five days set aside to honor the neteru. These discoveries could not have occurred without a disciplined approach and thousands of years of practical experience. The Earth's 24-hour rotational frequency, the length of the year, the Sothic Cycle, and the much longer cycle of the Precession of the Vernal Equinox occurred because ancient Africans made

---

21   Schwaller de Lubicz. *The Temple of Man.*
22   Gadalla, Mustafa. *Egyptian Cosmology*, p. 89. Surviving Egyptian records show that the Sothic year was fixed in 4,240 B.C.E.

continuous observations. The discovery of the 25,920-year precession cycle and the zodiac invention would require practical knowledge spanning the epochs long before humans first left Africa.

In 3100 B.C.E., at the beginning of written history, all the necessary methodologies for running a civilization were already in place in Kemet. The implication is that the culture is substantially older than implied by Western scientists. Out of Kemet came the blueprint for complete medical diagnostic methods, a full set of surgical tools, and many techniques used in modern surgical procedures, medicines, and prescriptions for use. They also created the cubit, which is the same as the metric system. Our current educational system originated in the lodge system, where Africans taught the world's first Liberal Arts curriculum. Most musical instruments originate in Africa, as did alchemy, architecture, mathematics, writing, natural philosophy, religion, and many notable achievements to which modern science and crafts all owe their origins. Evidence of the old philosophy exists in the plethora of artifacts, hieroglyphs, and metaphors, and it persists in the esoteric traditions in African secret societies that mirror Kemetic thought. Hundreds of years of deciphering the information have shown the black African origin of culture, yet widespread obfuscation about these origins continues in the modern era.

The Holocene Cycle and Africa's Great Migration

The race of the builders of Kemet is considered an unsettled question. Many in the popular culture feign surprise or anger at the notion of the African origin of civilization. Media portrayals continually feature aquiline featured Egyptians overseeing black African types bound as *slaves* to reinforce the belief in a hereditary enslaved African population. Nevertheless, Bruce Beyer Williams, PhD presented archaeological evidence that traces Egypt's origins to Nubia. He used archaeological evidence he obtained in Qustul, Lower Nubia, 5,800 years ago. However, no identifiable Hamite or Aryan race of builders in Africa exists anywhere globally, as some Western scientists postulate.

On the contrary, empirical evidence points to peoples from vast distances within Africa who cooperated or shared ideas and built great civilizations.[23] Their examples are more typical of the species than the idea of separation

---

23   Some Geographical and Political Aspects to Relations between Egypt and Nubia in C-Group and Kerma Times, ca. 2500 – 1500 B.C. - Journal of Ancient Egyptian Interconnections (egyptianexpedition.org)

and conflict held by white supremacist speculation. The last great migrations within Africa during the Holocene Cycle of wet and dry climatic conditions at the end of the previous glaciations, 12,000 years ago, merged into the Kemetic civilization. Author Ivan Van Sertima describes the transference of knowledge and culture throughout Africa's north region in prehistory in *They Came Before Columbus*. Van Sertima wrote of connecting rivers, now covered by desert sand that once tied Egypt to the lower part of the continent. Satellite photography later confirmed the theory of a much wetter Sahara delta with interconnecting waterways leading to and from the interior.

At the beginning cycle, from 14,000 B.C.E. to around 4- or 3-thousand B.C.E., the Sahara Desert was in its wet phase. Cave paintings radiocarbon dated to 7,000 B.C.E. show Africans using horse-drawn chariots[24] and reed boats for fishing and hunting the hippopotamus. As dry periods followed wet, it precipitated mass migrations towards the Nile River and prompted the consolidation of a large population and the world's highest civilization in the Nile Valley.[25] These early Africans had a divinity concept and well-organized civilized societies in prehistory. Skeletal evidence of the prehistoric Sudanic population and linguistics gauge the crucial development of the ancient worldview during the pre-dynastic periods of the late Stone Age to the Bronze Age in 255 B.C.E). Uncovered skulls from Northeast Africa exhibit a characteristic tribal mark of an extracted lower incisor tooth that delineates the geographical range of this early civilization. The Root words and concepts for God, names of plants, geographical locations, and the first domestication of animals originated by early Africans are traceable throughout Africa and beyond. The skull studies help to delineate migratory patterns and, consequently, the spread of agriculture, language, and ideas throughout the region of Africa that today encompasses Chad, Kenya, Sudan, Ethiopia, and Egypt.[26]

In *The African Origin of Civilization,* Author Cheikh Anta Diop establishes linguistic ties between Africans of the Nile Valley and those as far west as Senegal and Nigeria on the west coast of Africa.[27] In *Egypt Revisited,* author Ivan Van Sertima asserts that:

> It is important to understand from the outset that ancient Egypt was not a sudden and miraculous flower of the African genius.
>
> As we have shown in previous journals, the fragmentation and devastation

---

24 Gadalla, Moustafa. *Egyptian Cosmology: The Animated Universe,* p. 87.

25 Christopher Ehert. *The History of Africa up to 1800,* p. 71.

26 Ibid. *The History of Africa up to 1800.* pp. 72–73.

27 Cheikh Anta Diop. *The African Origin of Civilization,* pp. 182–183.

of Africa over the centuries, our belated knowledge of other African centers of sophisticated culture and technology, have led to the assumption that, if indeed it were African, it were a solitary rose among the thorns. Egypt was the node and center of a vast web linking the strands of Africa's main cultures and languages. The light that crystallized at the center of this early world had been energized by the cultural electricity streaming from the heartland of Africa.

—Ivan Van Sertima. *Egypt Revisited*, pp.3–4

Regardless of the facts concerning the rise of civilization in Africa, a persistent racial science permeates the study of culture in North-East Africa. Historians, anthropologists, and scientists such as Diop, who, for example, irrefutably established that ancient Egyptians were black Africans, did so to counter rampant fabrication, which is still prevalent in scientific circles. Diop presented ample evidence, including wigs of African hair worn by Egyptian royalty with hairstyles similar to the modern Senegalese.[28] Diop referenced cranial analysis of some Africans that European scholars identified as Caucasians, but that, in reality, typifies a large percentage of the skulls of black Africans.[29] He references the historical record of "The Table of Nations," a relief of Egypt's population types showing a black-skinned African carved on the walls of the tomb of Ramses III from the 20th Dynasty. Conclusively, Diop shows that Egyptians differentiated themselves from the Indo-European and Semite types depicted.

Further evidence of the Kemetic civilization's African heritage exists in Mali, Niger, and Burkina Faso's geographical area, where Dogon priests share a similar cosmology and writing system with the early Egyptians. The Dogon people state that their ancestors arrived in Mali from ancient Egypt to escape religious persecution. They have detailed knowledge of the invisible dwarf star Sirius B, including information on its composite matter and orbital frequency, and these facts remained unknown to modern scientists until 1968. There is a shared cosmology in regions much further to the south among the Bantu peoples in central Africa and the furthest southern areas inhabited by the Zulus. The symbolism shown below represents the seed form of the universe, named *Atum*, by Kemet and *Amma,* by the Dogon and Bantu people.

The similarities between Bantu Philosophy, the Dogon, and Kemet are

---

28   Diop, Cheikh Anta. *The African Origin of Civilization: Myth or Reality,* pp. 10–42.
29   Ibid. *The African Origin of Civilization: Myth or Reality*, pp. 10–42.

unmistakable. The oral tradition of Africa's priesthood in the Congo region also acknowledges ties to *The Brotherhood of the Higher Ones of Egypt.* The priesthood dates back to the reign of Cheops 2,589–2,566 B.C.E.[30] Throughout the continent, there are similarities in the cosmology, including symbols illustrating the seed of creation and the emergence of the four elements of water, earth, air, and fire that emerged from the universal spirit.[31]

Kemetic symbol of
the sun that also represents universal
consciousness.

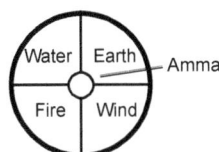

Dogon creator God Amma, the
womb of llife.

The shortlist of evidence of Africa's contributions to civilization is not a chauvinistic defense of the achievements of black-skinned Africans. However, it is illustrative of the earliest high culture, with evolved ethical standards that set all standards for civilization. Kemet's sacred science was a technology for transforming the spirit-body and achieving everlasting life.[32] The most enduring link between later cultures and ancient Egypt is the adoption of its ethics and spiritual beliefs, such as the transmutation of the soul. The Mysteries were critical to the spread of ethics to the rest of the world. The idea that the human being is a microcosm and the universe, the macrocosm, repeats throughout the culture. The same laws govern the universe above and human beings on the earthly plane below. That lesson occurs even in the pyramids' layout, which aligns with the Orion constellation. Miraculously, even the Nile River resembles the Milky Way and abuts it at the horizon.

Nevertheless, modern scholars attribute the widespread use of the microcosm/macrocosm concept to Greece based on an inscription in the temple of Apollo at Delphi. The banned book of Enoch quotes Jesus as the origin of the saying, *"Man, know thyself, and thou shall*

30 *The Ancient Wisdom in Africa,* an essay by Patrick Bowen: *Studies in Comparative Religion,* Vol. 3, No. 2. (Spring, 1969) Available at: www.studiesincomparativereligion.com . p. 6

31 *Bantu Cosmology & the Origins of Egyptian Civilization Notes.* Lecture by Asar Imhotep. December 15, 2007 S.H.A.P.E Community Center – Houston, TX. Available at: http://assets00.grou.ps/0F2E3C/wysiwyg_files/FilesModule/mtofolives/20100927224945-nyegvvqkpwdtsumnt/24552061-Bantu-Cosmology-the-Origins-of-Egyptian-Civilization-Notes.pdf . Pp. 16-18

32 Budge. E.A. Wallis. *The Book of the Dead,* p. 121

know the universe." However, due to its age and influence on world civilization, the Egyptian Temple of Luxor is the source that predates all other sources. Egyptologist Isha de Lubicz, the author of *Her-Bak: Egyptian Initiate,* reveals the translation of the original hieroglyphics on the temple walls:

> Man, know thyself . . . and thou shalt know the gods.

The universe as a stream of consciousness of the Father of Creation was the preeminent understanding of reality. Civilizations of the Mediterranean region remained faithful to principles of natural philosophy taught at Kemet's temples for more than 500 years after the Persian conquest in 526 B.C.E. The oldest documented funerary text, *The Book of Coming Forth by Light,* writes of the Creator's thought as the beginning of creation in the nun or celestial waters.[33] Implicit in the definition is that consciousness is the fabric of all reality. The neteru, or the forces of nature, fire, air, water, and earth, emanated from the undifferentiated mass that contained the essences of the material and immaterial world.

The Theory of Atomism by two Greek philosophers, Leucippus and Democritus, states that everything is made up of indivisible particles or atoms. Besides defining the atom as the basic building block of nature, they also speculated on the need for empty space that allows those atoms to move about. In doing so, Democritus discounted the more ancient idea of a universe permeated by the consciousness the Egyptians cite as the active, creative force sustaining the creation. Inevitably, ancient Greece, Rome, and a fledgling Europe discarded the ancient pantheist concept of the living universe and developed a theist concept compatible with the atomistic theory. Almost one hundred years after Niels Bohr developed the modern atomic theory in 1913, the idea of consciousness as the fabric of the universe was as obscure as during the ancient Greek discourse on the atom. Modern universities teach that 99.9 percent of an atom is *empty,* implying *nothingness.* Inevitably, science progressed beyond Newtonian Physics to Quantum Mechanics and became more in line but still short of the ancient concept of a universe permeated with consciousness. The belief that a universe is animated by a life force directly interacting with human beings is the basis for the *anima mundi* or world soul. The world soul and the human soul are self-similar according to the Law of Correspondence—

---

33   Budge. E.A. Wallis. *The Book of the Dead.* pp. 113-114.

As Above so Below. The immortality of the human soul emanates from the nature of the universe as consciousness. As the soul is a part of the tapestry of divine consciousness, it is immortal.[34]

Ancient Egyptians perceived the universal consciousness through the workings of celestial phenomena. Funerary texts refer to the flow of cosmic energy from the universe as the net.[35] The megalithic monuments, such as Stone Henge, the pyramids at the Giza plateau, and other monuments worldwide, sit on loci delineated by the directional lines extending around the globe. The Giza pyramid, for instance, originally marked the ancient Prime Meridian of the Earth, which is the center of the Earth's landmass at zero degrees longitude. The importance of the ancient Prime Meridian was dismissed by England following their military dominance of the Earth. The empire replaced the old Egyptian Prime Meridian with the Greenwich Meridian, passing through London. However, the Giza pyramid, which is located at the old Prime Meridian at Giza had perfectly delineated the movement of the sun and stars relative to the Earth's exact longitudinal axis. The location of the Giza pyramid at the ancient zero degrees longitude and latitude was a critical point of balance on Earth, which marks the convergence of metaphysical, celestial, and physical forces with the Earth's landmass's center of equilibrium along with Lake Victoria which is known as the Navel of the World. The message of harmony epitomized by the Great Pyramid also appears in most of the ancient Egyptian architecture.[36]

The ancients believed the living universe is a life force that animates physical reality. Indians on the subcontinent refer to this life force as prana. The Chinese refer to it as chi; the Greeks refer to it as ether or vitalism, and Quantum Physicists refer to it as the unity field or matrix. Plato's discourse on the Forms[37, 38] supports the idea of an invisible reality, which is more plausible than the material world. The forms exist in the universe independently of the physical world but are the basis for physical reality. Plato derived ideas on the Forms from Pythagoras, who mathematically systemized the wisdom of Egypt after his initiation into The Mysteries.

The ancient philosophy implies that humans directly access and experience higher levels of The Creation. The human body connects

34 Budge. E.A. Wallis. *The Book of the Dead.* p. 66..

35 Ibid. p. 45 chapter 153

36 Seiss Joseph. *Gospel in the Stars*, Available at: www.archive.org/details/ GospelInTheStarsSEISS/page/n1/mode/2up?form=MG0AV3

37 Havelock, A. Eric. Preface to Plato (History of the Greek Mind), p254.

38 www.africawithin.com/ani/excerpt_chap1.htm

directly to the cosmic net and receives and returns energy to the universe. Many of the original texts with references to ancient knowledge have disappeared. In the last 500 years, how human beings have come to view themselves as individuals, isolated from the universal consciousness and each other, is a radical departure from the original concept of the self as an integral part of a living universe. After the original inhabitants of Kemet had retreated from the large coastal cities and Greek pharaohs had ruled for three generations in the Hellenic era, the purpose of Kemetic spiritual objectives had diverged from its initial quest for everlasting life to achieving happiness. The change in ethics occurred as Greece's control of the trade routes in the Mediterranean region brought it considerable material wealth. A growing population gave rise to a class of educators known as Sophists, who profoundly influenced Athenian society. The Sophists introduced skepticism into the Greek culture, which began the trend of individualism and materialism. Under Alexander the Great, the communal gold stored in temples significantly financed Greece's military expansion. The Greeks advanced the cause of materialism and individualism and initiated the divergence from a prior age of spiritual righteousness and matrilineal society. However, while Greece has its place in history, it does not entirely displace Kemet, which even the Greeks acknowledged as the source of their wisdom and even their burial practices.

Chapter 3

The Origin of the Universe
Kemet's Creation Story

Western Rationalism emphasizes reason and intellect as the primary sources of knowledge. Based on René Descartes' rationalism and the scientific method, which emphasizes doubt and systemic reasoning, Western rationalism is sometimes cited as the only viable method of discerning reality. This exclusive mode of thought has often attributed key discoveries in the ancient world to Greece, overlooking the contributions of non-Western civilizations to the advancement of knowledge. History books have frequently perpetuated the belief that rationalization processes began with the ancient Greek rationalist philosophers, such as Socrates. Although ancient Greece was a significant hub of intellectual development, many of its philosophical and scientific concepts existed for thousands of years in other civilizations, such as those in Kemet, before being adopted by the Greeks.

In classical and Hellenistic Greek history (480–23 b.c.e.), which includes its conquest by Rome, many philosophical and scientific concepts that Western scholars automatically attribute to the Greeks originated in the Ancient Kemet (Egypt) 4,000 years prior. The Greek term philosophos, which translates directly to lovers of wisdom, originated from Kemet's mer-rekh (mr-rḫ) with identical translations. Without the work of the earliest sages who studied the first cause of creation, the most profound discoveries, such as the 25,920-year precession cycle, could not have occurred. The Pythagorean theorem emerged after Pythagoras studied in Kemet. Without his knowledge of the solution in the Rhind Mathematical Papyrus, it is questionable whether the theorem could have emerged when it did. Demonstrably, the sages of Kemet had found solutions to many mathematical problems, such as the 3.16 approximation of the value of π (pi) 4,000 years before the 3.14 value we have come to know.

The Zodiac derives from the precession cycle that could not be empirically verified had nature not fully revealed the entire cycle to Kemet. It is difficult to conclude that observations of the backward movement of the stars, revolving one degree every 72 years and observed over a short period, could result in a complete understanding of the entire precession cycle without the advanced, empirical data of the ancient Africans. A long list of innovations, including geometry, agriculture, monumental architecture, and medicine, could not have occurred as early as they did in Greece without the earliest studies that pointed the way. Nevertheless, biased research concludes that the idea for the Great Year is of Greek origin.

Thousands of years before the Greeks began their studies in Kemet, Africans had already resolved fundamental questions about reality. The origins of Kemet's creation story from Northeast Africa show that early humans, tens of thousands of years ago, hypothesized that the universe was a form of consciousness and that humans were a microcosm of a larger macrocosm. They concluded that an unknowable creator brought the universe into existence from nothing solely through the power of the mind. They revered the mother figure in various roles as creator and nurturer of life. They identified the nine parts of the soul, its functions, and its ultimate destination in the Pleiades in the northern sky. Amenta, where matter and spirit converge, and the sky meets the Earth on the horizon, evolved into a spiritual concept symbolizing inner peace. Similarly, concepts such as being and non-being, mother-father, and strong-weak are cognitively derived relationships that shape a unique perception of a reality composed of male and female forces. The belief that humans are connected to this universal consciousness and possess eternal life stems from ancient Kemetic metaphysics. This profound idea that humans have an immortal soul linked to universal consciousness has influenced every subsequent notion of the human relationship with the divine entity. Since the shift away from a pantheistic worldview, the concept of infinity is challenging for modern humans to grasp within a strict rationalist and empiricist framework.

> A hymn of praise to Osiris Un-Nefr, the great god who dweleth in Abtu, the King of eternity, the lord of everlasgingness, who tra-verseth millions of years in his existence.

> —E.A. Wassa budge translation

When Homo *sapiens* inevitably contemplated the sky, the lunar cycle became the most significant force deciphered. As early as 20,000 years ago, people in the Congo had derived number systems that they etched using lines on a femur bone of a baboon using an etching tool embedded in a wooden handle. The analytical thinking shown on the bone reveals the early human capacity to be proactive and create predictive models. Associating the lunar cycle with the menstrual period and fertility was a monumental leap that required such analytic thinking.

Ishango bone (20,000 b.c.e.), front and back—Discovered in the Democratic Republic of Congo by geologist Jean de Heinzelin de Braucourt. The markings represent clusters of various quantities that add up to even or odd numbers.

—Museum of Natural Sciences, Brussels.

The father figure, the great grandfather's reincarnation, became the pattern for the metaphysical concept of the infinite, unknowable lineage. *The Book of the Dead* states that The Father of the Creation is unknowable and is self-created. The people of Kemet derived a unique zoomorphic symbol using the male dung beetle's image pushing a round heap of dung containing its eggs to depict the self-created, creative energy that imbues all life. The male dung beetle is the exemplary zoomorphic representation of coming into being or Khepri. The Ra-Khepri symbol represents the creative energy that permeates all life. Ra has multiple aspects, but the most common depiction is the sun.

According to *The Book of the Dead*, the divine arose amid the chaos of the boundless primeval water. The divine primeval spirit, part of the primeval water, desired to begin the work of the creation. A passage from *The Book of the Dead* translates as follows:

> In the beginning, there existed neither heaven nor earth, and nothing existed except the boundless mass of primeval water which was shrouded in darkness and which contained within itself the germs and beginnings, male and female, of everything which was to be in the future world. The divine primeval spirit, which formed an essential part of the primeval matter, felt within itself the desire to begin the work of Creation, and its word woke to life the world, the form, and shape of which it had already depicted within itself. The first act of Creation began with the formation of an egg out of the primeval water, from which emerged Rā, the immediate cause of all life upon the earth. The almighty power of the divine spirit embodied itself in its most brilliant form in the rising sun. When the inert mass of primeval matter felt the desire of the primeval spirit to begin the work of Creation, it began to move, and the creatures were to constitute the future world were formed according to the divine intelligence *Maāt*.

> —*The Book of the Dead: The Hieroglyphic Transcript of the Papyrus of ANI.* Transl. by E.A. Wallis Budge. 1960. University Books, Inc., p. 119.

Benben stone from the Pyramid of Amenemhat III, Twelfth Dynasty. Egyptian Museum, Cairo.

The only conceivable means of creating the material world from nothing was through a conscious thought, which began with a desire. The creation followed irrevocable law as it emerged from the compressed and dormant seed that contained the essence of all things. The emphasis on order and logic in creation emphasized the ancient's high regard for Ma'at, the Goddess of law, and order, whose laws preside throughout the creation. As Ma'at was the creator's consort, her laws governed all aspects of creation.

The first stage of creation occurred with the transition from the chaotic and dormant phase to the first inkling of a conscious state described as Atum that settles on the mound known as the Benben stone.[1] The stone at the tops of pyramids and obelisks represents the mound referenced in ancient metaphysics as the universe's beginning. African Cosmogony organizes the forces of nature into male and female pairs. The self-begotten father and his consciousness are the first pair that tasks Atum with beginning the creation and bringing into being the male-female pairs of the Grand Ennead. Shu, the male energy that keeps the celestial waters above from inundating all life, is symbolized by the lion—the earliest representation of strength and power. Before there could be any life, Shu had to keep the sky separated from the Earth. In the pantheon of the neteru, Shu pairs with the female counterpart, Tefnut, the Goddess of moisture. Together, they create Nut (sky), Geb (Earth), and their offspring Ausar (Osiris), Auset (Isis), Set, and Nephthys. At times, Horus, the offspring of Isis and Osiris, is included as the ninth member of the Ennead.

Following the Grand Ennead, the preparation for the emergence of humanity begins with Ausar (water), followed by Auset (fertile earth), Set (fire), and Nephthys (wind). Heru, the son of Auset, was born of an immaculate conception and was the model for Divine Kingship as the first divine king who linked humanity to the father of creation. *The Bremner-Rhind Papyrus,* Book III, *Book of Overthrowing Apep*, from the 4th century B.C.E. housed in the British Museum, is the most explicit represen-

---

1   Massey, Gerald. *Ancient Egypt, the Light of the World*, p. 270.

tation of Kemetic Cosmogony. While the papyrus is from the Ptolemaic era, the ideas are from the Old Kingdom, 3rd Dynasty to the 6th Dynasty, or c. 2686 – 2181 B.C.E. The sources of these texts extend tens of thousands of years back to when ancient Africans created zoomorphic forms as representations of complex abstract concepts. The ancient endeavor to explain the universe's origin is the first occurrence of Natural Philosophy that the ancients defined as the study of the first cause of creation.[2] The zoomorphic forms in the ancient cosmogony do not imply that the people of Kemet worshiped animals or were polytheistic. On the contrary, they saw in nature the supernatural forces, or neteru, that they referenced using specific animal forms with the observed characteristics of the neteru.

The most prominent of Kemet's cosmogony is from its capital city, Memphis. The accepted founding date of the city in 3,100 B.C.E. marks the date of the unification of Kemet, although there is ample evidence that it had existed much earlier. Archaeological discoveries indicate that the Egyptians rebuilt Memphis multiple times as the Nile shifted its banks away from the encroaching desert sand.[3] The theology of Memphis is about the creative force Atum, who undertakes the actual work of creating the universe using the laws of Ma'at.

The Memphite Theology, which refers to the creation, is the oldest surviving theology from a primary source dated back to 4,266 B.C.E. The Nubian Pharaoh Shabaka (705–690 B.C.E) preserved the document by copying the original worm-eaten papyrus onto the stone artifact that bears his name. The Memphite Theology is the oldest known example of a natural philosophy that acknowledges one father of the creation and establishes the beginning of life in the universe. It states that all life is similar to Atum and that Atum's form flows through all living things, giving them shared characteristics of the heart and mouth or (word). According to chapter 20 of the Shabaka stone translation:

> There took shape in the heart, there took shape on the tongue the form of Atum. For the very great one is Ptah, who gave [life] to all the gods and their kas through this heart and through this tongue, in which Horus had taken shape as Ptah, in which Thoth had taken shape as Ptah.
>
> Thus heart and tongue rule over all the limbs in accordance with the teaching that it (the heart, or: he, Ptah) is in every body and it (the tongue, or: he Ptah) is in every mouth of all gods, all men, all cattle, all creeping things, whatever lives,

---

2 Natural philosophy or the philosophy of nature (from Latin *philosophia naturalis*) was the philosophical study of nature and the physical universe that was dominant before the development of modern science. It is considered to be the precursor of natural sciences.

3 Bernal, Martin. *Black Athena,* p. 28.

thinking whatever it (or: he) wishes and commanding whatever it (or: he) wishes.

Sight, hearing, breathing—they report to the heart, and it makes every understanding come forth. As to the tongue, it repeats what the heart has devised. Thus, all the gods were born and his Ennead was completed. For every word of the god came about through what the heart devised and the tongue commanded.

—M. Lichtheim: *Ancient Egyptian Literature*, Vol.1, pp.51-55

Observations and accumulated knowledge about the celestial sphere resulted in a practical science that produced the world's first accurate calendar and metaphysical concepts such as *transmutation, regeneration,* and *salvation.* In *The Divine Pymander of Hermes Mercurius Trismegistus,* the Egyptian Philosopher, explains the ancient view that "no man can be saved before regeneration."[4] The discourse in Pymander, written in hieroglyphics, is strikingly similar to the Sermon of Jesus on the Mount.[5] The concept of regeneration began in the African mapping of the sun's cyclical pattern, culminating in the December Solstice on the 21st, signifying the idea of regeneration after death.

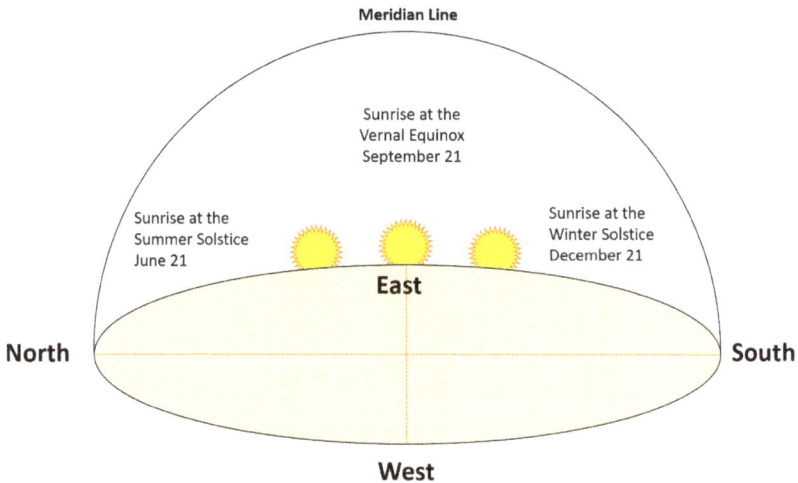

Position of the Sun during Equinoxes and Solstices at the latitude of Giza at sunrise. On the Summer Solstice, the Sun rises at the furthest points to the Northeast, and on the Winter Solstice, it rises in the opposite southeast extremity before it reverses. The midpoint, which is due East, measures the Equinox.

4   Massey, Gerald. *Ancient Egypt: The Light of the World*, p. 822
5   John 2:18—3:19. (3) Most truly I say to you, Unless anyone is born again, he cannot see the kingdom of God.

At sunrise, the sun's position on the horizon, each day from December 22-24th, moves further towards the south. On the third day, its advance stops and seems to die symbolically. However, it is reborn on the 25[th,] as its position at sunrise each day reverses direction and proceeds towards the north. The Earth's movement relative to the sun as it appears over the horizon over several days is a Kemetic concept symbolizing the savior Heru-ur's (Heru the elder's) rebirth.

The celestial observations that tracked the heliacal rise[6] of the star Sopdet (Sirius) on the horizon also led to the discovery of the 1,460-year cycle that the Romans named the Sothic Cycle. Sopdet is the brightest star in the east. It is prominently featured in folklore as the messenger that appears before December 25 in its significant alignment with three stars of Orion's belt, as the star of the annunciation. The Greeks and Romans changed Sopdet to Sothis and Sirius, respectively. The alignment of Sopdet on December 25 marks the virgin birth of the divine King Heru, who brings the light of salvation to humanity.[7] The allegory of Auset, Ausar, and Heru has recurred throughout history. In India, Isis's Immaculate Conception and the Virgin birth of the male child, Heru, are the same as the story of Krishna. The most recent of these historical recurrences is the biblical account of the virgin birth, death, and resurrection of Jesus Christ. We know there are 24 hours of the day because African people tracked the Sun (Heru), measured its passing, and depicted the twelve hours of daylight and twelve of the night using the twenty-four coils of the snake Apophis. The Kemetic idea of spiritual rebirth also derives from the renewal process in the Nile River's seasonal inundation and the beginning of the growing season.

Sopdet (Sirus) in the lower-left aligns with the three stars in Orions belt on December 25 and marks the rebirth of the savior.

---

6   The heliacal rising of a star occurs annually when it first becomes visible above the eastern horizon for a brief moment just before sunrise, after a period of time when it had not been visible.
7   Massey, Gerald. *The Natural Genesis*. Williams and Norgate, 1883, p 438.

Western Adoption of Egyptian Concepts

When the pre-Socratic philosophers traveled to Kemet to study the mysteries, Greece did not exist as a nation. Western historians place the beginning of ancient Greek history at 1,100 B.C.E. However, there was no unified Greek nation. Before Alexander the Great, Scholarly discussions by the pre-Socratic Greek philosophers occurred when the area was not united but consisted of independent and warring city-states—Mycenae, Minoa, Macedonia, Athens, and Thebes. The unification of these city-states in 337 B.C.E. created the Greek nation that lasted until the Roman conquest in 146 B.C.E. The philosophers Heraclitus and Pythagoras of the pre-Socratic era were not Greek but were from Iona (Asia Minor) and the island of Samos, respectively. Pythagoras's philosophical extrapolations on the transmigration of the soul are those of Kemet.[8] Although he had traveled widely throughout the Mediterranean, acquiring knowledge of the mysteries and seeking wisdom from other mystery systems in the Mediterranean region, his primary goal was to study in Kemet because he knew it was the center of learning. Pythagoras modeled his academic institution in Crotone, Southern Italy, after Kemet's mystery schools. He went as far as mimicking Kemet's secrecy and dedication to upholding the ancient cosmogony.

Pythagoras receives credit for discovering the Pythagorean theorem, harmonics, and universal application in music, architecture, medicine, and ethics. The Pythagoreans used numerical and geometric concepts to illustrate the unity and supreme importance of the One or the Monad. They devised *The Pythagorean Pentacle,* representing the soul's transmutation. Nevertheless, Pythagoras' familiarity with these ideas shows that he was aware of the Kemetic concepts that predated his arrival in Egypt. In *Stolen Legacy,* author George Granville Monah James states that:

> Another noticeable characteristic of Greek philosophy is the fact that most of the Greek philosophers used the teachings of Pythagoras as their model; and consequently they have introduced nothing new in the field of philosophy. Included in the Pythagorean system we find the doctrines of (a) opposites (b) Harmony (c) Fire (d) Mind, since it is composed of fire atoms, (e) Immortality, expressed as transmigration of Souls, (f) The Summum Bonum or the purpose of philosophy. And these of course are reflected in the systems of Heraclitus, Parmenides, Democritus, Socrates, Plato and Aristotle.

> — George G.M. James, Ph.D, *Stolen Legacy*

---

8   Transmigration refers to the cycle of reincarnation. Salvation according to ancient Egyptian cosmogony is the cycle of birth, death and rebirth that results in achieving a purity that makes the soul worthy of interacting with God.

The questions "What is there?" and "What is it like?" reputedly gave rise to Western Philosophy and led to profound insights into the fundamental nature of reality. However, theories such as the Theory of Atomism, attributed to two pre-Socratic philosophers, Leucippus and Democritus, are more aptly a derivative of the Kemetic doctrine of opposites. In Stolen Legacy, G.M. James posits that the Egyptians viewed the soul as composed of various elements, including atoms of the human soul and fire atoms of the universal soul.[9] Democritus' interpretation of atoms early on shows an acceptance of a purely material world. He sees these atoms as permanent aspects of the material world—odorless, colorless particles of various sizes existing in the *emptiness,* allowing them to be perpetually in motion.

Democritus' use of the term fire-atoms is similar to Kemet's knowledge of the soul's composition as a fire that ascends to the celestial regions where it originated. In the passage below, the author cites these concepts as Egyptian-conceived ones that connect the immortal human soul and the cosmic soul of the universe.[10]

> In death, the personality disappears, the senses also disappear; but the atoms live on for ever. The heavier atoms descend to the earth: but the soul atoms, which are composed of fire, ascend to the celestial regions, whence they came.

— George G.M. James, Ph.D, *Stolen Legacy.* 1954, p. 66

In his definition of reality, Democritus overlooked the knowledge that space was not empty but permeated by divine consciousness. His idea of *nothingness* had diverged from understanding consciousness as the fundamental construct of the universe. Democritus's atomist construct lasted until quantum mechanics replaced Newtonian Physics in the 20th century with Albert Einstein's confirmation of the quantum hypothesis that quantum particles make up light.

The Divine Trinity and Wisdom Cross

The works of the pre-Socratic philosophers and Plato are the most comprehensive reinterpretation of ancient philosophy. They are closely associated with an independent Kemet and The Mysteries' original objectives. Pythagoras was the last of the Pre-Socratic philosophers to attend the mysteries school in Thebes (Diospolis in Greek) in an independent Kemet before the Persian conquest (525 B.C.E.) He was allowed access to the

---

9   G.M. James. *Stolen Legacy*, p. 65-75.
10   ———. Ibid. 1954, p. 90

school only after undergoing a rigorous spiritual cleansing, which realigned his strict intellectual focus to a Kemetic perspective that demanded a lived experience as the only viable learning methodology. After studying for 22 years, the Pharaoh Amasis, the last ruler before the Persian conquest, approved his initiation into the Mystery School.

After its conquest, the plundering of Kemet's treasures and sacred documents led to the repurposing and reinterpretation of Kemet's sacred science. The plagiarizing and reinterpretation of these documents and secret knowledge taken from Kemet's temples, without the necessary rigorous initiation rites associated with the mysteries, resulted in erroneous translations and half-truths. From the early years of Plato and Aristotle, one had to study the Mysteries for up to 44 years in Kemet. However, after the Greek conquest, the Mysteries school initiation rites occurred on an accelerated schedule after seven years. The rejection of the Kemetic preference for a lived experience of its initiates and its aversion to writing the nation's secrets occurred as Greek rulers ordered Egyptian priests to compile and record their knowledge. Under orders from Ptolemy I, the High Priest Manetho was the first to write the history of Kemet, including a complete list of its kings. Most of Manetho's volumes perished in the burning of the Library of Alexandria.

Translations of some of Egypt's secrets into Greek set the course for modern Europeans' absorption and reformulation of philosophy and science. Greek sophists adopted a functional approach, taking what they needed from Egypt for mundane and worldly purposes. Their narrow and practical approach to teaching the mysteries precipitated a distortion of the divine purpose of the Lodge Educational System. For example, the Pythagorean theorem, widely credited to Pythagoras, was commonly known in the ancient world of Babylon and Kemet. The Greek essayist Plutarch describes the Egyptian knowledge of the process, which modern historians redefined as the Pythagorean theorem:

> "The upright, therefore, may be likened to the male, the base to the female, and the hypotenuse to the child of both, and so Ausar may be regarded as the origin, Auset as the recipient, and Heru as perfected result. 3 is the first perfect odd number, 4 is a square whose side is the even number 2, but 5 is in some ways like its father and in some ways like its mother, being made up of 3 and 2."

—Plutarch's Moralia Volume 5. By Plutarch, Frank Cole Babbitt, 1927

Plutarch has also simultaneously described the widespread African symbolism, which ascribes gender and numerology to a Divine Trinity of father-mother-child. Freemasons have also confided that Pythagoras's theorem is a derivative of Kemet's Divine Trinity and Wisdom Cross, a symbol from their ancient tradition. If we assume that no such mathematical formula existed in Egypt, it would be correct to attribute to Pythagoras his rationalization of the secrets he had learned in Kemet or Babylon. His work resulted in a mathematical equation easily replicated on paper without the essential Kemetic symbolism. Pythagoras's triangle, consisting of two sides of lengths 3 and 4 that form a third side, referred to as the hypotenuse of five, was a significant symbol in Kemet.

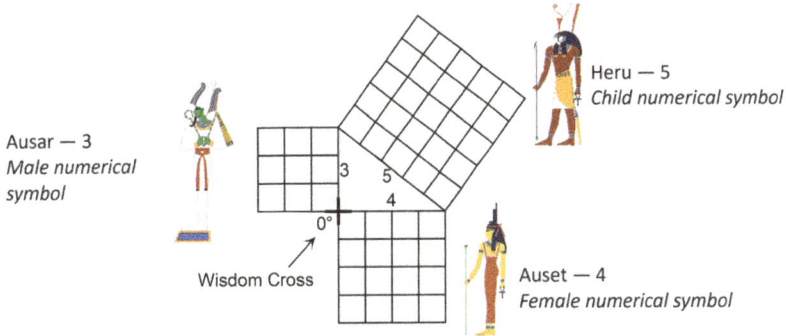

Heru — 5
Child numerical symbol

Ausar — 3
Male numerical symbol

Auset — 4
Female numerical symbol

Wisdom Cross

Father-Mother-Child grouping: The Egyptian concept of the Divine Trinity and the Wisdom Cross

The hypotenuse of the triangle equals the square of the base plus the square of the height. All masons are familiar with this essential method used in constructing square corners, although it lacks the original spiritual connotation depicted above. The methodology was indispensable in producing the most accurately squared building ever created—the Great Pyramid, situated at the ancient zero degrees meridian mark, the exact geodetic center of the Earth.

Other commonly attributed Greek discoveries, such as the platonic solids, are from a much older tradition. The key to these solids is inscribed on the temple wall at the antediluvian temple of Osiris at Abydos. The Platonic solids are all traceable within the form of the Seed of Life—the Kemetic lotus flower. In reality, an inscription in the coffin text, as it relates to Atum, describes creation in terms of the seed of life shown in the figure on page 52:

I am One that transforms into Two
I am Two that transforms into Four
I am Four that transforms into Eight
After this I am One

— (Coffin of Petamon, Cairo Museum no: 1160)

As shown above, the progression from unity to multiplicity and back to unity, depicts a fractal. The egg division in the womb follows a similar

Illustration of the Coffin Text

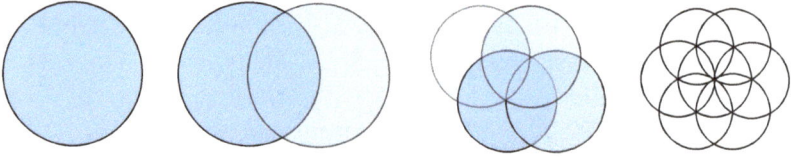

The Seed of Life derived from the text in the Coffin of Petamon. The 5 Platonic Solids can be derived by connecting the various nodes in the seed of life where the circles intersect.

pattern. The division into two, four, and eight parts result in a new life representing unity. The lesson revealed in sacred geometry is that the universe is a consistent and structured progression in the abstract and material worlds. During the influx of Greeks into Kemet, Sacred Geometry that linked the world of spirit and human beings became devoid of its spiritual connotation. Platonic solids became meaningless forms, separated from their sacred meaning. In architecture, principles of harmony and proportion became functional tools used to achieve arbitrary aesthetic objectives.

The advanced architectural methods that eloquently depict The Divine Man of the ancient Egyptians at the Temple of Luxor became repurposed to pay homage to the Greek ideals of beauty, heroism and war. As Greece militarily and politically dominated the Mediterranean basin under the rule of Alexander the Great, the Greeks dissociated the newly acquired customs of Egypt from its original spiritual mission. They derived the Parthenon in 495 B.C.E. from Egypt's Luxor temple constructed in 1,400 B.C.E.[11] as a symbolic representation of the Divine Man to suit the newfound ideals of Greece's patriarchal society. Kemet had experienced thousands of years of spiritual tradition, evident in their intricate but functional temple designs dedicated to their profound metaphysical concepts.[12] Greeks repurposed these ideas of temple construction to serve as a home for Athena, the Goddess of wisdom and warfare. She epitomized the female sexual purity required by the Greek patriarchal society. The Parthenon's proportions have survived as a testament to the Greek aesthetic ideals. However, as ancient Greeks buried their dead and looked forward to the final judgment and transmutation of the soul, their burial practices reminded the modern world that adopting Egyptian religious beliefs was the ultimate homage they could pay Kemet.

---

11   See Schwaller deLubicz: The temple Of Man. P. 113.
12   The pillars of the Egyptian temples represented the 9 planets. (from Stolen Legacy)

The Structure of the Universe
The Genesis of Cosmology

In the 25th and 24th centuries, B.C.E., Ra's universal, creative force was one of the most revered symbols in Kemetic society. Approximately 75 aspects of Ra are all neteru who participated in the creation.[13] Ra ruled over the three spheres of reality—the sky, Earth, and the underworld. As the scarab beetle (Khepri), Ra was the epitome of divine Kemetic consciousness. Ra, as the sun, became the symbol of regeneration, a universal symbol of love, and the source of all energy flowing through the universe. Ra's ultimate representation is the link to Atum, the father of creation, as Atum-Ra. These varying pairs of Ra's forms do not signify different gods but imply that Ra's energy imbues these forms.

In the unfolding universe, one force precedes all others. The ancient texts acknowledge that the self-created force is unknowable except by the attributes existing in the universe. In the unique African tradition, the creator is a male force, and his creation, the universe, is female. Africans recognize him as Atum, Atmu, Atem, or Tem. The *Book of the Dead* describes Him as possessing a dual soul, a Khu (heart), and Ba that manifests in the nun.[14] The nun contained all aspects of the universe in its seed form of undifferentiated mass. The Dogon, who trace their ancestry to ancient Kemet and who possess ancient knowledge, describe *Amma,* shown below, as the densest material possible and the dormant state of the universe.

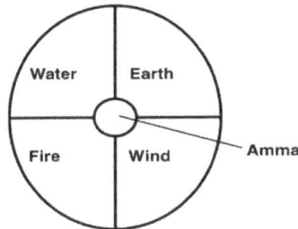

The descriptions of the beginning and structuring of the universe differ according to its city of origin. The cosmology existed in four different cities, each with its variation of the neteru. The two most famous centers of religious thought were Hermopolis (the city of Toth) and Heliopolis (the City of the Sun). These forces in the figure shown

---

13   Gadalla, Moustfa. *Egyptian Cosmology: the Animated Universe*, p. 70.
14   Book of the Dead, p. 113–120.

below combined to form the cosmic egg from which Intelligence (Tehuti or Toth) is born.

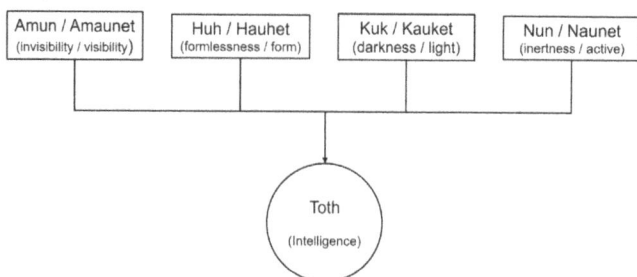

Amun / Amaunet	Huh / Hauhet	Kuk / Kauket	Nun / Naunet
(invisibility / visibility)	(formlessness / form)	(darkness / light)	(inertness / active)

Toth

(Intelligence)

The Ogdoad of Hermopolis: In the cosmology of Hermopolis that dates back to the Old Kingdom, the four pairs of the primordial forces of creation (the Ogdoad), categorized by male/female pairs, are Amun-Amaunet (invisibility and visibility), Huh-Hauhet (formlessness–form); Kuk-Kauket (darkness–light); Nun–Naunet (inertness–active).

In the cosmology of Heliopolis shown below, dryness and moisture are the first pair of neteru to emerge in the creation. They are the intermediaries that created Nut–Geb (sky and earth). The union of Nut and Geb produced four children—Set, representing fire; Ausar (Osiris), meaning water; Auset (Isis), representing the fertile earth; and Nebt-Het (Nephthys), representing wind.[15] These eight deities, including Atum, comprised the Grand Enneads of the material world, observed at Heliopolis.

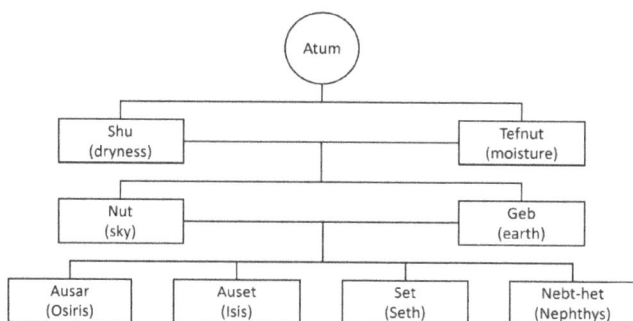

Atum

Shu (dryness)		Tefnut (moisture)

Nut (sky)		Geb (earth)

Ausar (Osiris)	Auset (Isis)	Set (Seth)	Nebt-het (Nephthys)

The Enneads of Heliopolis, showing the elements before the creation of Heru. Ausar (water), Auset (earth, Set (fire), and Nebt-Het (wind).

Natural Processes as the Beginning of Structure

Knowledge of the universe's structure began with observing natural phenomena. As the sun had perilously disappeared in the underworld and

---

15   *The Book of the Dead*, pp. 118-120.

reappeared on the horizon at dawn, it further validated Heru as the savior. Heru vanquishes the darkness with his redeeming light. In the pre-historic pantheon of the neteru, Heru is also synonymous with a continuous natural process of combining water, earth, air, and fire. Ausar (Osiris), as the embodiment of agriculture and the power responsible for moisture and renewal, is often depicted pictorially with a figure pouring water on 28 stalks of wheat growing out of his resting body. Auset (Isis), like the great mother Earth, is the healer and Goddess of fertility, who is the more critical deity and the kingmaker who gives birth to Heru. The Greek historian Plutarch writes in Moralia, Volume V:

> The Egyptians simply give the name of Ausar (water) to the whole source and faculty creative of moisture, believing this to be the cause of generation and the substance of life-producing seed; and the name of Set (fire) they give to all that is dry, fiery, and arid, in general, and antagonistic to moisture.
>
> As the Egyptians regard the Nile as the effusion of Ausar; so they hold and believe the earth to be the body of Auset, not all of it, but so much of it as the Nile covers, fertilizing it and uniting with it. From this union, they make Heru to be born. The all-conserving and fostering Hora, that is the seasonable tempering of the surrounding air, is Heru.
>
> The insidious scheming and usurpation of Set, then, is the power of drought, which gains control and dissipates the moisture which is the source of the Nile and of its rising.
>
> —Plutarch. Moralia, Vol. V

Over thousands of years of reference to the natural processes controlling their lives, African priests immortalized the trinity of Ausar, Auset, and her son, Heru. In Kemetic cosmology, the story concerns the creation of Mankind after the creation of the four primordial essences. The tale of Auset and Ausar follows the African tradition of ascribing duality and gender to each deity. The matriarchal tradition honors the feminine aspect of the creation and presents Auset as more potent than Ausar's male figure. To Auset, they ascribed the powers of magic, fertility, motherhood, healing, and rebirth. Auset resurrects her dead husband, and humanity receives the gift of salvation through her child, Heru. He conquers his enemy, the evil Set, to maintain the natural order and bring the redeeming light to humankind.

In cosmic reality, the battle between Heru and his uncle Set occurs when natural forces are in opposition, whether day and night, during seasonal changes, or during the lunar eclipse when the moon obscures the solar disc (Heru). Thus, ancient cosmology relays the connection of Heru to the fabric of the universe—the celestial waters—as he floods the world with light.

> The evil Apap, who drinks the water cubit by cubit at each gulp as the sun goes down, is slain by Heru at daybreak, when he once more sets free the waters of light which are designated the waters of dawn.[16]

Heru, as the child of Isis and Osiris, forms a triadic relationship consisting of mother-father-child. Thus, the child Heru is the first known symbol of resurrection. Symbolically, Heru was the pharaonic principle dedicated to upholding the natural order and the laws of Ma'at.

Precession of the Vernal Equinoxes, the Basis of the Zodiac

One of the most significant archaeological finds in Africa that reveals the ancient knowledge of the universe's structure and the Earth's position is the site at Nabta Playa in Egypt, near the Sudan border. The site is on the Tropic of Cancer north of the equator. On the Summer solstice, which occurs in the Northern hemisphere on June 21, the shadows of the stones disappear entirely as the sun's rays are directly overhead. The site was a significant point where humans from a vast region of Northeast Africa converged ceremonially for thousands of years. Researchers from Southern Methodist University, Texas, determined that humans had occupied the site from 12,000 B.C.E. to 6,500 B.C.E.[17] Egyptologist Robert Bauval later determined that the site was one of the earliest models of the cycle of precession. The Egyptians delineated these constellations using 12 Zodiac signs. Beneath the monument are several more layers of stone that refer to earlier times and history when Africans tracked the heavens.

Nabta Playa is the earliest archaeological evidence of a sophisticated cosmology in North East Africa that accounts for the sun and Earth's movement relative to the 12 constellations delineated by ancient Africans in the Zodiac. The ancient astronomers discovered the cycle[18]

---

16   Massey, Gerald. *Ancient Egypt Light of the World.* Book 9. p.547.
17   Fred Wendorf, Southern Methodist University Texas. Available at: www.wysinger.homestead. com/nabtaplaya.html
18   The Secret Calendar Codes: 2012 in the Cosmic Cycle of Time. Youtube. http://www.authorstream. com/Presentation/caterinas-427172-calendars-mankind-6-21-spiritual-inspirational-ppt-powerpoint/

Nabta Playa "calendar circle", reconstructed at Aswan Nubia museum

Source:By Raymbetz – CC BY-SA 3.0, https://commons.wikimedia.org/w/index.php?curid=7525976

while observing the sunrise each year in March at the spring equinox. Every 72 years, they would have noticed a 1-degree change in the constellations' position just before dawn until the cycle concluded after 25,920 years. This 360-degree cycle divides into the 12 Zodiac signs bearing the name of the constellations. Each of the 12 signs, observed and recorded, lasts 2,160 years. As they passed over the Giza plateau horizon, the constellations would have appeared to shift backward. For example, Taurus, the bull, would give way to Aries, the lamb, followed by Pisces, which preceded the dawn of Christianity with its antediluvian fish symbol.

The Ages of Man

The northern ecliptic, or The Pleiades, divides into seven sections that correlate in number to Man's sevenfold psychological and physical nature. The ancient Greeks had a similar classification but with five divisions or ages. The Great Pyramid marks Earth's position relative to the North Pole of the Ecliptic (NOPE) at zero degrees longitude using the north star Thuban (Alpha Draconis) in the Pleiades that lined up with the Earth's ecliptic when the pyramids were built. The Egyptians designated the Pleiades as the soul's destination because it is the most stable section of the sky. The Pleiades configuration and cycle relate to seven aspects of the soul that unify into the eighth *unit* of perfection, signifying the Christ within each individual. From Kemet and India to the Druids in England, many ancient cultures acknowledge seven aspects of the soul, mirrored by the stars in the northern sky. Six ecliptic stars are visible, and the seventh position is open space.

The cycle delineated by seven sections in the northern sky is a sec-
ondary component of the larger, more critical precession cycle. While
the Kemites associated each section of the Pleiades with a specific soul
quality, the Greeks associated only five stars with *The Ages of Man.* Each
of these five stars marks historical periods when human social evolution
moved from a Golden Age toward a Silver, Bronze, Heroic, or Iron Age.
The Greek Golden Age is a period of enlightenment and righteousness.
The Silver Age is impiety and dependence, and the Bronze Age is an age
of protracted wars. The Heroic Age signifies an improvement over the
Bronze Age of war, and the Iron Age is an age of pain and suffering.

Kemet marked their precession cycle's first sign as Leo and designated
it as The Golden Age, which they last experienced around 12,500 B.C.E.
when the pole star was Vega. They named their first golden age Zep Tepi, or
"The First Time," when humanity was in touch with the divine and Osiris
ruled over Kemet. Historical proof exists of at least one referenced changing of the pole star when half of the cycle of precession had concluded:

> *The Book of the Dead* (chs. 114 and 123) not only proves the ancient Egyptians
> to have been acquainted with the precessional movement, it also gives us an
> account of the actual changing of a pole-star. . . . There is a change in the
> position of the Maat, or judgment-hall, which in the stellar mythos was at the
> station of the pole, and was shifted with the shifting pole.
>
> —Gerald Massey. *Ancient Egypt, the Light of the World.* p. 582.

> In the Great year of precession, there are seven stations of the celestial pole,
> six of which are still identifiable in the constellations of Draconis, the Lesser
> Bear, Kepheus, Cygnus, Lyra, and Herakles. The pole changes, and its position
> is approximately determined by another central star about each 3,700 years.
>
> —Ibid. p. 580.

The 3,700-year duration of each of the seven Ages of Man, attributed
to Plato and Hipparchus in 160 B.C.E., is more extended than all the
Greek history. Herodotus wrote of the antiquity of African civilization
in *Histories*:

> Thus far went the record given me by the Egyptians and their priests; and
> they showed me that the time from the first king to that priest of Hephaestus,
> who was the last, covered three hundred and forty-one generations of men,
> and that in this time such also had been the number of kings, and of their

high priests. How three hundred generations make up ten thousand years, three generations being equal to a century. And over and above the three hundred the remaining forty-one cover thirteen hundred and forty years. Thus the whole sum is eleven thousand three hundred and forty years; in all which time (they said) they had no king who was a god in human form, nor had there been any such thing before or after those years among the rest of the kings of Egypt. Four times in this period (so they told me) the sun rose contrary to this wont; twice he rose where he now sets, and twice he set where now he rises; yet Egpyt at these times underent no change, neither in the produce of the river and the land, nor in the matter of sickness and death. . . .

. . . Of all this the Egytptians claim to have certain knowledge, seeing that they had always reckoned the years and chronicled them in writing.

—Herodotus, *Histories* Bk. 2, 142; 145

Drawing from the source Herodotus's *Histories,* Gerald Massey writes:

When Herodotus was in Egypt, the "mystery teachers of the heavens" told him that during a certain length of time which had been reckoned by the Egyptian astronomers, "the sun had four times risen out of his usual quarter; that he had twice risen where he now sets, and twice set where he now rises. Yet, that no change in the things of Egypt had been occasioned by this, either in the production of the earth 'or the river.'" And he adds, the Egyptians say, they know these things with accuracy because they always compute and register the years (B. 2, 142 and 145). Now there is no cycle in astronomy, save the circle of the precessional movement in which the phenomena thus unwittingly described by the faithful old chronicler could occur. One such cycle is certain, two are not improbable, and three are possible. After long study of the whole matter one sees perforce that the science of astronomy in Egypt, with its observed and registered cycle or cycles in precession, is actually older than any race of men on earth outside of Africa.

—Gerald Massey.[19]

Modern science has attributed the discovery of Precession to Hipparchus, who died in 120 B.C.E. Here, as in the cases of many other inventions and findings, the work of the ancient founders of civilization is attributed to those living outside of Africa tens of thousands of years

---

19 *Ancient Egypt, Light of the World*, by Gerald Massey. pp. 581-582.

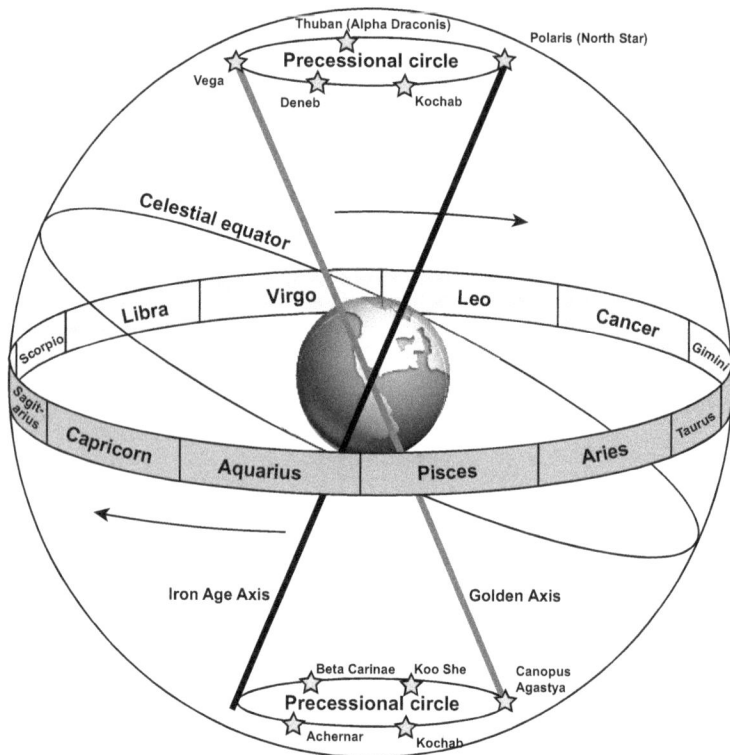

The Precession Cycle illustrated in a Vedic Geocentric Model of the Earth.

later. The evidence is overlooked or presumed not to exist. Ironically, the Great Year, which modern astrology renamed the Platonic Year, is based on Plato's references to the backward movement of the constellations in a conjectured 36,000-year cycle. Plato's life was more than 51 thousand years after ancient Africans had concluded the first of two observations of the 25,920-year cycle of precession that gave them their perfect Zodiac. In reality, Egypt's understanding of precession allowed them to know the beginning of the age of Pisces and to predetermine the fish symbols of Christianity. The Egyptians are known to have commemorated the new age in Alexandria. In reference to the Great Year, Massey writes:

> In the course of Precession, about 255 B.C.E., the vernal birthplace passed into the sign of the Fishes, and the Messiah who had been represented for 2,155 years by the Ram or Lamb, and previously for other 2,155 years

by the Apis Bull, was now imaged as the Fish, or the "Fish-man," called Ichthys in Greek. The original Fish-man--the An of Egypt, and the Oan of Chaldea--probably dates from the previous cycle of precession, or 26,000 years earlier; . . . [20]

The Age of Pisces was set for 2,155 with the birth of the mythical Christ, born as Ichtys in 255 B.C.E. According to Massey, the Age of Pisces ended in 1900. Humanity moved into the Age of Aquarius, the sign of the Waterman, in 1901. Massey writes that Equinoctial Christolatry has falsified the time of the world.[21] Nevertheless, even with the 255 or 2160-year inconsistency in the time-lapse, the world now believes that the concept of precession, which lasts for 25,920 years, fits logically into the theory of Precession's Greek origin based on Greek Rationalism.

Author Sir Norman Lockyer in *The Dawn of Astronomy: A Study of the Temple-Worship and Mythology of the Ancient Egyptians*, reveals conclusive evidence of the ancient Egyptians' knowledge of precession and shows how they aligned their temples to point at the spot on the horizon where they knew a star would rise each night. Lockyer explains that major Egyptian temples are aligned to the rising point of particular stars, and due to precession, this rising point changed over time, as did the orientation of temples. The Egyptians had built older temples that pointed to the stars at earlier times, such as at Dendera and Karnak, whose foundations lay beneath the later temples.[22]

The Ancient Texts

The oldest known funerary inscriptions are the Pyramid Texts recorded on pyramid walls at Saqqara 2350–2175 B.C.E. Like the Pyramid Texts, the Papyrus of Ani is a funerary rite of passage known as *The Book of Coming Forth by Light*. Both archaeological references depict the transference of consciousness from the living world to the afterlife. The inscriptions in the Pyramid Texts are dated to 2500 B.C.E. by the written reference in the tomb of Queen Khnem-nefert, wife of Mentu-hetep. Although the document's date is ancient, its origins predate the unification of Kemet. They are

---

20 Massey Lectures.pdf. p. 9. Available at: https://ia800304.us.archive.org/16/items/GeraldMassey-Lectures/GeraldMassey-lectures.pdf
21 Massey, Gerald. *The Historical Jesus and The Mythical Christ*. p. 184–185.
22 Lockyer, Norman, J. The Dawn of Astronomy. Available at: www.gutenberg.org/cache/epub/64849/pg64849-images.html

copies from a more remote era predating the 1ˢᵗ Dynasty,[23] 4,266 B.C.E. Thus, while the reference to this document is from 2,500 B.C.E, it was already an ancient document to the ancient Africans who possessed it. Its discovery in Antiquity places the written documentation of the Kemetic spiritual tradition at least six thousand years ago. Due to its complexity, the concept conceivably originated more than ten thousand years ago in the Neolithic era. That era marked the development of the essential elements of civilization, such as settled life, plant cultivation, animal domestication, pottery, sophisticated stone tools, metallurgy, and cosmology, that sought to explain the empirical world and man's place in it.

Faith as the Driving Mechanism of the Evolution of Spiritual, Social, and Philosophical Percepts

The early humans were undoubtedly awed by the creation from the outset and left a profound legacy about the species. Before the last migrations out of Africa and during humanity's isolation on the continent, the belief that humans are both physical and spiritual undoubtedly became hardwired in our genes. The idea of the spiritual nature of Homo sapiens arose from the belief that consciousness is the underlying structure of the universe. At the core of this understanding is a value system mirrored throughout creation. The *anima mundi,* or cosmic soul, is a macrocosm, and the human soul, a microcosm, both originate from one source of Divine consciousness.[24] Humanity fits into the structure of creation through the elaborate construction of the soul. That aspect of reality exists independently of the physical world, and as the human soul is an extension of the fabric of universal consciousness, it is immortal. Kemet named the eternal part of the soul, the *Ba,* and the spirit,

---

23   "The Book of the Dead", pp. 7-8. "The Wisdom of the Egyptians, Edited, and with an introduction by Brian Brown. New York: Brentano's 1923. --A hieratic inscription upon the sarcophagus of Queen Khnem-nefert, wife of Mentu-hetep, a king of the eleventh dynasty, c.2500 b.c., states that a certain chapter of the Book of the Dead was discovered in the reign of Hesep-ti, the fifth king of the first dynasty, who flourished about 4266 b.c. This sarcophagus affords us two copies of the said chapter, one immediately following the other. That as early as 2500 b.c. a chapter of the Book of the Dead should be referred to a date almost 2000 years before that time is astounding, and the mind reels before the idea of a tradition which, during comparatively unlettered centuries, could have conserved a religious formula almost unimpaired. Thus thirty-four centuries ago a portion of the Book of the Dead was regarded as extremely ancient, mysterious, and difficult of comprehension. It will be noted also that the inscription on the tomb of Queen Khnem-nefert bears out that the chapter in question was "discovered" about 4266 b.c. If it were merely discovered at that early era, what periods of remoteness lie between that epoch and the time when it was first reduced to writing?
24   Scranton, Laird. *The Cosmological Origins of Myth and Symbol: From the Dogon and Ancient Egypt to India, Tibet, and China.* P. 63

responsible for the body's physical animation; they named *ka*.[25] The human personality's eight parts are the natural body, spirit-body, heart, double, heart-soul, shadow, spirit, and soul. The Egyptians considered the name the ninth part of the soul, which completes the unitary life.[26]

The miracle of creation appears in divine proportions the ancients discerned in nature. These patterns appear in the growth patterns of the snail's shell, the sunflower seed, the growth of trees, and the physical proportions of the human body. These all exhibit the ratio of Phi (1.681), signifying growth or the fourth dimension. This secret was known and taught in Kemet more than two thousand years before Fibonacci used the sequence of numbers that gave rise to the Golden Ratio. These principles of harmony and proportion are physically encoded in the temple at Karnak, in the pyramids' proportions, in sculpture, vases, harmonics of musical notation, and in the design of musical instruments. They all conform to principles of harmony and balance encoded at the temple at Karnak, a template from which initiates of the Mysteries learned.[27]

Origins of Egyptian Ethics

The history of Africa's contributions to world civilization is significant. However, developing a moral code and a philosophy that leads to everlasting life is the continent's most enduring and venerable achievement, and it established a sound basis for civilized people. The success of each individual in attaining a place in the Pleiades rested on their moral standing. In *The Papyrus of Ani*, discovered in 1888 C.E. in Thebes and dated to 1,250 B.C.E., relatively late in Kemet's history, there is a glimpse of the ancient ethical system. The papyrus contains *The 42 Negative Confessions*, the evidence of a moral code existing in Africa long before Ani's death. The confessions of Ani are affirmations recited at the judgment of his soul, affirming that he broke none of the laws of Ma'at. *The 42 Negative Confessions* are not a finite moral code of the laws of Ma'at but affirm that the deceased had not violated the laws of the creation listed in the papyrus explicitly written for him. The laws of Ma'at are innumerable and cover all aspects of the creation, visible and invisible. Other examples of negative confessions show different affirmations. Although these differences suggest an arbitrary nature to the laws of Ma'at, they are snippets pertinent to each individual's life experience.

---

25   *Book of the dead*, p. 76
26   *Ibid.* p. 80
27   Alexander Badaway, "Architectural Design in Ancient Egypt"

The Judgment—From the papyrus of the scribe Hunefer (19th Dynasty). The jackal-headed Anubis leads Hunefer to the scale as the monster Ammut crouches beneath, waiting to swallow the heart if it weighs more than the feather of Ma'at, and proves a life of evil.

The celestially aligned pyramids, temple complexes, elaborate tombs, and funerary relics depict an unwavering faith and high regard for Ma'at in ancient Kemet. Immorality was such an affront to Ma'at that the priesthood believed it necessarily invoked chaos or *Isfet*. As Ma'at is true, right, and eternal, as are the laws of creation, *Isfet* is the opposite. Isfet is the result of injustice, and it brings about a horrific deluge where the *nun* or the watery ceiling of the Earth crashes down and destroys all life.

The Objective of Moral Philosophy in Ancient Societies

The concept of Ma'at coincides with the most compelling idea handed down through the generations—that of the divine-human being who is loyal to Ma'at. Cultivating the divine man makes real the promise that consciousness within human beings transforms into the sacred flame of immortality. The historian and Egyptologist Ivan Van Sertima, who recounted the promise of ancient Kemet, summarized this point:

> The Egyptians tell you of an initial world, which was just primal matter slowly growing to consciousness. God is consciousness. As the super consciousness, He was able to reconstitute matter, to fertilize it, to give it a direction; to give it a purpose; to give it a moral principle; to give it a structure so that it could begin to move out of motionlessness to achieve time out of timelessness; to perceive shape out of shapelessness; to achieve order out of chaos; Man is like that. [28]

—Ivan Van Sertima

28 Ivan Van Sertima. Kemetic Science 5.mov. Available at: http://www.youtube.com/watch?v=zC1jHcANPrU&feature=related. Accessed 12/8/2011

Figure 10.2: The emergence of the Divine Man from the Temple of Luxor.

Egyptologist René Schwaller de Lubicz, in *The Temple of Man,* reveals the model of the human body in the temple of Luxor and its role in cultivating the Divine Man.[29] The temple reproduces the human form and psyche with all the vital organs, functions, and psychic centers metaphorically represented in its architecture. The temple is a lesson in ancient metaphysics that guides the initiate to the highest spiritual perfection through lessons encoded in the temple's structure and walls. Schwaller explains the Egyptian pharaonic symbolism as internally derived, abstract, and based on the natural laws of symmetry and proportion. Kemetic metaphysics represents principles of creation using a harmony that unites all the disciplines of religion, science, philosophy, mathematics, and physics.

In its totality, the conscious universe, manifested as the reality in the material world.

The extreme comparison for Being would be Non-being. For us a thing exists only because it can, in the final analysis, not be. Now, presence is susceptible to changes; but absence—non-being—is immutable.

This reasoning of absurdity however, underlies any philosophy of Unity—that is to say, "God." Within this Non-being of Nature, which comprises all

---

29 Schwaller deLubicz: *The Temple In Man,* p.114. Available at: http://ia700608.us.archive.org/27/items/TheTempleInMan-R.a.SchwallerDeLubicz/TheTempleInMan-R.a.SchwallerDeLubicz.pdf. Accessed 12/20/2011.

"things," is summarized like a seed—everything that can be. Ancient Egypt accords the entire value of this Cause and not the object that emanated from it.

—René Adolphe Schwaller DeLubicz. *The Temple in Man*, p. 113.

Western Links to Ancient Kemetic Depictions of Virtue

The study of The First Cause or the mind of God, as the ancients referred to metaphysics, predominates in pre-Socratic philosophy. Moral philosophy focused on attaining spiritual purification in line with the nature of God. For example, the Ionian philosopher Heraclitus (535–475 B.C.E.) believed that man's highest purpose was to cultivate the divine reason or fire in him—his approximation of the life of the pure primal element.[30] Heraclitus acknowledged the Egyptian concept of unity in the creation, as borne out by the fragment below.

> This LOGOS holds always but humans always prove unable to understand it, both before hearing it and when they have first heard it. For though all things come to be in accordance with this LOGOS, humans are like the inexperienced when they experience such words and deeds as I set out, distinguishing each in accordance with its nature and saying how it is. But other people fail to notice what they do when awake, just as they forget what they do while asleep.
>
> —(Diels-Kranz, *22B1*). From the collection of Hermann Alexander Diels.

Heraclitus upheld the ancient Egyptian expression of man's subordination to a pre-existing order in the universe. He uses the term logos to suggest cosmic law, which he regrets, exists despite the tendency to ignore it. Heraclitus later lamented the failure of the Greeks to understand the meaning of logos. In his statement above, we sense a divergent materialist tendency growing among Greeks that Heraclitus casts into one class—those who hear the Logos but remain ignorant of it.

Among these pre-Socratic philosophers, Pythagoras (582–496 B.C.E.) was Western civilization's most critical link to ancient Kemet. He and his students defined a numerical classification process for uniting with the One. Pythagoras's interpretations and transference of Kemetic cosmogony were crucial developments in Greek moral philosophy. While in Kemet, he learned of Atum and the first four elements of the lower realms depicted in the Tetractys on page 67. The Greeks referred to the process that created

---

30   Philosophy and Popular Morals, Archibald E. Dobbs Jr, p. 103

		•		Flower	The One	Union
	•		•	Nous	2 Faculties	{ Love Intuition
•		•		• Psykhê	3 Faculties	{ Noetic Soul / Unreasoning Soul
•	•	•	•	Body	4 Elements	{ Fire / Air / Water / Earth

The Tetractys.

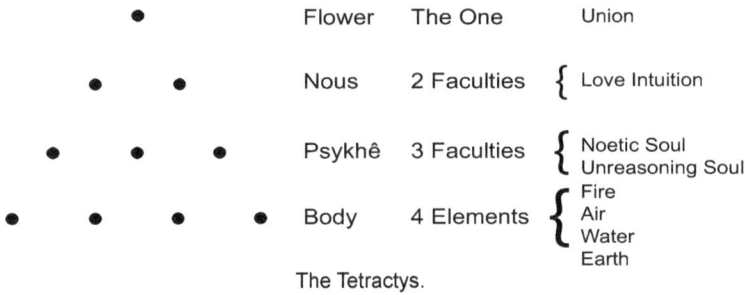

the universe as nous,[31] which translates to the mind of God. Pythagoras's studies of the living universe are a systemic approach that combines numbers and attributes in geometric sequences that approximated ancient beliefs on the transmutation of matter to spirit (immortality).

The knowledge Pythagoras acquired in Kemet evolved into the cornerstone of Greek virtue ethics emulated by Plato and Aristotle. Aristotle formulated the Doctrine of the Mean in his *Nicomachean Ethics*. According to Aristotle, a moral virtue is a mean between two extremes of excess and deficiency. There can be no meeting of opposite extremes, and a third intermediary that joins the two extremes at the mean becomes necessary. On a spiritual level, virtue enables a harmonious state of the soul by balancing the disparate elements of spirit and matter.[32]

Pythagoras influenced Plato's tripartite formulation of the soul, which he defines in *Phaedrus*, his book on the soul.[33] Plato highlighted the nature of the soul by equating the flawless operation of three parts of the city and those of the soul. He defines the three parts of the city, beginning with the ruling class responsible for decision-making, followed by the warrior class characterized by courage, and the merchants and citizens with competing interests. The corresponding parts of the soul are the reasoning facility, the spirited part, and the appetite subject to earthly temptations. Justice ensues when the three parts of the city and soul are balanced.

The Ancient Worldview

The ancient world of Kemet witnessed the transition from a typical matrilineal African social system with agricultural abundance to conquest and slavery. The significant differences between the two periods are

---

31   The first emanation is *Nous* (Divine Mind, logos or order, Thought, Reason), identified metaphorically with the Demiurge (the craftsman) in Plato's *Timaeus*.
32   Philosophy and Popular Morals, Archibald E. Dobbs Jr. p. 103)
33   *Phaedrus* 246a–b

abundance in the old system and scarcity in the latter, which typifies the transition from communalism to feudalism and colonialism. The prolonged shortages in conquered Egypt did not stem from natural causes like drought. Still, it developed from foreign control of the land, its people's subjugation, and its agricultural produce's appropriation. After the Greek and Roman conquests, the Egyptian peasants continued producing wealth. However, the taxes on their production increased dramatically to sustain the Roman army and the cities of Alexandria and Rome. With Egypt as the breadbasket of the new society, the father figure and the soldier emerged to become the new archetype, where courage, as the new virtue, became the redeeming factor in the quest for everlasting life. The transition from a matrilineal society to a patriarchal one occurred amidst the Classic period wars, and the accompanying violence did not favor the women enslaved by conquering armies. The mindset of cooperation, a characteristic of matrilineal civilizations, gave way to slavery and repression of women, which remained a characteristic of modern culture.

The literary works of Antiquity show a strong dislike for the spiritual decay generated by avarice and material corruption. The Hermetic scholars in Egypt's Hellenic culture (Egyptian-Greek) associated the material world with the source of spiritual depravity that would deny the ultimate quest for everlasting life. The search for spiritual purification was the predominant force in society. Ancient Egyptian burial scripts of the judgment depict the rigorous effort in the negative confessions required for eternal life. These ideas remained vibrant until the old matrilineal systems gave way to the patriarchy of Greece and Rome.

Chapter 4

The Transition to Hellenic Civilization

The Roots of Western Morality

Hellenic civilization, the combination of Greek and Kemetic cultures, is pivotal to the cultural diffusion and economic expansion that sparked the emergence of Western civilization. Alexander III of Macedon's conquest of Persia in 331 B.C.E. ended 132 years of Persian rule over Kemet. Egyptians welcomed his victory, and he demonstrated a traditional respect for the customs of the ancient and venerable land, which he renamed Agyptos (Egypt). Before Egyptian priests could coronate him as the divinely appointed Pharaoh, Alexander needed the approval of the Egyptian deity Amun. The ancient Egyptian god of the sun and air is one of the most important gods of ancient Egypt who rose to prominence at Thebes at the beginning of the period of the New Kingdom (c. 1570-1069 B.C.E.). At the Siwa Oasis, the most sacred temple and home to the Oracle of Amun, Egyptians crowned Alexander with the double crown of Egypt. They named him the son of God (Amun)—a title reserved only for the divinely appointed Pharaoh responsible for preserving Ma'at.

Egypt's prominence as an ancient and venerable culture in the Mediterranean region resounded with Alexander as it had for the Pre- Socratic, Greek scholars. Although he was a native of Macedonia, Alexander built his capital city of Alexandria in Egypt. Egyptians planned and constructed the city at the old port city of Rhakotis and completed the Pharos Lighthouse, one of the seven wonders of the ancient world. They created the Temple of Serapis, part of the Library of Alexandria complex. In the image on page 70, Serapis, the new hybrid god of the emerging culture, appears like a Greek god but in Egyptian attire. The combined Grecco-Egyptian deities of the Apis bull and Osiris, demonstrates Greek assimilation and the transformation of Egyptian culture. The deity was suitable for the emerging Hellenistic patriarchal society with spiritual links to ancient Kemet. While the emerging culture saw advances in science, medicine, and a burgeoning economy, it experienced unique developments in religion notably the transition from pantheism to theism.

Under Ptolemy I, the Greco-Egyptian culture created the Serapis deity in the rendition at the Rome Colosseum. Serapis appears as a Hellenized god with the Modius crown and the Egyptian, sacred Apis bull that transforms into Osiris-Apis after death.

After Alexander died in 323 B.C.E., The Greek Empire, which had expanded to the borders of the Indian subcontinent, split among his generals. The Ptolemy Dynasty, founded by one of Alexander's generals, ruled Egypt for three centuries until the death of the last Ptolemaic ruler, Cleopatra VII, in 30 B.C.E. The Greek occupation of Egypt started the Hellenic Age when Greeks assimilated Egyptian culture and built Alexandria into the world's largest metropolis. Alexandria became a cosmopolitan city, the home of multiple religious practices, peoples, and beliefs. It was the world center of learning that kept more than 700,000 books with knowledge from the cultures of the known world.

At Left: A Nineteenth-century rendering of the Library of Alexandria by the German artist O. Von Corven.

The Erosion of the Kemetic Worldview

Greek assimilation and transcription of Kemetic culture developed rapidly under the Greek Pharaohs. The writing of Kemetic knowledge combined with Greek ideas became the sources of Hermeticism[1] attributed to Theuti (Thoth). The wisdom of Thoth, the Ibis-headed Kemetic God of magic, writing, and knowledge, references several thousand years of Kemetic history. From 300 B.C.E to 1200 C.E., the Hermetic writings expounded on Kemetic themes of spiritual rebirth, belief in the supremacy and unknowable nature of the universal consciousness. Although the Greeks living in Egypt kept the original Kemetic purpose of spiritual rebirth through mummification, the growing rationalism in the Hellenistic culture began to erode traditional Kemetic beliefs. A materialist mindset cultivated in the economically vibrant Greek society arose from the ranks of ordinary Greek citizens—the plebeians or commoners—who had grown to outnumber the noble class in Greece. Their influence on Greek society led to profound changes in attitudes towards the individual and Greek philosophy.

Greece's societal changes were due to its rapid expansion as an empire under Alexander. The empire grew wealthier as it changed from an agricultural economy to a trade-based economy. Democratic institutions arose with an assembly, senate, and courts. However, the most vital part of Greek society was composed of the sophists who educated the plebeians and public officials in rhetoric and the art of persuasion. As Greece grew wealthy, self-interested individuals seeking political and social advantages increased. The sophists who taught the mysteries favored dialectic (speaking) to document and express public policy. They became adept at providing educational services to their clients. An intellectual class arose due to the sophist's role in educating the people and awakening the ideals of Athenian Democracy. The newly formed class of educated commoners challenged the wealthy elite and became the driving force in Greek history,[2] shaping and focusing the empire's materialist ideas.

The sophists taught the ethics familiar to Socrates and Plato, but they did so for money and not for virtue's sake as Plato and those before

1   Kathleen Sutherland and Christopher Warnock. *Hermetic Gnosis: Secrets of Spiritual Hermeticism.*
2   Archibald Edward Dobbs. *Philosophy and Popular morals in ancient Greece: An examination of popular Morals in Ancient Greece.* An Examination of Popular Morality and Philosophical Ethics, in their Interrelations and Reciprocal Influence in Ancient Greece, down to the close of the Third Century B.C. p 76

him had done. As Greece expanded economically and militarily, the progression from an older form of morality associated with divine unity to a more practical, Aristotelian virtue ethics occurred, intending to achieve eudaimonia or happiness. The sophists' aims coincided with sentiments in popular culture based on materialism, hero-worship, and courage as a virtue in the face of adversity. They understood integrity as a material advancement that diverged from Plato's ideas in his dialog of *Meno and The Republic*, which defined virtue as the activity of the rational soul. To Plato, the achievement of moral and intellectual excellence was paramount. Plato pursued the good because it was the right thing to do, while the sophists did so strictly for profit. During Plato's time, popular opinion had already replaced the established traditions of Kemet to follow Ma'at with the cultivated desire for social status in Greek society.

The effects of sophists on Greek popular culture were more widespread than we can infer based on Plato's popularity in modern times. Currently, Plato's writing receives universal acclaim that surpasses the achievements of sophists in ancient Greek society. However, they played a crucial role in diluting the Egyptian Mysteries and revolutionizing Greece's educational system. Before sophists diminished it, the study of the Egyptian Mysteries lasted 44 years and aimed to cultivate a lived experience and mastery of body, soul, and spirit. However, due to the influence of the sophists, initiation occurred quickly among the plebeians, who were a broad section of society seeking upward mobility by mastering specific skills in rhetoric and the Socratic dialectic. Besides their penchant for superficiality, the sophists succeeded in imposing an enduring skepticism into the culture that questioned all reality, particularly the basis of the concept of the *anima mundi* or living universe, which was central to Kemetic metaphysics. Greece's best-known skeptic, Sextus Empiricus, fervently doubted all knowledge and beliefs not acquired directly through experience. The sophists' systemized methodology redefined education in Greece but lessened the initiative to discover truth through innate wisdom and the lived experience that the Egyptian Mysteries required of the true initiate.

With the advancement of materialism and individualism, sophists succeeded in promoting disinterest in the universal consciousness that Plato referenced as the Good. The ordinary Greeks, or plebeians living in an increasingly wealthy nation, focused on social advancement and attaining the means to achieve wealth and happiness. The transition in Greek society from the worldview that focused on the afterlife to the more mundane concerns of the material world gave a broader acceptance of materialist ideas of happiness and wealth acquisition. In prior decades, even Plato, who rejected materialism and had an orthodox view of a highly ethical past based on the Good and the forms or the ultimate source of all ideas, was isolated in his opposition to the emerging moral philosophy from popular sentiment and the political class.

The Struggle Against Avarice and Usury in Ancient Greece and Rome

In ancient Greece, economic expansion and social upheaval saw temples to Isis become repositories of citizen wealth, inadvertently fostering financial manipulation. Priests often used Greece's gold reserves to finance wars of plunder, while the rise of banking and overseas trade introduced the earliest forms of usury in the Western world. However, Greeks recognized the dangers of usury and its potential to fuel avarice. To curb its excesses, they imposed strict controls, limiting usury to high-risk overseas trade and capping interest rates. The restrictions on usury reflected a broader ethical stance against wealth accumulation at the expense of communal well-being.

When Rome conquered the Mediterranean, it inherited Greece's philosophical ideas on avarice and usury, such as Aristotle's denunciation of usury as an unnatural and unethical practice of exploiting others for personal gain. Aristotle believed that charging interest on loans was contrary to the natural purpose of money, which was to facilitate exchange and not generate profit through lending. However, the restraints on usury were largely eroded under Roman rule as wealth accumulation through conquest and exploitation was statecraft. Rome's ascent to power—marked by the subjugation of Greek city-states in 146 B.C.E., the destruction of Carthage, and the pacification of vast territories—was driven by imperial ambition rather than ethical governance. With Egypt's annexation in 30 B.C.E. under Augustus Caesar, the Roman Empire secured immense wealth and food supplies, reinforcing Rome's dominance but deepening social and economic inequalities.

In cities like Alexandria, elite Hellenized Greeks and Romans enjoyed tax exemptions, while indigenous Egyptians bore the burden of labor and taxation. This stratification and the cultural and religious pluralism allowed under Roman rule sowed discontent. Babylonian-Jewish religious influences and the rise of Gnostic thought began to challenge the materialistic ethos of Roman society, laying the groundwork for ideological shifts that would culminate in Christianity's emergence.

Roman demands for emperor worship clashed with Jewish monotheism, fueling resistance in Alexandria and Judea. Jewish belief in a messiah who would liberate them from Roman oppression grew amid these tensions. This hope for divine redemption eventually contributed to a profound split within Judaism, giving rise to Christianity. Early Jewish sects, such as the Ebionites and Marcionites, debated the nature of Jesus's divinity and his role as the messiah. The Ebionites viewed Jesus as a righteous human chosen by God. At the same time, the Marcionites saw him as a spiritual savior sent by a benevolent deity to counter the Old Testament's harsh demiurge.

Amidst Roman oppression, the apostle Paul played a pivotal role in shaping Christianity by redefining Jewish beliefs and promoting a new interpretation of Jesus's teachings. His efforts laid the foundation for Christianity to evolve as a distinct faith, diverging from its Jewish roots. Over time, theological disputes regarding Jesus's nature and mission led to accusations of heresy, the exclusion of certain texts, and the eventual establishment of an acceptable Christian canon.

The historical struggle against avarice and usury, intertwined with religious and ethical debates, highlights the tension between those advocating for accumulating material wealth and those upholding spiritual ideals. While ancient civilizations grappled with the corrupting influence of greed, the emergence of Christianity offered a vision of redemption and moral reform that challenged Rome's imperial legacy.

Philo of Alexandria

Philo of Alexandria (20 b.c.e–50 c.e.), the Jewish philosopher of the Hellenistic period, expressed the sentiment of his fellow Jews in stark terms that supported their rebellions against Augustus Caesar (27 b.c.e.–14 c.e.). Philo was a contemporary of Jesus and was vital to developing Jewish philosophy in Alexandria. He discovered similarities between the Jewish Pentateuch—the five books containing the laws given to Moses, and two of Plato's works—Laws and Timaeus, his creation story. Alexandria, Philo's objective was to popularize Jewish heritage among the Greeks by using a narrative style and the subject matter of the ideal state, which Plato and Aristotle wrote. Philo's brand of Judaism, written to endear the religion to the Greek-speaking Jews, evoked critical responses in two biblical texts, *Colossians* and *Hebrews*, written in retort to his Messianic philosophy.

During the reign of Augustus Caesar (27 b.c.e.–14 c.e.) and around the time of the historical Jesus Christ's life, Philo harmonized the Torah with Pythagoras, Plato, and Aristotle, as well as Stoicism, which was the Roman religion of the day and also a derivative of Platonism. Philo's central theme is the Logos—the emanations of a central God flowing down in a hierarchy of creation from the angels down to man. Philo's visions are similar to Platonic and Aristotelian hierarchical concepts in the creation, where God emanates various levels of beings from the highest spiritual entities (angels) and descends to the material world and man. Since his literary influences are from the classical Greek period, his themes include virtue, the soul as the heart of virtue, the soul as a prisoner in the body, sexual piety that depicted the woman as a temptation, and themes of imprisonment of the soul by a defective body.

Titus Flavius Josephus

Titus Flavius Josephus was a second and more prominent Roman Jewish historian who influenced Christian thought (37 c.e. – 100 c.e.). Josephus left written evidence of Jewish history under Roman authority, like his predecessor Philo. Before the outbreak of the Jewish rebellions, the Jewish experience in Rome had been amicable. Julius Caesar, who preceded Octavian or Augustus, his adopted son, had treated Jews kindly. However, as the Jewish population increased during Augustus's reign, rebellions frequently occurred because the Roman Senate had made a god of Julius Caesar and began the imperial cult that declared all succeeding Roman emperors and their family members as gods. The Roman authorities decreed the Jewish violations of these Roman traditions as treasonous. The Jews were in a precarious position of being forced to violate their religious prohibition against worshiping idols in their temples. They saw their predicament and suffering under Roman tyranny as validation of their belief that Earth was a place of suffering that required a messiah and a redeemer sent by God to cleanse away the evil and bring about His world.

Jewish influence on religious beliefs in Alexandria and the rest of the Roman Empire introduced a newfound dualistic cosmogony that included a male god opposed by a demiurge who created the material world. The more ancient ideas, particularly that of the first divine king Heru, representing humanity's salvation and transmigration of the soul, merged with Babylonian-Zorastrianism and Apocalyptic Judaism. Traditional beliefs, or the orthodoxy, told of a messiah from God that would liberate the Jews from suffering under Roman tyranny. Judaism acquired its patriarchal customs and theology that saw the material world as a temporary place of suffering that the kingdom of God would replace. The religion became infused with Babylonian thought around 570 B.C.E. following the destruction of the first temple and enslavement of the Jews in Babylon. The Jewish religion's Messiah—The Anointed One—shares characteristics similar to Heru. They are both born of an immaculate conception, and in the Kemetic tradition, Heru is the savior who brings the redeeming light of salvation. In the period preceding Christianity, a wide-ranging group of ancient religions shared beliefs that included a messiah and shunning of the material world. The Jewish Messiah was Joshua, the sun god and an emissary sent to establish God's earthly kingdom. The Gnostic Messiah was corporal—within each individual, similar to the divine self of ancient Kemet.

On the other hand, some Jews believed the messiah was an actual person, just like the Jews suffering under the yoke of Roman tyranny, who looked forward to a king and a redeemer sent by God. In the Gnostic cosmogony, a perfect god presides over the spiritual world and a demiurge rules over the imperfect material world he created. While the idea of a demiurge appeared in Alexandria with the rise of the Jewish sect, the Marcionites, it was not part of an African tradition but emanated from Babylonian-Zoroastrianism. Enslavement of the Jews in Babylon began around 597 B.C.E. and ended in 537 B.C.E. when the Persians conquered Babylon and freed the Jews. The Persians then permitted the rebuilding of the second Jewish temple in Jerusalem.

The Jewish experience of Roman tyranny in Rome's conquered territories made it seem like the material world of the demiurge from which Jews believed the coming messiah would free them. These religious beliefs began the era of Apocalyptic Judaism, which anticipated the coming of the messiah, destined to be anointed as the king who would free Jews and bring God's world into reality on Earth. Apocalyptic Judaism and its competing sects are synonymous with the religion modern writers have named early Christianity. Although Roman historians had an extensive historical writing tradition around the dates of Jesus's life and crucifixion, direct knowledge and references to his birth, life experience, and crucifixion do not exist. The first writing of Jesus's life in the bible occurs long after his death. Scholars estimate the gospels evolved from an oral tradition 40–100 years after Jesus's crucifixion. Thereafter, writing about Jesus began in the Patristic Era 100 C.E. Christian literature emerged from a cultural melting pot and recirculated

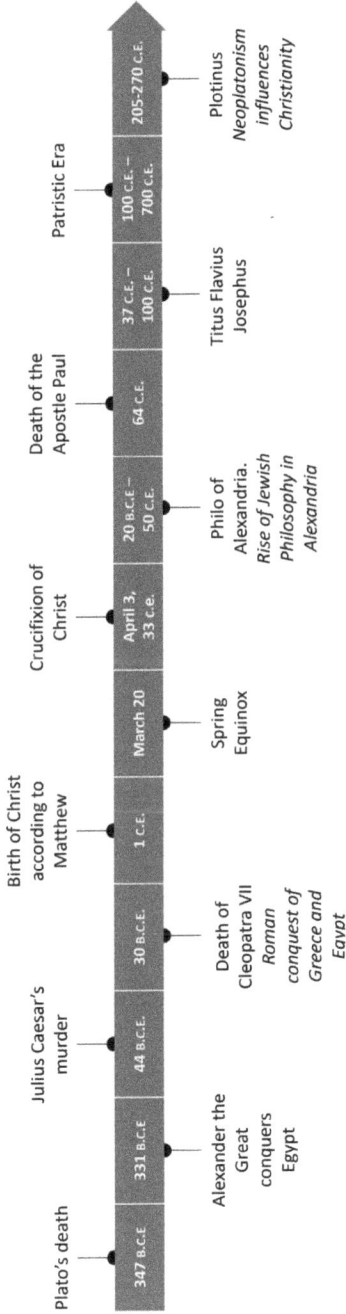

Timeline of Greece and Roman rule over Egypt and evolution of religion in the Mediterranean region

oral and written ideas in the Mediterranean region that often relied on pagan sources of Greek Philosophy that the Christian priests and theologians did not acknowledge. Instead, these pagan sources were believed to be biblical sources and vehemently defended as Christian philosophy.

Errors of the Patristic Era

The Patristic Era, when Christian theologians and writers wrote about Christianity from an intellectual point of view, spans the centuries from 100 C.E. to 787 C.E.. Writers such as Saint Augustine grappled with the writing of Christian theology based on themes such as the divinity of Jesus Christ, the holy Trinity, and the Incarnation. Other themes included establishing the New Testament canon, interpreting the Scriptures, and providing guidance on how Christians should live according to their faith. The Christian writers believed that their sources of information were all of biblical origin. However, despite these beliefs, their sources were the pre-Christian Greek and Latin texts derived from Platonic and Egyptian philosophy, Hermetic texts, and Neo-Platonism, which is a reconstituted Platonic Philosophy developed by Plotinus (205–270 C.E.). These texts were not of any Christian origin and ordinarily would be condemned as paganism. For example, the concept of the Trinity existed in Kemet and other ancient cultures of Babylon and India long before it occurred in Christianity. In Kemet, the Trinity was a divine concept, first elucidated in the story of Auset, Ausar, and the child Heru, who was born of an immaculate conception. The use of Pagan sources suggests that the idea of a triune deity was not unique to Christianity and was influenced by earlier religious traditions. However, the Christian doctrine of the Trinity is distinct in its formulation and theological implications.

The Egyptian-born Greek writer Plotinus's pupil Porphyry edited and published his original work in *The Six Enneads*, 270 C.E.[3] The three fundamental principles of Neo-Platonism, The One, the intellect, and the soul,

---

3   Works of Polinus, "The Six Enneads" www.ccel.org/ccel/plotinus/enneads.ii.i.html Plotinus is often accredited as the founder of Neo-Platonism. In an attempt to revive Platonic thought, this third century philosopher and mystic wrote about issues such as virtue, happiness, reason, body, and soul, with Plato's philosophy as his guide. Like Plato, Plotinus had much disdain for material things and instead embraced the idea of a higher realm of immaterial intelligibility. Plotinus located the source of creation in a supreme "One." Plotinus believed this "One" transcended being, nonbeing, multiplicity, and division. The Enneads were compiled by Plotinus' student, Porphyry, who gathered together his teacher's essays and arranged and edited them himself. These writings had a significant impact on the religious metaphysicians and mystics from the ancient world. Plotinus has also influenced many thinkers of Islam, Indian Monism, and the Eastern Orthodox Church.

as published in *The Six Enneads*,[4] are Plotinus' examination of Platonism's central themes. Plotinus's work became a source of Christian theology[5] as the emerging Christian theologians copied these themes, believing they were original Christian theology. Consequently, Neo-Platonic Philosophy became acceptable as a unique Christian theology because the Church Fathers believed the bible was the source of all ancient philosophy.[6] St. Augustine, the father of Christian theology, was thus heavily influenced by the ancient Platonic thought and Cicero's writings. St. Augustine's writing influenced a broad section of the Christian world, notably Coptic Christians and Catholics.

The Arian Controversy

Belief systems like Stoicism, Gnosticism, and religions such as Judaism and the Coptic faith upheld ancient views from various Mediterranean religions that further destabilized the Roman Empire simultaneously as it had begun to disintegrate from tribal attacks in the 6th-century C.E. Emperor Justinian banned The Mysteries in Greece and Egypt and closed Plato's Academy in 529 C.E. to end the ancient Kemetic and Hellenistic influence in the Roman Empire. Nevertheless, the competing religious sects perpetuated the widening schism over the validity of Christian claims that the Son of God is equal to God the Father. The ancient traditions of Greece and Egypt supported the beliefs of Gnostics and Copts that Christ could not be equal to the Father. The ancient pantheist worldview was contrary to that of Christians who believed in a literal Christ as a god who was equal to the Father.

The controversy about the nature of God crystallized in the argument between Arius, a Christian priest of Alexandria, and Athanasius, the Bishop of Alexandria. Their debate centered on the true nature of God the Father and the Son of the Father. Arius's belief about the substance of Christ contradicted that of the early Christians but aligned with his ancient wisdom, summarized below:

> "If the Father begat the Son, he that was begotten had a beginning of existence: hence it is that there was when the Son was not. It follows then of necessity that he had his existence from the non-existence".[7]

---

4   The Six Eneads, available at: www.classics.mit.edu/Plotinus/enneads.html
5   Polinus as a Platonist: www.plato.stanford.edu/entries/plotinus/
6   www.plato.stanford.edu/entries/christiantheology-philosophy/ . accessed 11/1/2020.
7   Bettenson, Henry, ed. (1963). Documents of the Christian Church (2nd ed.). New York: Oxford University Press. p. 40.

Emperor Constantine (306–337 c.e.) convened The First Council of Nicaea in 325 c.e. to unify the opposing religious views and preserve unity in his empire. The Council of bishops from around the Roman Empire ruled that Jesus, the son of God, was equal to God. Constantine, who converted to Christianity in 312 c.e., decreed one God and one Emperor and declared the Gospels of Mathew, Mark, Luke, and John the only viable gospels. He outlawed Gnostic writings as heretical and ordered books such as *The Life of Adam and Eve* and *The Book of Enoch*, consisting of 108 chapters, removed from the bible. Enraged by the opposition from Arius, Constantine evoked his oracle and cursed the bishop, his followers, and their daughters from the North African coast to a life of ruin. He issued a death sentence to anyone found with the writing of Arius.

> Lend your ears and listen a little, impious Arius, and understand your folly. O God, protector of all, may you be well – disposed to what is being said, if it should admit of faith! For I, your man, holding to your propitious providence, from the very ancient Greek and Roman writing shall demonstrate clearly Arius' madness, which has been prophesied and predicted three thousand years ago by the Erythraean Sibyl. (19.) For she indeed says: "Woe to you, Libya, situated in maritime regions, for there shall come to you a time, in which with the people and your daughters you must be compelled to undergo a terrible and cruel and very difficult crisis, from which a judgment both of faith and of piety in respect to all persons will be given, but you will decline to extreme ruin, for you have dared to engulf the receptacle of celestial flowers and to mangle it with a bite and you have polluted it with iron teeth."[8]

Amid the destruction ordered by Constantine, the Nag Hamadi Gnostic scrolls, hidden in the deserts of Egypt, survived and are rare examples of the forbidden texts. Nine of the declared heretics fled Rome to Ethiopia and established the Ethiopian Orthodox Tewahedo Church in 480, c.e.

The Nicene Creed remained vibrant throughout the Middle Ages as the Roman Catholic Church, the only remaining institution in existence after the collapse of Rome, reinforced the creed through its theology and rituals of baptism and holy communion. Based on Aristotle's Substance Theory,[9] the Church and its followers believed that the bread and wine

---

8   Emperor Constantine to Arius. Available at www.faculty.wlc.edu/thompson/fourth-century/index.htm?http&&&faculty.wlc.edu/thompson/fourth-century/Urkunden/trans34.htm
9   Substance Theory categorized all reality into substances—The actual things like people, rocks, etc. On the other hand, accidents are things that happen to substances such as walking, skin color etc.

at the Last Supper and the sacraments served in the Church during holy communion were the actual body and blood of Christ. During the Middle Ages, the Church used Aristotelean Substance Theory to defend its transubstantiation doctrine, which supports the conversion of the actual blood and body of Christ into bread and wine. The argument of the Council of Bishops was about the substance of the son of God that they claimed was: ". . . *Begotten not made, consubstantial to the Father, by whom all things were made.*"[10] In using the term "*consubstantial with the Father*" to describe Jesus, the bishops implied that they were of the same substance—identical. Their conclusions were based on the Aristotelian Substance Theory, which states that substances make up all things in the universe and that accidents are all external occurrences applied to substances that make them look and feel as they appear. Accidents could make substances identical, although they would appear different.

Constantine's Christianization edicts attempted to add a layer of divine authority and universality to morality, creating a system that aimed to confront evil through theological doctrine. However, it led to divisions like those between Eastern Orthodoxy and Western Christianity that persisted into the contemporary period.

The collapse of the Roman Empire in 576

About midway through the Patristic Era, the Western Roman Empire collapsed into multiple kingdoms, and the Middle Ages began. Faced with the historical persecution of Christians and the difficult life they lived, the main question considered by the Church was the importance of being a Christian. The Christian Church of the Medieval era evolved towards a theology deeply rooted in Hellenistic philosophy after Roman authority over the Church had collapsed. Standing alone amid the chaos after St. Augustine's leadership and the collapse of the Roman Empire, the main question before the Church was how to be a good Christian. It found answers in the existing Christian monasticism prevalent in Egypt, where the lived experiences of the Anchorite and Coenobite monks became the example the Church followed.

The ethical values of the desert monastics came primarily from the teachings of St. Anthony, the founder of organized Christian monasticism.

---

10   Excerpt from the Niceno-Constantinopolitan Creed—a translation of the original where the 'consubstantial' is used to replace 'one in being with the Father.

His example and those of monastic monks show that they were generous and lived simply and ethically according to the standards of Patriarchs of the Hebrew Scriptures such as Abraham, Jacob, and Isac. Other sources include Aristotle's *Nichomachean Ethics,* and the New Testament Gospels. Saint Anthony proposed a list of Christian virtues that became the model for Christian piety, conforming to the best in Hellenistic moral values of prudence, justice, temperance, courage, understanding, love, concern for the poor, freedom from anger, hospitality, and faith in Christ. [11] Over the centuries, these all merged to form the ethical values of the Christian Church. However, contrary to the Church's beliefs, these were based on Hellenistic morals that sought the soul's liberation based on social responsibility, self-reliance, graciousness, earnestness, prayer, even-temper, philanthropy, study, endurance, vigils, fasting, meekness, and long-suffering. For most of the early years of the Middle Ages, the Church's theology was shaped by these examples.[12]

The Christian Church's integrity remained unchallenged until after the Muslim conquest of Constantinople in the 15th century. As refugees from the war carried hordes of ancient documents of the Classical Period into Europe, scholars such as the Italian humanist Lorenzo Valla (1407–1457) began critically examining the old manuscripts. Besides sparking a cultural revolution, the discoveries and new knowledge revealed inaccuracies in the Catholic Church's core beliefs. In 1475, Lorenzo Valla discovered that Christian theological claims of an eclipse occurring at Jesus's crucifixion were doubtful because the ancient astronomical records did not record any eclipse at that time. Valla's revelations cast doubt on Matthew 27:45, Mark 15:33, and Luke 23:44. The ancient astronomical observations studied by Valla had no record of darkness occurring up to the ninth hour of the day of Jesus's crucifixion as the biblical passages imply.

The translated documents exposed the dubious nature of the Church's claim that the bible, as the word of God, was the source of Classical Philosophy and Christian theology. The evidence for the erroneous crucifixion narrative led to one of the authors of Christianity's emerging theology, Dionysius, who had placed himself in the vicinity of Jesus's crucifixion when he claimed to witness the eclipse that had coincided with the crucifixion date while he was in Egypt. Dionysius, whom St. Paul converted to Christianity,

11   Ferris, Doug. "The Ethics of Early Christian Monasticism: Symbol and Reality." The Annual of the Society of Christian Ethics, 1981. Available at: www.youtube.com/watch?v=Bw5SZ8eIquE
12   Ferris, Doug. "The Ethics of Early Christian Monasticism: Symbol and Reality." The Annual of the Society of Christian Ethics, 1981. Available at: www.youtube.com/watch?v=Bw5SZ8eIquE

traveled with him to preach the gospel and convert souls to Christianity. However, although the error in the Church's theology appeared to be from Dionysius, who lived in the 1st century, the scholars of the 15th century determined that the writings were not from him but from an unknown author from the late 5th century to the early 6th century, who fraudulently attributed them to Dionysius. Due to the uncertainty about the forger's identity, scholars referenced his name as Pseudo-Dionysius, the Areopagite, to denote his false identity. Pseudo-Dionysius wrote extensively on Christian theology in *Divine Names, Mystical Theology, Celestial Hierarchy*,[13] and *Ecclesiastical Hierarchy*. In *Celestial Hierarchy*, Pseudo-Dionysius writes about the nine heavenly beings and the order of angels—themes that are not original Christian theology but are derived from the works of the ancient philosophers. Pseudo-Dionysius's writings profoundly influenced Saint Thomas Aquinas (1225–1274 C.E.), the most renowned Scholastic Christian theologian. Although Pseudo-Dionysius' writing relied on Platonic philosophy, he writes that the source of his knowledge for his hierarchical organization of the heavens was divine revelations or angelic visions.[14]

The Neo-Platonic writings of the Hellenistic philosopher Plotinus and his student Porphyry's work on the *Six Enneads* heavily influenced Pseudo-Dionysius' work.[15] Neo-Platonists relied on Plato's philosophical works that expounded on the nature of the One, the intellect, and the soul. These were critical themes of the Egyptian Mysteries taught by Africans in Egypt and by Classical Philosophers such as Pythagoras, Plato, and Aristotle in Greece. Even *theoria*—the essential contemplative method used by Christian theologians for acquiring truth and revelation—was based on ancient philosophers' dialectic method and was preferred by Aristotle. Pseudo Dionysius's Christian theology, widely accepted by the

---

13   www.tertullian.org/fathers/areopagite_13_heavenly_hierarchy.htm
The Hierarchy of the Angels: (1) Seraphim, Cherubim, and Thrones; (2) Dominations, Virtues, and Powers; (3) Principalities, Archangels, and Angels.
14   Dionysius the Areopagite, Works (1899) vol. 2. p.1-66. *The Celestial Hierarchy*
15   Works of Polinus, "The Six Enneads" www.ccel.org/ccel/plotinus/enneads.ii.i.html Plotinus is often accredited as the founder of Neo-Platonism. In an attempt to revive Platonic thought, this third century philosopher and mystic wrote about issues such as virtue, happiness, reason, body, and soul, with Plato's philosophy as his guide. Like Plato, Plotinus had much disdain for material things and instead embraced the idea of a higher realm of immaterial intelligibility. Plotinus located the source of creation in a supreme "One." Plotinus believed this "One" transcended being, nonbeing, multiplicity, and division. *The Enneads* were compiled by Plotinus' student, Porphyry, who gathered together his teacher's essays and arranged and edited them himself. These writings had a significant impact on the religious metaphysicians and mystics from the ancient world. Plotinus has also influenced many thinkers of Islam, Indian Monism, and the Eastern Orthodox Church.

Christian church as authentic, was nurtured in Mediterranean civilizations long before the birth of Christ.

The scholarly revelations of the forgery of Christian theology by Pseudo-Dionysius and the non-biblical sources did not dissuade the Catholic church from enforcing acceptance of a biblical origin of Christian theology. On the contrary, Valla's revelations unleashed an era of religious persecution against classical philosophy that affected the intellectuals of the period and led to the papal bulls enslaving pagans. The inquisition's extreme tortures, used to extract confessions from heretics and enemies of Christ, were a critical method to impose the church's decrees on an unwary public. Working in concert with the monarchy, the Church began a new era of capital accumulation premised on arbitrary accusations of anti-Christ sentiments, supported by tortured confessions and seizure of property as Europe descended into a legally sanctioned embrace of avarice.

Chapter 5

The Foundations of the Western Legal Tradition

The transition from the grandeur of classical Rome to the dawn of the Middle Ages profoundly shaped a Western European spiritual, ethical, political, and legal landscape. As the economy of the region faltered with the collapse of Roman authority, the western territories fragmented into warring kingdoms, feudalism, and enslavement of the poor peasants. Despite the enduring influence of Rome's legal tradition, there was a marked shift from the ancient Roman ideals of Humanism, which elevated the human being as the source of all ideas, to a medieval theocratic order where God orders all reality. As the Roman era waned, the emphasis on virtue, rationality, and pragmatism gave way to a theocracy where God and Christianity became the central pillars of ethics and law. This evolving Western culture began to diverge significantly from the ancient values, particularly in the attitudes towards innocent, non-Christians, the lower classes, and the institution of slavery. As Europeans began to exercise their authority over the lower classes, an agricultural economy was all that remained of what was once Rome's vast international trade network and vibrant economy. Trade had diminished significantly, and the Church and self-sufficient manorial estates became the primary economic force. The use of coinage declined, and barter became common, with land being the predominant commodity.

In the prior Roman epoch of cultural development, social organization was hierarchical, allowing for social mobility through military service, politics, and economic success. However, during the early medieval period, society became more rigidly stratified. Feudalism established a strict hierarchy with kings, nobles, knights, and peasants that limited social mobility to those born of noble status. Medieval culture emphasized faith in God, religious devotion, and a strict adherence to Christian teachings. Papal authority was unquestioned, leading to the reforms that integrated local cultural and spiritual practices into the law. Feudalism and the rise of the Church led to a decentralized system of governance where Kings and lords held authority, and ethical obligations of the Church were tied to maintaining existing feudal relationships, often requiring slave labor.

While slavery was common in both Rome and medieval Europe, attitudes towards the enslaved differed. In Rome, slaves made up over two-thirds of the population, including educated and skilled captives who worked in vital state institutions and uneducated individuals sentenced to hard labor. Skilled slaves and those in domestic roles received more humane treatment and were integral to the state and family unit. As the Roman Empire declined and the supply of enslaved people dwindled, laws were enacted to maintain a viable slave population, prohibiting manumission and the killing of enslaved people by their owners. Towards the end of the empire, Roman Law recognized fundamental rights for enslaved people, including citizenship and the ability to seek relief for violations of their rights.

Roman Law persisted in medieval Europe but lacked the dialectic and interrogative processes that created it in Roman culture. The Holy Roman Empire, with its dwindling resources, did not significantly improve the law. As Europe declined into feudalism, its fragmented territories underwent wars of consolidation, culminating in the coronation of Charlemagne in 800 C.E. Although Charlemagne believed his empire was a continuation of the old Roman Empire, the ancient Roman civil authority and infrastructure had collapsed. Roads and aqueducts were in disrepair, and the Christian Church, the only surviving institution of the defunct state, became the center of economic activity. The Church preserved the libraries, educated its chosen flock—the Roman Catholic Christians—and administered the Canon Law. More importantly, the Church, which was the largest landowner in Europe, and the monarchy relied on the enslavement of the local populations.

Without a viable, currency-based economy, the monarchy's control of land was the only means of paying for the loyalty of barons and knights. During the Dark Ages, when the Christian Church became a central authority and economic force in Western Europe, poor peasants, who made up approximately 90 percent of the agriculturalists in Europe,[1] were indispensable to the manor's functioning. However, the Church condoned serfdom as the necessary result of sin, although it was a harsh, unjust system that initiated many rebellions, such as the 1381 Great Rising in England. While Rome's Stoic tradition had encouraged virtue, courage, wisdom, justice, and temperance, the medieval mind focused on the word of God

---

1   Tawney R.H. Religion and the rise of Capitalism, p. 55.

in the bible as the barometer of a humane society and ignored its vow to protect the poor and unfortunate.

When the Portuguese incursions into Africa began in the 15th century, the dignity of enslaved persons had vanished despite the efforts of the Church to adhere to Christian values. Innocent human beings were routinely condemned as subhuman chattels based on arbitrary religious percepts and unjust wars, evidenced by a series of Papal Bulls written by Pope Nicholas V between 1452 and 1493. These Papal Bulls comprise The Doctrine of Discovery, which is summarized by the following excerpt from Dum Diversas:

> ...invade, search out, capture, vanquish, and subdue all Saracens and pagans whatsoever, and other enemies of Christ wheresoever placed, and the kingdoms, dukedoms, principalities, dominions, possessions, and all movable and immovable goods whatsoever held and possessed by them to reduce their persons to perpetual slavery, and to apply and appropriate to himself and his successors the kingdoms, dukedoms, counties, principalities, dominions, possessions, and goods, and convert them to his and their use and profit.

> —Pope Nicholas V (Papal Bull Dum Diversas–1452)

As Vicar of Christ who believed himself empowered by Jesus's words to St. Peter in John 21:16-17, the Pope assumed the responsibility to care for Christ's followers in his absence from Earth. He declared non-Christian lands free for the taking and their inhabitants subject to seizure and perpetual enslavement. The Papal Bull was a departure from the old Roman law that recognized the taking of captives only under the just war doctrine of military ethics, which set conditions for declarations of war. In areas granting advantages to Europeans, the Canon Law remained linked to Roman Law, particularly in international relations, where it provided the precedence for military operations in foreign lands. While the new edicts saw innocent non-Christians condemned as chattel, and as their owners claimed absolute power over them, the old Roman laws, particularly the law of nature, allowed Europeans the right to sail any inland waterway and settle on land at the water's edge to conduct trade. As medieval society developed and transitioned to the early modern era, the capture and enslavement of non-Christians as chattel became the primary objective of explorers interacting with the blameless inhabitants of the lands beyond Western European borders.

The publication of *A Short Account of the Destruction of the Indies* in 1552 by Bartholome de Las Casas is the earliest account of the atrocities committed by the Spanish against indigenous populations in South America. The book, banned in Europe for 300 years, lists horrific tortures, killings, and abuses of the indigenous people. While these atrocities occurred during the early modern era, their root cause of avarice was in the medieval period when Europe's evolving legal system embraced a range of immoral behaviors driven by debt, usury, and war of plunder. These ethical violations had routinely violated the medieval Christian Church's taboo against usury, a recognized source of moral corruption in ancient Greece and Rome. Usury, which often led to the enslavement of debtors, marked the emergence of a new ethic during the Protestant Reformation when the Church openly embraced the role of usury in generating wealth. Papal bulls, such as Dum Diversas, provided the legal means for staggering profits of chattel slavery that made usury affordable to the elite debtors. Before the Protestant Reformation, the centuries of wealth accumulation through the legal enslavement of the peasants in Europe's feudal system and commercial trade generated the accumulated capital necessary for building the mechanisms of the chattel slavery that were to emerge in the modern era. These included sailing ships, navigation, cannons, and pistols for exploiting the unwary inhabitants of the new lands across the oceans with a brutality unknown in history.

Much of Western Europe's legal stance towards slavery originated from Rome's unique legal system that the Holy Roman Empire adapted to form a new Western legal tradition. There was no continuity between the older Greek Law and the Roman Law adopted by the Holy Roman Empire. While Roman jurists had used the Greek dialectical method to devise a practical, interrogative process among Roman citizens, the result was still their unique legal system. The categorized responses that became the basis of Roman civil law had come from the ranks of Rome's citizens. Through the dialectical process and over time, a legal standard arose that applied to each specific category of the law appearing in Classical Roman society.[2]

The Holy Roman Empire's reconstructed legal system was partially based on Roman customs combined with local European tribal traditions. Roman Law consisted of the Proclamations of Bishops and the Ecumenical Council of Nicaea, along with The New Testament and the *synods* or proclamations from bishops from North Africa. The New Canon Law of the Holy Roman Empire included Germanic tribal customs inherent in the Frankish kingdom of Charles I, particularly the system of patronage that rewarded loyal members of the tribe. The tradition of patronage became widespread in the Holy

---

2   Berman, J. Howard. *Law and Revolution: the Formation of the Western Legal Tradition*, pp. 123–135

Roman Empire during the Feudal era when the land was the principal means of rewarding the noble class.

Although the emerging Western Law lacked Classical Rome's intellectual rigor, The Holy Roman Empire developed a religious component of the law that equated pain and suffering to a Christlike redemption. Punishment for crimes was initially a tit-for-tat assemblage of penalties consisting of bones broken based on the crime committed and the local traditions of the different European tribes. There was no logic in the types of ghastly injuries inflicted on the guilty as punishment became linked with extreme pain. Over time, as Christian principles predominated, trial by ordeal inevitably reduced justice to painful, dangerous tests by fire or water, with the expectation that God's intervention would save the innocent.

Western Christianity's Distinguishing Feature

Christianity, which evolved from various religious ideas circulating in the large, cosmopolitan city of Alexandria under Roman control, is the most critical pillar of modern Western culture. In the old city, views from Egyptian Mysteries, Platonism, Zoroastrianism, Judaism, Stoicism, Gnosticism, and Coptic Christianity had developed and spread in the Mediterranean region. Under the Roman Emperor Constantine, Christianity acquired its unique brand where Roman civil authorities, its ecumenical councils of bishops, and the Church, acting as instruments of the state, generated and preserved the cannon. The most influential law passed by the Emperor occurred at The First Nicene Ecumenical Council, convened in 325 C.E., declaring Jesus as equal to God. This newfound belief contradicted the traditional beliefs of the Mediterranean region that had acknowledged the male child in the trinity as separate from the Father. Constantine's decree established the Nicene Creed that radically differentiated Western Christianity from Orthodox Christianity. Constantine initiated the split in Christianity in the 4th century with a violent campaign of death and destruction against all those who rejected his edict. The destruction extended to all religious symbols and temples across the Roman Empire.

The split in Christianity initiated by Constantine continued informally until the Church Fathers revised the Canon Law in 1054. The date marks the formal separation between the Christian sects of Catholicism and the Eastern Orthodoxy.[3] More importantly, it marked a break with tradition as the new laws

---

3   Berman, J. Howard. *Law and Revolution: the Formation of the Western Legal Tradition*, pp. 2, 85–119.

incorporated new customs and ideas from the evolving European society that continually formed a new canon. As societal conditions evolved, Canon Law adapted accordingly. Despite the Holy Roman Empire's efforts to curb avarice and usury, both the Church and State struggled to maintain control as society transitioned from feudalism to a capitalist economy. The acceptance of usury in commerce occurred as feudalism's land barter system became obsolete, and money, usury, and debt became the primary means of rewarding loyalty, accruing wealth, and achieving social status. As land for barter became scarce, the need for money increased, and money lenders, with their usurious fees, became more and more necessary for economic growth. Correspondingly, the canon became more accommodating to the vice.

The caste system in European feudalism restricted the membership of the nobility to land owners. However, as money accrual increased from usury, these restrictions changed to include anyone with money. The rush to accrue money began within Europe before the First Crusade in 1095, as bands of knights roamed the land, robbing the dispossessed peasants. The lust for gold led to the first attack on Constantinople, the capital of Byzantium and a landmark Christian city founded by Emperor Constantine. However, it was not the Muslims who sacked the town but Christian armies on their way to Jerusalem during the Fourth Crusade in 1204. With the increasing accumulation of money in the hands of capable individuals, the old guard—the oligarchy—could no longer deny a place at the altar of privilege to those among the landless majority, who resorted to pillage and plunder to acquire wealth first in Europe and later in the Holy Land during the Crusades, and in Africa.

The Origins of a Local Natural Law Theory in Europe

The Holy Roman Empire had no written legal system before the Benedictine monk Gratian wrote *The Concordance of Discordant Canones* in 1140. The book, also known as *The Decretum of Gratian*, is his collection of approximately 4,000 disparate texts issued by various monarchs and popes over the centuries that sought to standardize the differing laws of multiple groups in medieval society. Gratian separated law into categories of divine law, natural law, human law, the law of the Church, the law of princes or secular law, enacted law, and customary law.[4] By synthesizing and organizing the legal texts, Gratian provided a framework that addressed contradictions and ambiguities in existing laws.[5]

---

4   Berman, J. Howard. *Law and Revolution: the Formation of the Western Legal Tradition*, pp. 143–151.
5   Gratian and His Book: How a Medieval Teacher Changed European Law and Religion. Available at: www.academic.oup.com/ojlr/article/10/1/1/6271403

Gratian's compiled texts, known as glosses, became the medieval texts used by European universities to teach law. His adaptation of the law to European conditions disregarded the traditional universal consideration the defunct Roman Empire gave to the law. For example, the reinterpretation of the Roman law of nature, that had granted the old empire access to waterways, trees, and fruits in forests on foreign lands[6] empowered Europeans to lay claim to the newly discovered lands beyond Europe's borders, on coastal river banks and remote islands. The law, particularly in the early modern era, facilitated the English's seizure of these lands along the mouths of rivers and river banks in West Africa. The new interpretation of the Roman Law of nature was instrumental in creating the territory of The Gambia, which is made up of narrow strips of appropriated land on both sides of the Gambia River in West Africa.

In the late 17th century, a more devastating corruption of Roman Law occurred in the Virginia colony that redefined Africans as hereditary slaves. Although Roman Law did not discriminate against human beings by skin color and had never denied their natural rights as free human beings, the European adaptation and subsequent modification of *Partus Sequitur Ventrem*, which is the Roman Law used for tracking ownership of animals, to track the offspring of African women in the English colonies. In ancient Rome, the law initially controlled ownership of animals by monitoring the mother's offspring. However, under Europe's reinvigorated slave economies, the law became applicable to African people in stark violation of the traditional understanding of the natural rights of free-born human beings. The amended law played a decisive role in rejecting the citizenship of the children of Englishmen and African women. It branded African people as hereditary enslaved people, beginning in colonial Virginia in 1676 and Barbados in 1662.

Gratian's concept of natural law caters to the individual's perception of law based on historical experience. He summarized the law as "Do unto others as you would have them do unto you." However, The Golden Rule, which traditionally involved reciprocity and personal involvement in observing the law, became infused with local European traditions based on retribution. In the orthodox tradition, natural law comes from divine law, from God, and the ancients perceived natural law as eternal and unchanging. However, until the birth of the Holy Roman Empire, when individual perception based on local traditions influenced the interpretation of the law, the reclassification of Africans as chattel had no legal foundation.

---

6   The Ames Foundation. *Justinian, Institutes*. J.B. Moyle trans. (Oxford, 1911) p.19. Available at: www.amesfoundation.law.harvard.edu/digital/CJCiv/JInst.pdf

Most of the changes characterizing the modern era occurred during the changing times in Europe's Feudal era. The growing use of land to barter for the military services of warriors was the traditional tribal custom of patronage among Europe's tribal peoples. With this method, the monarchy seized lands and leased them to the barons, who provided money and knights to the king. The barons, in turn, leased land to their knights, who then subjugated the peasants and forced food and menial labor concessions from them to pay the baron. Wars for land rights occurring during the formation of the Holy Roman Empire persisted through its initial split into three competing territories. Charlemagne's son, the Co-Emperor, divided the empire among his three sons and unwittingly planted the seeds of personal ambition, war, and debt. Predictably, towards the end of the 9th century, the empire had fractured into three separate kingdoms: France, Germany, and the remaining territories of Burgundy. The collapse of central authority from the ambitions of competing monarchies sowed the seeds of debt, avarice, and slavery.

The chronic search for land, money, and power in the Feudal society led to a second prolonged conflict, rooted in the ambitions of the papacy seeking control over spiritual and state matters. The War for Investiture created shifting alliances among supporters of Pope Gregory VII against the various monarchies of the Holy Roman Empire under Emperor Henry VI. For a hundred years (11–12th century), a war continued between the papacy and the monarchy, seeking autonomous rule over the land. The papacy sought to control the appointment of bishops to various cities and principalities. Through control of the investiture process, it desired to manage construction contracts for churches and related offices that formed the core of the economy of the Holy Roman Empire.

On the other hand, the monarchy believed that the Divine Right of Kings gave the sovereign territorial control and the power to appoint bishops and even the Pope himself. The wars for investiture shaped the continent's character as predominantly Christian but with deep religious and political divisions that led to a separation of Church and State. The division between Church and State became formalized in the 1122 *Concordat of Worms* treaty between Pope Calixtus II and Emperor Henry V. The treaty allowed the state economic benefits, such as the right to tax subjects in lands not claimed by the Church. In addition, it prohibited the state from taxing church lands. More importantly, the treaty set the precedent for ending church control over state affairs. The wars for investiture resulted in the eventual creation of a legal framework where the bishops appointed by the monarchy swore allegiance to the sovereign in military and state affairs but maintained loyalty to the Pope in spiritual matters. Five hundred years after The *Concordat of Worms*, Europeans formalized the form of the modern secular state with the 1648 *Treaty of Westphalia*, which established the concept of sovereignty for the first time in Europe. War no longer had a religious foundation but became grounded in political and territorial ambitions and the right of the state to control its religious affiliation.

The culmination of almost six hundred years of war in Europe did not end the chaos that ravaged the region. Before an economic resurgence could begin, more wars and the Bubonic Plague (1346–53) claimed approximately 75–200 million lives.[7] Historians often cite the plague and Europe's unending wars as determinants of an economic boom in the 15th century that led to the Renaissance. Typically, the dramatic decrease in the labor pool caused by the plague and the corresponding wage increase correlates with creating a middle class of consumers that transitioned from feudalism and serfdom to a capitalist economy.[8] However, throughout the medieval era, with the increasing scarcity of land, economic and social conditions were more dependent on the accumulation of money from usury, war, merchant banking, and trade than reason.

Usury

From the earliest evidence, dating back to ancient Phoenicia (c. 1550 B.C.E. to 300 B.C.E.), the basis for wealth creation in the Mediterranean region was trading financed by loans with interest added to the principal. In ancient Athens, adding interest to commercial transactions occurred first in overseas trade. Charging a small fee (interest) on loans was reasonable because of the inherent risk of losing cargo during storms. However, from its earliest beginnings, usury has had a negative connotation that originated with the misuse of ancient Athenian wealth placed in local temples for safekeeping. Unknown to the citizens of Athens, temple priests used their wealth to finance trade and war for profit. From these ancient times, the elites used money and interest rates to accumulate wealth and unfairly perpetuate cycles of debt and war. In early Mediterranean societies of Greece and Rome, a small charge for loans for ordinary purposes was legal.

The ancient meaning of associating usury with immoral behavior differs from the modern definition, which carries no moral value. Generally, usury, which is an English term based on the Latin *usuria*, was associated with

---

7   Austin Alchon, Suzanne (2003). *A pest in the land: new world epidemics in a global perspective.* University of New Mexico Press. p. 21.
8   David Herlihy, Samuel Kline Cohn. T*he Black Death and the Transformation of the West*, pp. 49–50.

the extortion and enslavement of debtors and their families. Plato believed usury was contrary to nature.[9] Aristotle[10] equated it to theft because the added interest charge for using money diminished its real value and thus robbed the owner of its fair exchange value. Aristotle defines *exchange value* as a proportional value between different categories of goods, and this value is in the trust people have for each other. In Aristotle's virtue ethics, injustice in pricing was any price exceeding the mean or what is fair value.[11] Aristotle equates usurers to tyrants and attaches harsh labels of wicked, impious, and unjust. The tyrant, he claims, seeks a base gain through sacking temples and the usurer through charging high interest rates.[12] In the Christian bible (Ezekiel 18:19-13), the punishment of death is deemed worthy for the usurer. Until the fourth century, the ecclesiastical writers and clergy believed it was inhumane to demand interest from a poor and needy man.[13]

While the late Middle Ages had begun to normalize usury, traditionally, there have been numerous efforts to curb or abolish the practice. In ancient Athens, while it was appropriate to charge an added fee for the use of credit involving risky overseas trading, transactions that did not include the risks of sea voyages were exempted from interest charges. In ancient Rome, a one percent monthly interest rate cap, or 12 percent per year, was legal. The Roman Empire used simple interest, where interest is paid only on the principal, and did not use compound interest rates, where interest is paid on the principal plus interest. Eventually, the Christian theocracy outlawed usury altogether as the empire collapsed. In 1290, King Edward I issued an edict expelling all Jews from England for charging interest in their money-lending operations. In 1311, Pope Clement V made the ban on usury absolute and declared all secular legislation in its favor null and void.[14]

Since the Athenians established the first repository for gold in the temple of Isis, the premise of controlling the risk associated with lending money through usury has not changed. However, the routine application of compound interest rates on loans plus interest to rapidly accumulate money has changed over the millennia as unethical and desperate actors

9   Plato (Laws, v. 742)

10   Aristotle (Politics, I, x, xi)

11   Browne, R. W. *The Nicomachean Ethics of Aristotle.* George Bell & Sons, 1889., Book 4, Ch. 5, pp. 131-132.

12   Browne, R. W., Tr.: *The Nicomachean Ethics of Aristotle.* George Bell & Sons, 1889. Book 4, Ch. 1, p. 92.

13   *New Advent: Catholic Encyclopedia.* Available at: http://www.newadvent.org/cathen/15235c.htm Accessed 2/25/2024.

14   Carlen, C. (ed.). 1990. *The Papal Encyclicals, Vol. I.* Raleigh, N.C. p. 15-17.

corrupted ethical standards. Loans with exorbitant interest rates financed the armies used by the European oligarchy to seize the commons and enforce slavery upon the peasantry. The oligarchy quickly reduced the peasantry's available European land in the emerging feudal system. It forced them to live as enslaved people, bound to their plots of land and indebted to the new lords of the manors.

Across Europe, the unending greed of the European aristocracy only exacerbated the peasant's plight. England and France, for example, fought The Hundred Years War (1337–1453) over the covetous territorial claims of the English King Edward III. The war led to unbearable hardships for the English peasantry. The pressing need for money to execute the war and pay off exorbitant loans with interest forced the English Monarchy to levy crushing taxes on an already burdened population living a rugged and severely restricted feudal existence. While the impoverished peasants had survived serfdom, the draconian policies of the English king left them no alternative but to begin the Peasant Revolt of 1338. The peasant rebellion sought to reduce the tax burden and end serfdom. Their dilemma of unbearable impoverishment, their violent reactions, and the reforms that followed resulted from the revolving door of the greed of powerful state actors, their indebtedness, and ensuing wars that were complicated by the scourge of compound interest rates as high as 150%.[15]

The expansion of England's wool industry, a monopoly that supplied wool to Europe, best exemplifies the rapid adoption of revolutionary finance methods in medieval Europe. As the wool industry came under the control of Italian bankers of the English Crown, they provided regular revenue for the English Monarchy (Edward I, II, and III). Customs charges to the bankers became the premier source of England's national wealth. The taxes collected far surpassed the antiquated medieval feudal financing methods of seizing land and wealth. The Italian bankers, foreign buyers, and investors paid England's taxes on wool. They relied on letters of credit, which allowed them access to the financial resources of the entire European continent. During Edward I and Edward II's reigns, the Royal debt to the Italian bankers reached £420,650, which outstripped England's national wealth considerably. The wealth of the bankers far surpassed the combined wealth of ordinary citizens.

Without the newfound source of wealth, the English Monarchy could not have conducted the Hundred Years' War. The meager resources of

---

15   A.R. Bell, C. Brooks and T.K. Moore. *Interest in Medieval Accounts: Examples from England, 1272–1340, p. 7.*

the English peasants, already severely taxed at the start of the Hundred Year's War in 1337, were insufficient to clear the previous year's debts. As Edward I prepared for war against the French, the English Crown experienced a credit crunch that would have proven detrimental to his reign if not for the loan services of the Italian bankers. For their services, the bankers gained access to England's wool industries and tin mines and control of much of the Crown's financial affairs.[16] Due to greed and the desire to compound wealth, the role of money changers, pawnbrokers, and merchant bankers grew in importance. A burgeoning financial system emerged in medieval Europe that relied increasingly on usury. However, as beneficial as banking was to the economy, it evoked the illegal practice of compound usury that the ancient writers of the Classical Era and the early Christians had compared to the most heinous crimes in their time.

The moneychangers increasingly relied on rapidly multiplying their wealth despite the Church's opposition. Usury provided increasing wealth for the profiteers as they financed avaricious, warring factions shaping medieval society's religious and economic course.[17] By the early to mid-medieval era (11-12 centuries), the primary driver of European economic development was European merchant banking, which first emerged in Northern Italy in Lucca. The increasing use of money and usury coincides with medieval Europe's first notable emergence of merchant capitalism and the financial panic of 1294. The Italian bankers failed to pay their debt obligations.

At various points in European history, usury was either reduced or outlawed completely, but the underlying principle of avarice that perpetuated the practice remained vibrant. Christian writers formulated Christian theology in the patristic era. The 3rd-century theologian St. Augustine preached and wrote exclusively on the importance of Christian virtue and piety, and he relied on biblical writings to oppose usury. In the 13th century, St. Thomas Aquinas also condemned the practice because it distorted the exchange value of money, as Aristotle had shown. St. Thomas's premise espousing Aristotelian virtue derives from the revered tradition, which associated spiritual purity with the reward of everlasting life.

---

16   Terry B. Schuyler. *The financing of the Hundred Year's War 1337–1360.* pgs. XIII–XV. www.archive.org/stream/financingofhundr00terrrich#page/4/mode/2up

17   A.R. Bell, C. Brooks and T.K. Moore. Interest in Medieval Accounts: Examples from England, 1272–1340.   www.books.google.com/books?id=-Og4DQAAQBAJ&pg=PA223&dq=Interest+in+Medieval+Accounts:+Examples+from+England,+1272%E2%80%931340.&hl=en&sa=X&ved=0ahUKEwiSyaqrkabaAhXRs1kKHYUUDJAQ6AEIKTAA#v=onepage&q=more%20and%20more%20common%20&f=false

Nevertheless, Middle Age ethics routinely accommodated money lenders and traders who ignored the canon law in pursuit of forbidden profits. The Catholic Church viewed usury as a practice that deprived the needy of their sustenance. The fifth Lateran Council (1512–17 C.E.) defines usury as follows:

"Some of these masters and doctors say that the credit organisations are unlawful. After a fixed period of time has passed, they say, those attached to these organisations demand from the poor to whom they make a loan so much per pound in addition to the capital sum. For this reason they cannot avoid the crime of usury or injustice, that is to say a clearly defined evil, since our Lord, according to Luke the evangelist, has bound us by a clear command that we ought not to expect any addition to the capital sum when we grant a loan. For, that is the real meaning of usury: when, from its use, a thing which produces nothing is applied to the acquiring of gain and profit without any work, any expense or any risk."[18]

The Church associated the practice with avarice and deprived usurers of Christian burial. Canon 13 of The Second Lateran Council (1139 C.E.) denounced usurers as follows:

Furthermore we condemn that practice accounted despicable and blame worthy by divine and human laws, denounced by Scripture in the Old and New Testaments, namely, the ferocious greed of usurers; and we sever them from every comfort of the Church, forbidding any archbishop or bishop, or an abbot of any order whatever or anyone in clerical orders, to dare to receive usurers, unless they do so with extreme caution; but let them be held infamous throughout their whole lives and, unless they repent, be deprived of a Christian burial.[19]

Canon 29 of the Council of Vienne (1311 C.E.) declares that,

"Furthermore, since money-lenders for the most part enter into usurious contracts so frequently with secrecy and guile that they can be convicted only with difficulty, we decree that they be compelled by ecclesiastical censure to open their account books, when there is question of usury. If indeed someone has fallen into the error of presuming to affirm pertinaciously that the practice of usury is not sinful, we decree that he is to be punished as a heretic . . ."[20]

---

18   The Fifth Lateran Council available at: www.ewtn.com/library/COUNCILS/LATERAN5.HTM
19   From H. J. Schroeder, Disciplinary Decrees of the General Councils: Text, Translation and Commentary, (St. Louis: B. Herder, 1937). pp. 195-213.
20   www.ewtn.com/library/COUNCILS/VIENNE.HTM

Liber Abaci

Despite the Church's legal restrictions on usury, by the 14th century and the aftermath of the Black Plague, an enormously enriched class of bankers routinely extended credit and charged interest throughout Europe. The methodology that made the minute interest rate calculations possible arrived in Italy from the Near East before the Renaissance. It allowed the use of fractions in a way that had been impossible with Roman numerals. The system relies on Arabic numerals and mathematics. Leonardo Bonacci (c. 1170–c. 1250), more widely known as Fibonacci, described the new methodology in *Liber Abaci* (Book of Calculations). The new math included using the double-entry ledger that gave rise to the modern banking system.

The growth of commerce, urbanization, and economic development occurred as ever-increasing sums of accumulated money became available to more and more borrowers. Bankers such as the Medici family openly circumvented the law against usury and, in the process, accumulated unparalleled sums of money as they charged small fees for converting international currencies and lending money. The Medici argued that their fees were not interest charges and did not conflict with the law against usury. The compulsion to accumulate wealth was strong enough that the execution of 5 of Medici's family members for capital crimes in preceding years did not deter his quest. By 1437, barely a generation after the end of the plague, The Medici family became the wealthiest and most powerful bankers in the 15th century, and the Republic of Florence had come under their financial and political control. Labor, production, and wages played less of a role in accumulating capital and the city's economic development than did usury and international trade that came in its wake. The success of The Medici bankers made usury the basis of capital accumulation and economic development throughout Europe. The city of Florence, The Medici base of operations, became European banking operations' financial capital of European banking operations..

The early Florentine bankers had a far reach, supplying money to the monarchs of Europe as far away as England. Incidentally, these monarchs were all engaged in European wars financed by bankers as money accumulated in banks such as The Medici and the Fuggers banks and commercial traders such as the Bardi and Peruzzi banks. Its uses went towards shipbuilding, financing war, slavery, and the lucrative spice and luxury trade throughout the Mediterranean region. Their money played a part in corrupting influential institutions such as the papacy and the monarchies of Europe. The Bardi and

Peruzzi bank and trading companies traded high-quality cloth, oil, and wine. Records show that in the 14th century, King Edward III of England was heavily indebted to them for £250,000.

The Fuggers Bank in Venice extended the financial domination of Europe. It controlled the throne and the money supply of the Holy Roman Empire and the shipping industry, trade, and banking in the Mediterranean region through credit control. Venice's control of the money supply and the trade routes made it a worthy adversary and a superpower by medieval standards despite its tiny size. The Venetian Empire (10th–18th century) was the primary beneficiary of Rome's maritime power. Venetian bankers controlled trade from as far north as the Black Sea to the ports on the Silk Road in Constantinople and North Africa. They had the most significant shipbuilding industry globally, located at Arsenal in Northern Italy. The facility that began in 1104 C.E. grew into Europe's most important industrial complex. The Venetians had once supplied the Roman Empire with galleys operated by enslaved people from the Mediterranean region and Northern Europe. Venice's maritime legacy stemmed from the remnants of the Western Roman Empire's naval power. Near the end of the Middle Ages, Venice had over 300 ships, each capable of carrying over a hundred tons, while its larger ships carried up to 400 tons of cargo.[21] While the power of the Medici declined, the demand for increasing sums of money, credit, usury, shipbuilding, and trade did not. The need for finance was an ever-increasing necessity, which the Fuggers Bank in Venice fulfilled.

At the start of the Middle Ages, usury sustained the papacy's and European monarchies' appetite for wealth and power for more than five centuries. Maintaining standing armies during that period of shifting political alliances and prolonged wars between the Church and the Holy Roman Empire was the only way to triumph. The House of Hapsburg came to rule over 20 different kingdoms through wars, bribery, and marital alliances. Within their territories of the Holy Roman Empire, there was intolerance for the taboos of the prior age against usury and a rejection of the Church's religious authority. As waring escalated and the Church's jurisdiction over commerce weakened, the Church's moral authority was diminished, particularly in regions where banking and trading were most concentrated—in the large cities and financial centers of the Middle Ages. While the respectable society of church followers frowned on the sins of the trader and money lender, their increasingly tolerated moral corruption occurred out of sight in the ghettos.

---

21   Parry, John Horace. *The Discovery of the Sea*, p. 20–21.

The violations of canon law sanctioned by the Church of Rome and scholars of the School of Salamanca had an impact far beyond the confines of the ghettos. As banking, trade, and the accumulation of money increased, the medieval era became fertile ground for the barbarism of chattel slavery.

While it had percolated before the 15th century, the devolution of morality became a normalized affair, particularly after the Crusades had sufficiently angered the Muslims. Their retaliation made trade extremely difficult for Europeans, who had established a lucrative trade with the Orient. The search for wealth became a priority as the Portuguese King Jao began a strategy that included gaining financial support and a legal pretext from the papacy to conquer Muslim territory across the straits of Gibraltar.

The wars between Christians and Muslims gave urgency to searching for an alternate trade route to the Orient. However, the more critical historical development in the systematic enslavement of African people was the 400 years of contact Europe had with Near Eastern culture. Revolutionary ideas in science from the Orient changed European culture, notably how they conducted business. Among the earliest beneficiaries of the early contact with the Near East were The Knights Templar, who used the newfound knowledge to become Europe's earliest bankers and primary financiers of the European monarchies in the 12th century. They grew wealthy with vast landholdings while financing Europe's Christian armies. They remained in control of European banking until they fell victim to the seizure of their assets by the French and English monarchies, (King Phillip of France and King Edward II of England), beginning in 1307.

The newly acquired science to compound wealth was exploited without interruption for at least 200 years before the Muslims began interrupting Europe's trade with the Orient. The allure of compound interest was strong enough to compromise the existing ecclesiastic laws condemning usury. Bankers and traders used innovative methods to circumvent existing canonical laws prohibiting usury. The new math copied from the Near East made it possible for money lenders to charge minuscule amounts for exchanging international currencies. The fees were small enough that bankers such as the Medici could claim it was not usury, thereby circumventing canon laws.[22] The new method of double ledger accounting and letters of credit allowed Europeans to conduct business in faraway ports without carrying large amounts of gold. The double ledger accounting method accurately tracked profits and losses to fractions of a penny. In addition, letters of credit

---

22 www.ehistory.osu.edu/articles/medieval-banking-twelfth-and-thirteenth-centuries

allowed repayment of loans in distant cities and in different currencies. These methodologies were so efficient that they remain the basis of present-day international finance and banking.

The trade blockade sharpened hostilities between Christians and Muslims in the Iberian Peninsula and exposed a stark reality for Europeans. They could not grow their wealth without the lucrative trade of gold in exchange for the precious silk cloth, jade, ceramics, and spices of the Asian markets. The religious wars and the ensuing cash crunch exacerbated the feudal fundraising method of seizing available land assets, and the oligarchy began a frantic search for gold and silver. Queen Isabella reformed the Inquisition as a tool to extract confessions and plunder the wealth of the newly converted Jewish Christians, Jews, and Muslims who were finally driven from al-Andalus in 1492. Before Queen Isabella's reign, the Inquisition had operated as a court that traditionally issued mild rebuttals for heresy. During her reign, the Church and the Spanish Monarchy re-purposed it as a court to extract wealth, using extreme tortures to elicit confessions from its wealthy victims.

The tide of history had turned decidedly against the Muslims, whose conquest of Spain had endured for several hundred years, beginning in the 8th century. However, by 1250, Christians had conquered almost all territory in Spain. In 1492, Queen Isabella finally conquered Grenada's remaining Muslim enclave in southern Spain. Granada was the southernmost territory in the Iberian Peninsula, ruled by the Moorish Sultanate of Abdul Hassan. Arab historian Leo Africanus (1485–1554) describes the Sultan as a tyrant he blames for attacking the Christians in the neighboring territory of Castile to bolster his declining popularity among his people.[23] Leo Africanus was a Muslim captive of the Spanish whom Pope Leo X baptized in 1520. His writing presents a Christian view of the causes of the war. Other authors point to Queen Isabella's failure to receive tribute from Granada upon her coronation as a cause of the invasion of Granada. The Spanish enslaved many of the Moors of Granada in gold mines in Peru, where Spain had established its first colony. They expelled the remaining population to Morocco, where their fellow Muslims further victimized them.[24]

Portuguese actions in Africa show that an unprecedented level of greed motivated the early sea voyages and drove changes in the perception of the

---

23   Leo Africanus. *The History and Description of Africa, 1550–1600.*
24   Leo Africanus. *The History and Description of Africa.* Vol I. (translated in 1600 by John Pory p. x. Available at: www.play.google.com/books/reader?id=PwU7AAAAIAAJ&printsec=frontcover&output=reader&authuser=0&hl=en&pg=GBS. PP9

law. Avarice had become a permanent fixture in the culture accustomed to political rivalries, usury, debt, and war. The Portuguese King's determination to establish a trade monopoly motivated the attack on Ceuta. After achieving that objective, the king prohibited Africans of the Maghreb from trading with each other without a Portuguese intermediary. Divergences from traditional Christian ethics went beyond avarice and included St. Augustine's Just War Doctrine and chattel slavery violations. The divergent ethics challenged life's longstanding, unquestionable moral purpose from the Hellenistic idea of The One. Moral corruption grew to the extent that it swayed the Catholic Church from its mission of salvation and became embroiled in the quest for wealth. The evolving moral decline became the incubator of social upheavals, economic destabilization, famine, and prolonged genocide unleashed in Africa and the Americas. The European policy at the root of Africa's demise and Europe's economic expansion is termed benignly as trade. However, trade, as an ancient human capacity to agreeably interact, barter, and prosper, contrasts sharply with the European Oligarchy's activity in Africa and the Americas. In effect, their prosperity depended on a counter-trend to the noble achievements of the classical civilizations in the Mediterranean that had, at the very least, attempted to maintain ancient spiritual ideals based on virtue.

Debt obligations of the oligarchy were at the core of European greed. The Portuguese King João (John) I ruled over the poorest territory in the Holy Roman Empire, founded in 1135 C.E. He needed increasing sums of money for his kingdom. In Spain, Queen Isabella assumed the throne of the newly formed kingdom in 1474 and inherited enormous debts incurred from the wars in the Holy Roman Empire under the reign of Charles V. The papacy also succumbed to the economic practices of the time and cooperated with the monarchy. Pope Martin V had a vested interest in the Monarchy's promise of wealth. He supported their first military campaign against Ceuta with an unusual Papal Bull urging support for the war.[25] The Pope reasoned that the fight against the Muslims would bring converts into the fold of the Christian Theocracy and save souls.[26] He appointed Prince Henry as Ceuta's Administrator and authorized him to operate as the Church's instrument of salvation while conducting Portugal's war of appropriation in the Maghreb lands to the west of Egypt. The papacy acquiesced to the Portuguese demands, legitimizing the slave trade for political expediency, as it stood to profit from Portugal's conquests in Africa.[27]

---

25   Housley, Norman. *Religious Warfare in Europe* 1400-1536, Oxford University Press, 2002, p. 182.
26   (Housley, Norman p. 184)
27   Burton, p. 197. Pope Martin V launched the Africa Crusade in 1418.

Chapter 6

From Natural Law to Positive Law

The Problem of Legal Positivism

Natural law refers to a set of timeless philosophical principles that suggest inherent laws of morality and justice common to all humans originate from a divine source rather than societal rules.[1] Humans do not write these laws and the moral principles that emanate from them. Plato wrote that we can grasp these laws instinctively, and Aristotle believed reason and experience were the means to perceive them. Aristotle's natural law theory, which cites natural law's origins in nature, became a source for the writings of St. Paul, St. Augustine, and St. Thomas Aquinas. Legal experts believed that natural law originated from a divine source until the 18th and 19th-century legal theories of David Hume and Anthony Bentham. Hume and Bentham's arguments against natural law lay in their mistrust of the divine source of law, which natural law proponents referenced without any empirical evidence. Without concrete evidence from natural law proponents, Hume and Bentham claimed that natural law percepts are strictly from local observations and are not reasoned moral propositions originating from the divine.

Despite Aristotle's belief in nature as the source of natural law, his conclusions about enslaved people as natural-born slaves, were based on his observations of Greek society, where women, children, and enslaved people were subordinated to the Greek male citizens. Based on his senses and experiences, which are technically void of moral sentiments, Aristotle concluded that some people in Greek society were natural-born slaves because they lacked the rational capacity to govern themselves and were better off being ruled by others.[2] However, he did not provide a moral justification for their enslavement. In the 17th-century, the legal theories of David Hume and

---

1   Natural Law. Britannica. Available at: www.britannica.com/topic/natural-law
2   Aristotle. Politics, Book I.

Jeremy Bentham both emphasized the importance of distinguishing between facts and values. They argued that moral principles should be based on human experience and rational analysis rather than an assumed natural order or divine source. They believed natural law should be based on facts, not on presumptions of morality from an unsubstantiated divine inspiration.

The concept of natural law as a derivative of the environment is an idea that discounts the role of divine power in human affairs. Since the replacement of natural law, the basis for viewing reality depends on reason and experience as the source of inspiration and truth. What is often perceived as divine natural law is instead seen as rooted in the social customs practiced by societies over time. Philosophers like Hume and Bentham argued that the soul's supernatural connection to God was unnecessary and could result in moral principles lacking justification through reason and evidence. Nevertheless, the most fundamental natural laws—such as the preservation of life, the drive to procreate, and the desire to understand the world and seek truth—are deeply ingrained instincts that predate the emergence of Homo sapiens. These laws arguably did not originate from human reason but are innate to life forms on Earth. Their origins are intertwined with the process of creation, as the ancient Egyptians believed.

Kemet

The oldest reference to the divine source of law is from the ancient Kemetic civilization that traces its history to prehistoric times. References to natural law in nature originate from the word nTr or Netjer, the Kemetic term for divine power or God. The term stems from an era when pantheism predominated, and God was believed to be the active and animating force in all things. All life was believed to be self-similar to the Creator, sharing similar features and the processes perceived as natural law.[3] Kemet believed that the Goddess Ma'at governs the natural world, and her laws and universal principles are truth, balance, order, harmony, law, morality, and justice. Ma'at is described in Kemet's creation story as the Creator's consort. The implication is that Ma'at was in effect at the beginning of creation, suggesting that the divine is the source of natural law, and the divine law which is known only to God. The Egyptians believed that Ma'at regulated the stars, seasons, and the actions of mortals and deities.

By definition, Ma'at is an early form of natural law, referring to a body of

---

3   See Shabaka Stone Theology.

unchanging moral principles regarded as a basis for all human conduct. One of the earliest uses of a moral principle emanating from Ma'at is the Golden Rule, which is the principle of treating others as one would like to be treated. It originated in Kemet, around 2040 B.C.E. where the Maxims of Ptahhotep advises, "Do for one who may do for you, that you may be sure when he does for you that he shall do it right."[4] Other principles of natural law include The Code of Hammurabi, a Babylonian legal text composed around 1750 B.C.E.

Ancient Greece and Rome

Natural law played a significant role in the legal systems of ancient Greece and Rome. Plato did not have a natural law theory, but set the groundwork for its development. His student Aristotle believed in inherent, universal moral principles derived from nature and he made the distinction between natural law and written law."[5] The Roman Senator and Philosopher Cicero also distinguished natural law from civil law, which he states that Roman citizens were bound to obey. In the 4th and 5th centuries C.E., Saint Augustine developed the Christian version of natural law. Augustine believed that natural law was based on the universal principles of justice and fairness that govern the behavior of all beings. He derived these principles from the nature of God and believed that they were evident in the natural world. St. Augustine argued that natural law was a universal principle that applied to all people, regardless of their religious beliefs or cultural backgrounds.

Despite being inspired by Aristotle's works, Saint Augustine believed that the church's canon law, which is the body of rules that govern the practices and beliefs of the Christian church, was based on natural law. He believed that the church's laws should be in harmony with natural law and guided by the principles of justice and fairness:

> The ultimate sources of the Church's Canon Law are God recognized through natural divine law (as found in the nature of things) and Revelation (positive divine law) found in tradition. Canon law also includes positive law formulated by the legislator that conforms to divine law. Philosophic speculation does not give rise to canon law that the Church considers emanating from God through the holy books, Apostolic writings, and living tradition.[6]

---

4 Fontaine, Carole R. "A Modern Look at Ancient Wisdom: The Instruction of Ptahhotep Revisited." The Biblical Archaeologist 44 (1981), pp 155–60.
5 Britannica. "Early formulations of the concept of natual law. www.britannica.com/topic/natural-law
6 Source: New Advent. Accessed 1/5/2022. Available at: www.newadvent.org/cathen/09056a.htm

Romans had a view of *The Law of Nations (Jus Gentium)* which governed the behavior of all humans, as an extension of natural law that protected the rights of all humans and governed their behavior wherever they may be. The law of nature or natural law governed the rights of animals and humans and under the law of nations, it also granted all humans access to air, running water, the sea and its shores. The Romans perceived these rights as universal and common to all, giving them equal access to foreign lands via rivers, seashores, and to the fruits and wild game from those lands. Although Romans thought that *The Law of Nations* was universal, they nevertheless created limitations that respected the human rights of all people. However, although natural law respected that all are born free, *The Law of Nations* did not reject slavery which fell under civil authority.

Near the end of the Roman Empire, apparent violations of natural law emerged as Saint Augustine addressed the issue of slavery in his writings. In "The City of God," Saint Anthony acknowledged the immorality of slavery and emphasized it was a consequence of sin rather than a natural or just condition. He believed that slavery was a result of the fallen state of humanity and saw it as evidence of the moral disorder in the world. However, he did not advocate for its abolition but urged enslaved people to endure their condition patiently and virtuously while striving for spiritual liberation.

Saint Augustine's view towards slavery emerged as he faced the calamity of Rome's impending collapse. In appeasement of angry Roman citizens who blamed Christianity for the Visigoth sacking of the city, Saint Augustine distinguished the religion the material concerns of the world. Saint Augustine did not specify a separation of Church and State, but stressed that the two worlds he equates to the city of God and the earthly city, existed by different rules. His explanation for the evil that befell Rome was to account for the sin in the world as irrelevant to the city of God.

Slavery, although immoral, thrived in Europe's feudal era throughout Western Europe, despite the Church's moral directives of Saint Anthony's monastic Christianity that sought the soul's liberation through good works. Natural law violations persisted in Europe under Papal authority. The European use of the old Roman law of nations in the 15th century to sail up rivers and to establish trading posts on the shores of Kingdoms in Africa expanded to include unwarranted ownership rights of all foreign lands and perpetual enslavement of their non-christian populations in stark violation of the universal rights of all humans the Romans had observed.

The Western Legal System

After the collapse of Rome's strong central government and prior to the 11th-century Papal Revolution, law in the Holy Roman Empire was disorganized and had merged with the local feudal customs of Europe's isolated populations. Due to the lack of a standardized law, the Pope sought to produce the first Western system of Canon Law, which incorporated remnants of the old Roman Law alongside tribal, mercantile, and unique European traditions. This legal system was independent of both the state and feudal lords. The Papal Revolution facilitated the development of integrated legal systems, including Canon Law, Royal Law, and Urban Law, laying the foundation for modern Western legal institutions and concepts.

However, the New Canon Law, contrary to natural law concepts, ignored critical issues such as the removal of local populations from their traditional lands and their enslavement under the manorial system, which severely limited their freedom of movement. Combined with the obligations of feudal lords to maintain food production and service the manor, the Church tacitly accepted slavery as part of the natural order because it stood to benefit from the enforced labor of impoverished peasants.

As non-clerical sectors of society largely disregarded Canon Law and focused instead on the emerging hybrid legal systems, the Church struggled to assert authority. It was relegated to a junior position relative to the feudal system, which was dominated by regional populations and territories. During the wars over the investiture of bishops sparked by Pope Gregory VII's reforms, feudal, manorial, mercantile, and urban laws coexisted uneasily with Canon Law. Mercantile Law, for example, served the interests of merchants engaged in local, interregional, and international trade.[7] Christian ethics, which had first succumbed to the rules-based ethical requirements of the state as early as 313 CE when Christianity was legalized in Rome, no longer adhered to the intellectual rigor of the ancient Roman tradition.

The Gregorian Reformation—also known as the Investiture Controversy—arose from Pope Gregory VII's declaration of the political and legal supremacy of the Church. His reforms sought to establish the independence of the clergy from secular control, including the authority to depose emperors and kings.[8] To secure ownership of the land, agricultural produce, and tithes of its Christian flock and to protect them from greed, the

---

7   Berman. J. Howard. *Law and Revolution: The Formation of the Western Legal Tradition,* 1983, pp.84–86.
8   ———. Ibid. p. 87.

Church demanded control over the bishops and their domains, including their agricultural and economic outputs.

Slavery—or serfdom—did not become a central issue until after the wars of the Gregorian Reformation ended. By then, the lives of the serfs had become increasingly complex under exploitative feudal legislation. Harsh conditions frequently led to rebellions, which were brutally repressed. The 1381 Peasants' Revolt in England was the most notable of these uprisings. Historians often point to the culmination of these events during the feudal era as the beginning of the modern period, marked by the gradual separation of Church and State and the rise of sovereign rule driven by political and territorial ambition. This trend ultimately gave rise to the nation-state in the 17th century.[9]

However, the influential Catholic Church committed a foundational moral failure by compromising with Roman civil law, which legitimized slavery—an act deemed ungodly by St. Augustine. Worse yet, it failed to curb the growing power of secular crafted by avaricious monarchs, feudal lords, and merchants, who sought to permanently enslave the commoner, both on the manor and, starting early in the 15th century, on overseas plantations.

The Western Legal System and its Global Influence

The Western world had no written legal system with a unique set of guiding principles until the Benedictine monk Gratian wrote *The Concordance of Discordant Canones* in 1140 c.e. Also known as *The Decretum of Gratian*, this work is a collection of approximately 4,000 texts issued by various monarchs and popes over several centuries. Gratian standardized these laws and categorized them into divine law, natural law, human law, the law of the church, the law of princes or secular law, enacted law from legislators, and customary law, which is based on tradition. Like many before him, Gratian regarded natural law as the pinnacle of law from which all other laws derive.

Even earlier, in 1075 c.e., Pope Gregory VII initiated a series of reforms after declaring the legal and political supremacy of the papacy and its independence from secular authorities. His reforms centered on the Church, particularly the investiture of bishops, which was a focal point of Investiture Controversy. Around the same time, the rediscovery of Roman law, particularly Justinian's

---

9   Berman. J. Howard. *Law and Revolution: The Formation of the Western Legal Tradition,* 1983, pp.84–86.

codes, influenced European legal thought and the teaching of law. These rewritten laws were pivotal in shaping Western jurisprudence for centuries, persisting in influence well into the 20th century.

The systemizing of the laws under Gratian marked the beginning of an original Western legal framework. As legal principles began to conform to Gratian's methodology, a distinctive legal system emerged that was increasingly independent of local tribal influences. By placing natural law at its pinnacle, Gratian reaffirmed a universal truth that natural laws originate from God. However, the concept of natural law—much older than ancient Rome—evolved alongside the changing legal codes of Western Europe. While the Romans understood the premise of natural law, their application of it reveals the Roman state's dominance over natural law principles in crafting laws that have persisted in Western legal traditions.

The ancient Romans had a broad understanding of natural law, which gave rise to *The Law of Nations*. This body of law governed interactions with other human societies on an international scale. While natural law—or the law of nature—dealt with universal rights shared by all living beings, such as access to air, water, and procreation, the Roman *Law of Nations*, grounded in natural law principles, also granted Romans access to rivers and seashores. Although they claimed these laws were universally applicable, they were formulated exclusively by the Roman state, often disregarding the differing conclusions and perspectives of other cultures. Excerpts from the *Corpus Juris Civilis* reveal the intrusive and authoritative nature of Roman Law:

Roman Law of Nations

1. Thus, the following things are by natural law common to all—the air, running water, the sea, and consequently the sea shore. No one therefore is forbidden access to the sea shore, provided he abstains from injury to houses, monuments, and buildings generally; for these are not, like the sea itself, subject to the law of nations.

2. On the other hand, all rivers and harbours are public, so that all persons have a right to fish therein.

3. The sea-shore extends to the limit of the highest tide in time of storm or winter.

4. Again, the public use of the banks of a river, as of the river itself, is part of the law of nations; consequently every one is entitled to bring his vessel to the bank, and fasten cables to the trees growing there, and use it as a resting-place for the cargo, as freely as he may navigate the river itself. But the ownership of the bank is in the owner of the adjoining land, and consequently so too is the ownership of the trees which grow upon it.

5. Again, the public use of the sea-shore, as of the sea itself, is part of the law of nations; consequently every one is free to build a cottage upon it for purposes of retreat, as well as to dry his nets and haul them up from the sea. But they cannot be said to belong to any one as private property, but rather are subject to the same law as the sea itself, with the soil or sand which lies beneath it.

6. As examples of things belonging to a society or corporation, and not to individuals, may be cited buildings in cities—theatres, racecourses, and such other similar things as belong to cities in their corporate capacity.

— The Ames Foundation. *Justinian, Institutes.* J.B. Moyle trans. (Oxford, 1911) p.19. Available at: www.amesfoundation.law.harvard.edu/digital/ CJCiv/JInst.pdf

The transition from natural law to positive law during the period of European exploration and colonization marked a significant shift in legal and philosophical thinking. Natural law, rooted in universal principles derived from a Christian God, reason or the lived experience of social circumstances, initially provided a theoretical framework that guided early European actions in foreign lands. Historically, natural law had informed the legal systems of ancient Greece and Rome. While thinkers such as Cicero clearly distinguished between natural law and civil law, Roman law often remained subordinate to natural law principles, as evidenced by the Roman *Law of Nations*. However, following the collapse of Rome, and the subsequent power struggle between Pope Gregory VII and the Holy Roman Emperor, the content and meaning of natural law began to change.

Under this evolving framework, Europeans justified exploration and expansion by invoking principles such as the right to navigate rivers and settle unoccupied lands. As European powers sought to exert greater control on indigenous populations, distant territories, and local labor forces, they increasingly turned to positive laws enacted by human authorities to legitimize their actions. This shift is exemplified by papal bulls such as *Dum Diversas (1452)* and the *Doctrine of Discovery*. These legal proclamations granted European monarchs the authority to claim and colonize lands inhabited by non-Christian peoples. Although grounded in religious doctrine and natural law arguments, these bulls effectively transformed natural law principles into positive legal mandates, justifying European conquest and domination.

The legal concepts codified through positive law facilitated the expansion of European empires, enabling them to establish colonies, exploit resources, and subjugate indigenous populations. Additionally, the Church incentivized such actions by offering plenary indulgences— promises of forgiveness for sins to fulfill the Pope's military orders of conquest in regions such as North Africa. The newfound power of the papacy contributed to the erosion of traditional notions of natural law as a universal and immutable moral code. Instead, positive law became increasingly tailored to serve colonial powers' political, economic, and territorial ambitions.

The transition from natural law to positive law played a crucial role in legitimizing European exploration and colonization. While natural law provided initial justifications for expansion, positive legal instruments such as papal bulls institutionalized and codified colonial domination, marking a stark departure from earlier concepts of justice and morality.

Under the *Doctrine of Discovery*, from the *Dum Diversas* bull, European explorers were granted the right to claim sparsely populated lands and assert dominion over their inhabitants, relying on the questionable logic of the Pope as God's representative on Earth. While Roman natural law had traditionally governed interactions with foreign cultures—such as rights to navigate rivers freely, settle on seashores, or inhabit river mouths— European acquisitions in Africa and the Americas rested on papal mandates. These mandates, purportedly grounded in natural law derived from God, were aimed at protecting Christian interests against non-Christian pagans.

In this context, the divergence from traditional natural law concepts becomes evident. Unlike the Roman framework, which upheld some degree of universal applicability, the colonial application of natural law subjugated it to human-created legal constructs, often for exploitative purposes. Compared to ancient African concepts of law—which emphasized a clear delineation between the laws of nature and human obligations to truth—the corruption of natural law in European colonial practices is both evident and perplexing, as violations of its principles were allowed to persist unchecked.

The Theory of Legal Positivism

From the 11th century to the legal changes in the 18th century, when the Theory of Legal Positivism was formally articulated by John Austin, the

Western legal system relied heavily on the laws of ancient Rome and a Roman dialectic method for creating and integrating new laws. Over time, there was a growing separation of secular law, or civil law, from natural law. This trend escalated with the changing political and economic landscape as powerful rulers enacted laws to serve their material aspirations. The distinction between natural and secular law was recognized as early as ancient Rome, with Cicero noting their differences. However, during Cicero's time, secular law was still closely tied to natural law, and this connection was widely accepted and adhered to.

The hypocrisy surrounding the evolving legal framework in Western Europe came to a head with the emergence of legal positivism, which marked a complete rejection of natural law. The theory of legal positivism posits that the existence and content of law are determined by social facts rather than moral or divine merits. The theory was a stark departure from the medieval Canon Law, which Saint Augustine had described as being derived from natural law and ultimately from God.

In reality, however, Canon Law was heavily influenced by the practical needs of the Roman state. Roman law incorporated elements of Aristotle's *Nicomachean Ethics*, older canon laws, synods from North Africa, and Roman civil law. As a result, aspects of the Roman *Law of Nature* merged with the Canon Law of the Holy Roman Empire. This synthesis produced a flawed interpretation of natural law, which Europeans often exploited by presenting it as God's will.

Positive Law: A Historical and Ethical Analysis

The Displacement of Natural Law by Positive Law

Civil laws in the early modern era became increasingly disassociated from natural law and the aim of fairness. As the law succumbed to the whims of commercial traders and profiteers, it prioritized economic gain over moral purpose. This marked a departure from traditional canon law, which emphasized divine and natural principles. The monarchy, property-owning elites, and even the Church benefited from these changes, exploiting commoners and marginalizing the principles of fairness and justice.

One notable example of this shift was the use of vagrancy laws to conscript impoverished Europeans as indentured servants or enslaved workers in overseas plantations. As Europe's population grew, such laws criminalized poverty and enforced a system of servitude, benefiting an emerging oligarchy. The Church, aligned with these elites, profited alongside them, further entrenching inequities.

The Role of Positive Law in Perpetuating Slavery

The 17th-century colony of Virginia demonstrates how positive law institutionalized racial discrimination. Following Bacon's Rebellion in 1676–1677, where indentured servants and enslaved people united against the ruling elite, the colonial governor amended laws to criminalize African ancestry while exempting Europeans from hereditary slavery based on maternal lineage. Adapting Roman civil law—which linked livestock ownership to the mother's status—colonial authorities applied this principle to humans, determining a person's legal status solely by their mother's criminalized African ancestry.

These Virginia Colony's laws had no basis in natural law or English Common Law. Instead, it guaranteed the profitability of the colony's tobacco enterprises. The racially biased statutes reflect a Machiavellian philosophy as it prioritized the state's economic interests and the king's profit objectives above justice. Consequently, children of white men and African women could no longer be freeborn in the colony, although it was mandated by English Common Law still operating in England. Western ethics, rooted in the precedents of English Common Law, were systematically negated as the profit motive of the oligarchy took precedence.

The philosophy of Niccolò Machiavelli (1469–1527), which emphasized the supremacy of the state's power, underpinned the Virginia governor's actions that handed the oligarchy a lifeline at the expense of innocent Africans. Machiavelli asserted that any state action to ensure its survival was justifiable and that all such actions were morally correct and enforceable. This shift in legal philosophy, favoring state interests over moral considerations and natural law, began with the criminalization of African people and their condemnation of perpetual slavery.

Modern society largely disregards the diminution of natural law as the foundation of all legal systems despite natural law embodying the seed of universal rights. Positive law displaces natural law and often attempts to supplant divine law—understood as the Creator's mind—by marginalizing the historical reverence for an omnipotent God's role in shaping the law. The pursuit of profit and the abuse of power by secular states suppress the historical objective of achieving the highest ideals of justice. Philosophical theories supporting rule by force obscure the morality rooted in divine and natural law. Nevertheless, the universal principles of natural law—self-preservation, freedom, and justice—are eternal, having evolved through millennia of reverence for their divine origins.

While natural law emphasizes fairness, justice, and brotherhood, glaring racial disparities persist within the framework of positive law, as evidenced by statistics. In the United States, for example, data consistently show that African American communities face disproportionately worse conditions—whether in income, incarceration, crime, poverty, or child mortality rates—than the national mean. In contrast, European American communities fare significantly better. Such disparities cannot occur naturally and reflect the corrupting influence of positive law on justice.

Somerset v. Stewart and the Clash of Legal Traditions

The suppression of traditional reverence for natural law is further clarified by a 1772 English court ruling on *Somerset v. Stewart*, which inspired the Abolitionist Movement. Lord William Murray, 1st Earl of Mansfield (1705–1793), presided over the case involving Somerset, an enslaved African in Virginia who was brought to England by his owner, Stewart. After escaping, Somerset sought protection through the English courts. In his decision, Lord Mansfield ordered Somerset's release, asserting that chattel slavery had no precedent in English Common Law and was fundamentally unnatural.

English Common Law, rooted in unwritten customs predating the reign of Richard I in 1189 and codified through acts of Parliament, rejected slavery as incompatible with its ancient traditions. Mansfield argued that slavery was not supported by England's unwritten and ancient traditions, as Parliament wrote them down, and that it could only be derived through positive law. The avaricious claims of the slave traders in colonies beyond England's borders, such as Virginia, were upheld by such positive law. The new laws deviated from English Common Law in England. Still, they were allowed in the Virginia colony by a secular authority with a vested interest in profiting from the stolen labor of other human beings.

The legal precedent in England based on Common Law as written by Parliament decided the Somerset case. It occurred at a time when the Enlightenment ideas of John Locke and other social contract theorists such as Thomas Hobbs and David Hume, had already displaced the classical worldview that had established the precedent inherent in the English Common Law. In the throes of the Atlantic Slave Trade and the Enlightenment, Lord Mansfield, a contemporary of Locke at that time, could still rely on English

Common Law that maintained allegiance to the earlier concepts of the law as fair and impartial.[10] Although he considered slavery an evil and unnatural practice that deviated from natural and canon law, he could not use these much older sources of the law as the precedent for his decision. English common Law, as written by a secular Parliament, had become the precedent of English law. Fortunately for Somerset, the English jurists had, as yet, gained no lasting appetite for chattel slavery. They had no opportunity to write into the Common Law the odious briefs we see in colonial Virginia, which criminalized people of African ancestry for profit.

In the newly emerging European society of the early modern era, under the domination of government and wealthy commercial interests, chattel slavery and racial discrimination increasingly violated the basic premise of natural law and English Common Law. Nevertheless, it became entrenched as a precedent in Europe's colonies. Natural law had been observed in Europe since the 13th century when Roman Law was reconstituted in Venice, but it carried little weight in the 17th century. The foundation of natural law found in the study of the nature of God had begun to shift during the Religious Reformation in the 16th century. For example, in the Calvinist era, determinism had pervaded popular sentiment, making it easier to accept the plight of the unfortunate, the poor, and the enslaved as acts of God against the unfaithful.

The shift away from the basic premise of principles of Christianity occurred as popular sentiment increasingly relied on empiricism to support deterministic conclusions on the poor and enslaved. Determinism from the Latin *(de plus terminus)* implies that all events happen in a predetermined order. Determinism inevitably leads to fatalism—the idea that God has ordained all occurrences to happen. At the start of the Calvinist religious reformation, it had become fashionable to accept the plight of the unfortunate, the poor, and the enslaved African peoples as consistent with God's word in the bible. It was a complete inversion of truth. Calvinism was a movement that began in the urban centers of Europe, but it was spread from country to country by traders and workers who paid little attention to traditional canonical laws restricting their business. Businesses required funding, which was the task of the moneylender who found it reasonable to demand interest. The great urban centers of Europe, Geneva, Amsterdam, and London, supported the ideas of Calvinism. These included condoning the search for profits and usury—the very sins that the Catholic Church opposed. [11]

---

10   An Argument in the Case of James Sommersett, a Negro (Sommersett v. Stewart Court Case).

11   Tawney, R.H. Religion and the Rise of Capitalism, p. 92—95.

The process of co-opting the ethics of the Medieval Church occurred in the 16th century. For example, John Calvin and Martin Bucer were both theologians and reformers of the faith, who were singled out in the 16th century as supporters of extortion (usury)[12] that in the prior era, when Luther pinned his thesis on the church door, was a crime. The basic premise for the condemnation of usury lay in Aristotle's definition of the term written in Politics in 350 B.C.E. as one of the most hated means of trade, which makes a gain out of money itself.

The larger European society viewed usury and slavery as onerous practices, but that did not stop practitioners from carrying on the relentless drive for unfair profits. These commercial interests formed a counterculture dedicated to perpetuating their trade. For example, the cotton manufacturers in Liverpool, England, grew wealthy from the African Slave Trade but kept it secret from the average Englishman. In addition, Thomas Jefferson, the 3rd president of the United States, and enslavers in the Southern United States also shared similar sentiments based on self-preservation. They believed that slavery could not be relinquished. Jefferson sums up the sentiment of the enslaver earning his livelihood from slavery by equating the practice to holding a wolf by the ear and being unable to hold him or let him go.

As the business of Europe's commercial centers had turned to dependence on the African Slave Trade, Calvinist determinism acquired an additional layer of empiricism and circular logic. The victims, African families, fathers, mothers, and children in impoverished and emaciated conditions became the villains who deserved their dreadful fate. By the 19th century, derogatory beliefs about the suitability of African people as slaves had gone beyond conjecture in 17th-century Europe. They became based on the flawed science of Samuel George Morton in Pennsylvania, with physical categorization by cranial size and race. In the 21st century, the scientifically founded basis for racial discrimination, which advocates for species differentiation of the human family, continues to provide the premise for racist beliefs. However, chattel slavery, the fundamental reason for the fabrication, was abolished in 1863 in England and in 1865 in the United States.

Positive Law and the Divergence from Natural Law

The Roman senator and historian Cicero defined two types of law for posterity—The Law of Nature (Natural Law) and civil law, which demands

---

12   Tawney, R.H. Religion and the Rise of Capitalism, p. 75.

obedience to the state's laws. In ancient Rome, divine law (the mind of God) and natural law (The Law of Nature) were fundamental to Rome's concept of law and the emperor's power. The earliest idea of divine law is in the Kushite story of Horus, the first divine king who was born of an immaculate conception. The story tells of the creation from the mind of God, and the significance of the first divine king, Heru, as a template for the first pharaoh. Divine law was the basis of African kingship—the communal organization that supported Africa's large cities and nations and empowered the king. The ancients revered God sincerely, and their view of the Pharaoh and his obligation to the moral order stemmed from God's will. Divine law became one of Europe's sources of canon law, and it also legitimized the concept of absolute monarchy that misapplied power and dominated Europe until 1648.

The ancient and early Christian worldviews on slavery originated from natural law and Retributive Justice theories that advocated for a proportionate punishment of wrongdoers and additional punishment for defiance of the law. The ancient Romans, while their system of slavery was brutal, saw slavery as a service to repay a debt but did not brashly disregard the human right to life of an enslaved person. The penalty for violations of that law shows the Roman regard for the sacredness of life, and high regard for the law. The Law called for the death sentence for the murder of an enslaved person by an owner. St. Augustine, who was Christianity's first theologian in Rome, believed that slavery was a means of providing service to purge sin. St. Thomas Aquinas also believed that criminal and civil offenses required punishment, but there should be additional punishment for violating the law.[13] Usury, which led to the enslavement of poor debtors, was despised by the Romans at various times in their history and by Emperor Charlemagne of the Holy Roman Empire because it violated the spirit of Christianity. Christian theology opposed usury up to Martin Luther's Religious Reformation in the 16th century. Generally, usury was an unfair means of profiting from the pain and suffering of the poor. In effect, the ancient laws deemed compensation for labor as fair, but using money to make money without a corresponding outlay of work was a violation.

Ethics in modern Western societies are shaped almost exclusively by new laws that impinge on the concept of natural law. Positive law inevitably became tools of an Oligarchy that ignored the creation and purpose of these civil laws as inevitably emanating from God's will and with a moral

---

13   Berman. J. Harold. Law and Revolution: The Formation fo the Western Legal Tradition, p183.

objective as the earliest Christians had understood the process of forming the law. Race-based social structures in western societies are reinforced through positive law to control their populations' behavior and fulfill the requirements of an elite controlling the government apparatus.

The U.S. Constitution, for instance, was written in opposition to the absolute rule of the monarch empowered by divine law and tradition. The newfound proclamations of the founding fathers in the Constitution elevated the positive law as supreme, above divine and natural law. Roman Law, Scholastic theories on natural law, and Enlightenment social contract theory became the essential replacement for the rule of the hereditary monarch. However, these aspirations became positive laws in the Constitutions of the modern era nations intertwined with the moral corruption of the elites of the secular state—the landowning nobility in search of profits. Modern-era oligarchs spoke eloquently of life, liberty, estate, and the pursuit of happiness yet could not find a single human from Africa deserving of these natural rights. They were far from sympathetic to African people suffering a ghastly fate under the yoke of Western positive law. The U.S. Constitution diverges from natural law because Article VI makes the Constitution the supreme law of the land:

Article VI

All debts contracted and engagements entered into, before the adoption of this Constitution, shall be as valid against the United States under this Constitution, as under the Confederation.

This Constitution, and the laws of the United States which shall be made in pursuance thereof; and all treaties made, or which shall be made, under the authority of the United States, shall be the supreme law of the land; and the judges in every state shall be bound thereby, anything in the Constitution or laws of any State to the contrary notwithstanding.

The Senators and Representatives before mentioned, and the members of the several state legislatures, and all executive and judicial officers, both of the United States and of the several states, shall be bound by oath or affirmation, to support this Constitution; but no religious test shall ever be required as a qualification to any office or public trust under the United States.

One of the key accomplishments of the secular state in the effort to control the lives of its population is the rejection of the ancient reverence for salvation as the foremost objective of all social and economic activity.

Rejection of the divine basis of natural law conversely legitimized immoral modes of exploitation such as usury and chattel slavery, where the innocent became trapped in lifelong slavery. The emergent secular authorities who projected their profits from their slave enterprises into perpetuity owe that prosperity to positive law and military force. It was all undergirded by greed, money, and credit.

The Need for a Moral Reawakening

After the slave trade began, there was no discernible criticism against chattel slavery in Europe for at least two hundred years until Bartholome de Las Casas wrote about the atrocities occurring in the Spanish colonies. However, the trade's remote nature and the profit motive's resounding success were reasons to ignore the horrific human toll. So entrenched was the moral corruption during the early years of the slave trade that the powerful Roman Catholic Church was powerless. While it could wage war for more than 400 hundred against the Holy Roman Empire, it could not prevent the enslavement of its African Christian converts in the Canary Islands despite a Papal bull prohibiting the practice.[14] The aristocracy basked comfortably in the financial rewards they garnered from their accommodation with immorality.

However, those who fought for liberation throughout the African Diaspora did so because of the moral imperative every living thing understands—the universal right to self-preservation, freedom, and reparation. Their resolve emanated from an innate perception of natural law from the first instance of Portuguese kidnappings of African people along Africa's west coast in the 15th century. In the 19th century, European Americans such as John Brown (1800–1859)[15] understood that slavery was a grave moral affront against divine law. On the other hand, African Americans such as William Still (1821–1902) and Harriet Tubman (1822–1913) knew innately through experience that there could be no compromise with the enslaver. In Haiti, resistance was a moral imperative—a do-or-die situation that must be acted upon, as the Haitian Revolution of 1804 showed.

By the late 19th century, African-American Sociologist W.E.B. Du Bois, who studied the conditions of African descendants in America, believed that Sociology was a solution to the problem of racial discrimination— the legacy of slavery. In 1896, when his doctoral dissertation on "The

---

14   Stark, Rodney, For the glory of God, (Princeton University Press, 2003), 330
15   John Brown along with his followers seized the American Armory at Harpers Ferry in 1859, in an open rebellion against slavery.

Suppression of the African Slave Trade to the United States of America, 1838–1870" was published, the racial problem focused on the physical ramifications of slavery. Despite his efforts to solve the race problem through sociology, Du Bois concluded that the solution lay in mass agitation and protest. The reality of mass lynching and other gross violations of the rights of African Americans demonstrated that direct action was necessary. His conclusion has been the standard viewpoint on dealing with racism ever since. We see the theme of protest and agitation echoed in the work of Dr. Martin Luther King Jr. and the Southern Christian Leadership Conference (SCLC) on the one hand and those of the Black Panther Party on the other. While their methods were opposed, the fundamental principle remained one of protest and agitation aimed at the state.

The rising tide of progress appears to have lifted many people of African ancestry out of poverty, but conditions have worsened as the African remains in last place. Africa has more of the poorest people in the world, and more African Americans are imprisoned in the 21st century than were enslaved in 1865. The gap between the wealthy, privileged class and people of African ancestry has never been wider since abolition. It is proven that racism plays a prominent role in this vastly disproportionate statistical measures. Racism thrives and continues to inflict a very heavy price regardless of the work of the many advocates for freedom.

Chapter 7

The Modern Era

Early Modern Period–(1500-1700)

As the Middle Ages drew to a close in Europe, the people of that era were largely unaware of the profound transformation occurring in their understanding of reality. Historians later marked the end of the Middle Ages and the dawn of the Modern Era with events such as Columbus's discovery of the New World, which challenged long-held perceptions of the Earth as flat and the universe as geocentric. This new epoch was further divided into the early-modern, modern, and contemporary periods, with milestones such as the 1453 Muslim conquest of Constantinople, the capital of Byzantium—or the Eastern Roman Empire.

Mehmed II, the Ottoman sultan, cemented his victory over the Byzantine capital with symbolic gestures that reverberated throughout Christendom. As a final symbolic gesture to his conquered adversaries in the Christian world, the sultan converted the Hagia Sophia, Christianity's most iconic church, into a mosque. The towering structure shown on page 122, which was located on the European side of the Bosporus strait, had endured destruction and reconstruction since its original construction by Emperor Constantine, with its final form completed in the 6th century under Justinian I. The Muslim blockade of Constantinople forced Europeans to seek new trade routes, leading to discoveries that shattered the medieval worldview, including the realization that Jerusalem, as the city of God, was not the center of the universe.

Age of Discovery and The Renaissance

The fall of Constantinople disrupted European access to the Black Sea and the Eastern Mediterranean, cutting off vital trade routes like the Silk Road that had connected Europe to Asia's riches since Marco Polo's time in the 13th century. This disruption drove a frantic search for alternative

Hagia Sophia – Ayasofya Mosque — in Istanbul, the Ottoman Empire.

trade routes, and it sparked a cultural revival in Europe, fueled by Greek-speaking Christian refugees fleeing to Italy with ancient texts and knowledge. These refugees brought a treasure trove of manuscripts that revitalized interest in the classical works of Greece and Rome, laying the intellectual foundation for the Southern Renaissance.

This flowering of art, philosophy, and economic activity began in Italy and it emphasized Renaissance Humanism, which shifted the focus from the medieval idea of humans being made solely in God's image to a broader appreciation of human potential, reason, and culture. Figures like Petrarch, one of the earliest Renaissance scholars, rediscovered classical works by Homer and Cicero, initiating a wave of intellectual and artistic achievements. The Renaissance thrived in the peace following the Hundred Years' War, a period of relative stability that allowed for economic growth and major cultural projects, such as Michelangelo's Sistine Chapel ceiling and the domed St. Peter's Basilica.

Portugal and Spain spearheaded the search for new trade routes to bypass the Muslim-controlled Silk Road. The Portuguese, utilizing advanced navigational knowledge and shipbuilding techniques, focused on an eastward route around Africa, while Spanish explorers, led by

Columbus, sailed westward into uncharted waters. Columbus's discovery of inhabited lands in the Americas shattered medieval conceptions of the universe and the geocentric model, which had placed Earth and Jerusalem at the center of creation.

The Copernican Revolution marked a major intellectual shift. In 1508, Nicolaus Copernicus mathematically demonstrated that Earth and other planets orbited the Sun. Galileo Galilei later used his telescope to provide empirical evidence, such as the phases of Venus, further disproving the geocentric model. This paradigm shift emphasized empirical observation and mathematical reasoning over religious dogma, displacing God as the direct cause of natural phenomena.

The Northern Renaissance and the Printing Revolution

While the Southern Renaissance flourished in Italy, a parallel cultural awakening occurred north of the Alps in Northern Europe. Artists like Albrecht Dürer pioneered techniques for his woodcut printing that enabled the mass production and dissemination of art. Durer's process of segmented and specialized labor in an assembly process symbolized the rise of capitalism, as segmented labor and assembly-line production became central to the emerging economic system.

The invention of the printing press by Johannes Gutenberg further accelerated the spread of Renaissance ideas. For the first time, texts like the Gutenberg Bible were mass-produced and distributed widely, making knowledge accessible to common people. In Germany, the Bible was printed in the local vernacular, allowing laypeople to read and interpret it independently of the Catholic Church. This democratization of knowledge undermined the Church's monopoly on religious authority and contributed to broader cultural and intellectual shifts.

Military Power and European Expansion

The Renaissance was not just about artistic achievements. It also paved the way for European domination. Contact with the Orient introduced intellectual enrichment and critical technologies like gunpowder, firearms, and navigation tools. These innovations allowed European monarchies to amass unprecedented military power, which they used to conquer and exploit new territories across the globe.

At the same time, the Catholic Church, threatened by the new empirical worldview, resisted these changes and clung to traditional doctrines. The Spanish Inquisition, initiated in 1478, epitomized the Church's efforts to maintain control, using brutal methods to root out heresy. The monarchy also used the Inquisition as a tool to seize wealth from Jewish and Muslim converts and those accused of heresy. This period saw the Spanish monarchy, under Ferdinand and Isabella, amassing wealth by conquering Muslim lands in southern Spain and expanding their exploitation to the Americas.

Spanish explorers, conditioned by the brutal tenor of the times, viewed indigenous peoples not as equals but as resources to be exploited. Despite the generosity and hospitality of the native peoples they encountered, the Spanish dismissed them as savages whose primary value lay in their utility for labor and profit. The church and monarchy's dual motives of Christian zeal and economic gain often blurred, but the underlying driver was clear: the accumulation of wealth to meet mounting debt obligations.

The Role of Usury in European Expansion

The war between Christians and Muslims and the persecution of Jews in the Iberian Peninsula culminated with the first Spanish Monarchy's control of the land. The monarchy began the wealth accumulation that financed the expansion of the Spanish Empire through expulsions of Muslim populations and seizure of their wealth. It launched the Inquisition in Spain in 1478, and in keeping with traditional medieval practices, it worked together with the church using torture as a standard cross-examination method. The prevailing Christian belief based on Middle Ages thought was that the almighty God would intervene to save the innocent from death. The church and monarchy worked to purify the ranks of Christians by torturing, expelling, and seizing the wealth of former Jews who had converted to Christianity, Jews, Muslim converts, Muslims, and anyone suspected of harboring heretical ideas. As the appetite to acquire wealth had infiltrated the church, the Spanish Inquisition quickly became a re-purposed tool to seize vast land holdings and accumulate vast wealth.

As Portuguese and Spanish explorers encountered new lands and peoples far beyond Europe's borders, the brutal tenor of the times had conditioned them into ruthless exploiters of the same people the Catholic Church had vowed to serve—the poor and the meek. The Church and monarchy's pressing need for wealth guided their Christian zeal. The conquest of Muslim lands in Southern Spain had added immensely to the wealth of Spain's first monarchs, Queen Isabella and King Ferdinand. However, in the newly encountered lands, the abundant kindness of the strangers Europeans met had no impact on the predetermined Spanish explorer's perceptions of their character as soulless savages. Their utility rested on the increased profits they could provide for the church and state. The immediate objective of the explorers was not discovery or mutually beneficial trade links, but Christian converts, slaves, land, and profits to fulfill debt obligations.

Centuries of experience acquired during the Crusades in trade across vast distances and international finance were crucial in facilitating the exploitation of new lands. European culture had grown dependent on usurious loans, the beginning of the process that, in the past, had funded medieval wars and international trade. Usury persisted in the Medieval Feudal system because the land used for barter had become scarce, and the use of money and the role of moneylenders had increased. Borrowing money to fund military campaigns was a win-win situation for the monarchy and moneylenders seeking to compound wealth. The monarchy found financing for their military conquests of new territory and people to reward their vassals and clear debts.

The pattern of pillage and plunder, extending from a Middle Age feudal worldview, is evident in 1411 when the Portuguese King João (John I) won a military victory against Castille (Spain). He needed money and recognition for his newly liberated but impoverished kingdom. With borrowed money and permission from the Pope to undertake a crusade against Muslims across the Straits of Gibraltar, he attacked and captured the city of Ceuta in 1415. In his quest for more land and gold, he financed a shipbuilding and exploration enterprise seeking a new sea route to the Orient to profit from its wealth. He funded the development of sailing and navigation technologies acquired from North Africa along with locally sourced shipbuilding methods, weapons, and fort technology. The Portuguese abilities in shipbuilding and military strategy allowed them to occupy and defend remote islands and to capture and enslave African people to create the earliest plantation systems copied by every succeeding European power. The emerging European monarchies had access to money with usurious charges using interest rate calculations, evolved finance and accounting methods such as letters of credit, double ledger bookkeeping, advanced military technology, and a seasoned compulsion for profits.

Mass Production

These innovations, including mass production, appear beneficial to early modern society. However, in 15th-century Europe, they posed ethical challenges to the teachings of the Christian Church. The methodology of interest rate calculations did not directly violate the canon law. However, when combined with the intentions of the moneylender, usury was a more egregious sin as a methodology for creating profit because it involved no labor, no production, and had a specific objective of illegally compounding wealth. In effect, it was theft to the medieval mind. With usury, the moneylenders of the era and the church and monarchy found a higher calling in the lure of profit than in Christianity's highest ideal of saving souls.

In the late Middle Ages, mass production, which enabled capital accumulation, began during the Northern Renaissance in Germany in the late 15th century. The region, across the Alps, is isolated from Italy, where the Southern Renaissance occurred in the 14th century. In 1491 German artist Albrecht Dürer began producing exquisite woodcuts, and Johannes Gutenberg built his printing press based on Chinese technology. Both men were from the flourishing guild tradition that relied on a labor division. Dürer produced the woodcut design, but specialized workers created the carvings and produced the prints that bore his name. However, more importantly, as the concept of mass production exploited technical skills, a new opportunity for wealth creation emerged that was unique to Europe. Gutenberg's press required special skills in metallurgy, engineering, and carpentry. Still, it helped reduce the cost of labor in book production and allowed for the mass production of the Gutenberg Bible. The Church could only open the gates of merchant capitalism under the guise of spreading the word of God. Indeed, ideas began to disseminate rapidly throughout Europe via printed books. The printing press led to the lucrative publishing industry and facilitated the accumulation of money in the specialized industry. In direct opposition to the merits of virtue in the Christian quest for salvation, the surplus wealth, far above what the canon deemed necessary to live, became accessible to the lower classes.

The infectious effects of avarice quickly exploited mass production to accumulate wealth far above what canon law deemed necessary to sustain life. Nevertheless, mass production involved labor and was more in line with the ecclesiastic laws against avarice. The accumulation of profits

Albrecht Dürer woodcut – The Four Horsemen. National Gallery of Art: online database: entry 1979.39.1. The earliest example of mass production occurred in Europe.

made it difficult for commercial interests to follow the canon law against avarice that restricted their retail business. This tendency continued since the Medici bankers conducted international trade by charging minute fees smaller than the Church decrees for exchanging money. Additionally, with promissory notes introduced to Europe in the 13th century by Marco Polo,[1] notes redeemable in gold became indispensable in conducting trade over vast distances, often patrolled by armed thieves who made carrying

1   William N. Goetzmann; K. Geert Rouwenhorst (1 August 2005). The Origins of Value: *The Financial Innovations that Created Modern Capital Markets*. Oxford University Press. p. 94. ISBN 978-0-19-517571-4.

large sums of gold impractical and dangerous. Promissory notes issued to depositors of redeemable gold or silver in faraway cities became the conventional means to facilitate transactions across international borders. Usury was the motivation that made it feasible. As profit was the incentive for lending money, it became the glue for the economy.

Papal Complicity

The Portuguese quest for gold started in 1411 with the attack against the city of Ceuta. The city surrendered in 1415, and while in Ceuta, the Portuguese learned of the lucrative trade networks that spanned the Sahara Desert to the interior of the African continent.[2] By 1443, Portuguese sailors had sailed a scant 1,700 nautical miles south of Ceuta. Near Arguin Island in modern-day Mauritania, Captain Nuno Tristao captured and enslaved 14 Africans.[3] That first, unprovoked act of military aggression violated the Christian Just War concept of Saint Thomas Aquinas, who listed the pursuit of justice as a worthy cause. The English author James Bandinel Esq. wrote that the Portuguese captain was elated at how easy it was to capture these Africans. He states further that Prince Henry the Navigator, Gilianez Lanzarote, and other followers of the prince formed an association that promised to pay Henry a portion of their goods.[4] Slavery had ceased being a service to erase debt or sin. With the Portuguese successes in Africa, it became a business enterprise that operated under the protection of the Papacy, with its fabricated Christian evangelical objective of saving souls. Like the accusations of heresy against Christians in Spain and the judgments of the Inquisitions, the African's curse was arbitrary and based on barbarous Middle Age ethics motivated by greed.

The weakness of the Papacy, given violations of canon law, such as usury and the seizure and enslavement of the innocent, emboldened the oligarchy. Their increasing reliance on usury and increase in wealth corrupted the Church's traditional role in society. When Pope Martin V gave the Portuguese permission to enslave African people in 1442, he relied on the evidence of those captured and enslaved along with the gold dust

---

2   Constable, John Ure, London 1977. "Prince Henry the Navigator."
3   Bandinel, James, Esq. Some Account of the Trade in Slaves from Africa As Concerned With Europe and America, pp .15–16.
4   Bandinel, James, Esq. *Some Account of the Trade in Slaves from Africa As Concerned With Europe and America*, pp .15–16.

brought back to Portugal before he unleashed the unparalleled brutality of the desperate men who cared nothing for the soul. Historically, while it had been illegal to trade captives between Christians and Muslims, Africans below the Sahara did not fit any religious category. They became the preferred source of enslaved people, who could be traded in either the Arabic Eastern Slave Trade or the Atlantic Slave Trade. The beginning of the early modern era saw a trickle of enslaved Africans entering Portugal. However, as the slave trade spread out of control throughout Europe and its colonies, Africa's population growth rate dropped precipitously as the trade expanded. The declining numbers imply the onset of population extinction, as Walter Rodney points out in *How Europe Underdeveloped Africa.* The incredible expansion of the slave trade coincided with the use of fraudulently printed paper receipts without corresponding backing in gold or silver, used to clear debts.

Besides its notoriety as a morally bankrupt practice of the early modern era, European chattel slavery was symptomatic of the unbridled greed that had escalated with the increasing use of credit and usury in Medieval Europe. Condemnation goes to the other forms of slavery as well, which, although morally bankrupt, were not totally out of control. The acceptance of usury emanated from centuries of accrued experience in a feudal society that exploited labor, land resources, and the peasantry. The former indigenous peoples who had established cultural norms of vassalage and patronage, which rewarded their heroes with land and wealth, became landless serfs under the domination of the aristocracy and armed knights. They were, in effect, European slaves—a cheap source of labor who, besides being the backbone of Europe's agricultural economy, worked wherever necessary to maintain the appropriated property of the new lord of the manor and provide food for all those of the upper classes.

Under the circumstances of serfdom, where profits accrued to the oligarchy, the corrupt trend of capital accumulation could only increase in Europe and grow more complex, with each opportunity to circumvent the law in conducting commerce. These opportunities occurred in rapid succession with contact with Africa and the Americas. While the church preached about Christian virtue and financed high art and culture during the Renaissance, the money lenders, commercial traders, and the monarchy established the hard facts. They determined the course of European history as one where credit with usurious charges and chattel slavery—the most profitable venture of all—would predominate. Ethics had no bearing on that outcome.

The Money Changer and His Wife," painting by Quentin Massys, 1514; Louvre Museum, Paris.

The efforts of the powerful Papacy to maintain allegiance to the law were half-hearted or non-existent. Although it was punishable by ex-communication, usury gained its approval in the 15th century when the wealth and power of the Medici came directly from usury and made the bankers wealthy enough to control Florence. The thin line between legal and illegal became ever more meaningless as the legitimacy of the profit motive, and usury advanced with the rise of the secular state and the institution of positive law. When the early modern era began in a frenzy of chattel slavery, even the Papal bull, Sicut Didum, issued by Pope Eugene IV in 1435 forbidding the enslavement of Christians in Cape Verde, failed to stem the rampant enslavement of the innocent African Christian converts. The slave traders who fought to defend their livelihood left their legacy of avarice, racial indoctrination, and the usurpation of power. However, the ethical digressions that led to the brutal human exploitation of the early modern era are obscured by Renaissance Humanism and even praised as a social good that introduced the savages to civilization, although they are the root cause of unparalleled destruction and social dislocations.

The frenzy of commercial speculation was of such magnitude that within 111 years after the arrival of Europeans on the shores of Ceuta, Northern Africa in 1415, the social fabric in Central Africa had collapsed. In a letter to the King of Portugal, Jao III, in 1526, the King of Kongo, Nzinga Mbemba (Afonso I), references the collapse that he writes has depopulated his kingdom. Kongo had converted to Christianity in 1491, yet it ended as Portugal's main source of enslaved people. The Portuguese had perfected techniques for corrupting the targeted populations with cheap material goods, used linen and guns that kindled avaricious tendencies, and widespread wars in Kongo that destroyed the cultural cohesion of the once peaceful kingdom. Africa's fate as a source of enslaved people and natural resources placed it in perpetual decline.

Despite the Church's role as the spiritual protector of the poor and dispossessed, the 1452 Dum Diversas Papal Bull established the Pope's authority worldwide in alliance with the Portuguese and Spanish monarchies, issued to support their profit objectives. Dom Diversas granted European powers the right to convert pagans to Christianity or enslave them for rejecting it. The bull served the pretentious purpose of saving souls, but it legitimized the brutal form of European chattel slavery under the banner of Christian Evangelism.[5] Beginning with the first trading outpost in 1443 in Arguin Island, Portuguese slave forts spanned approximately 10,000 miles[6] in a thin band along Africa's East and West coasts and across the Indian Ocean to Macau. Their early military success was an auspicious beginning of their fight to control sea routes from West to East that spanned the Mediterranean region, Coastal Africa, and east across the Indian Ocean to Macau, China. It stretched across the Atlantic Ocean to Brazil and the Americas to the West.[7]

The Portuguese forts were integral to the geopolitical and military strategy for conquest and imperial domination. They were conduits for guns, cheap European goods, and enslaved people and sheltered European ambassadors within their walls. They played a crucial part in dividing and conquering the various African kingdoms and were instrumental in conducting the slave trade. The most famous examples of these forts and transmission points are

---

5   The Papal Bull, Dum Diversas issued in 1452 by Pope Nicholas V, authorized Alfonso V of Portugal to reduce Muslims to perpetual slavery.
6   Tawney. Religion and the Rise of Capitalism, p. 66.
7   How Europe Underdeveloped Africa. Walter Rodney, pp. 76–82.

European ambassadors in the presence of the King of the Kongo, Musée Royale de l'Afrique Centrale, Belgium

the 1482 Elmina fort, the first European trading fortress in Africa, and Maison des Esclaves on Goreé Island, founded as a slave factory by the Portuguese in 1536. In 1776, the Dutch built the prison, which is now the location of *The Door of No Return Museum*. Dozens of such forts and captured ports on the mainland played a crucial role in disrupting Africa's regional economies to establish an African dependence on European trade.

The Portuguese occupied the unpopulated Madeira Island in 1419 and, by 1420, had begun to populate the island with enslaved Africans. Madeira is the earliest example of agrarian capitalism, with the first plantation populated with enslaved Africans to produce sugar for export to Europe. From this template of land ownership beyond Europe's borders coupled with agrarian capitalism, the plantation system, with its incalculable human toll, mushroomed out of control. Insatiable Oligarchic greed propelled the expansion of sugar plantations and increased sugar consumption in Europe, perpetuating the plantation system.[8] The combination of private land ownership and slave labor began with the allure of profits and investment capital, which

---

8   Estimates spreadsheet: 2010 estimates-excel.xlsx. Available at: http://www.slavevoyages.org/ tast/database/download.faces#namesdb. Accessed on 6/29/2013.

inevitably became the unsecured paper money or IOUs, put to work outside Europe and beyond the church's Canon Law.

The Modern Era (1600-1800)

Fractional Reserve System

In the mid-17th century, paper money payable in gold to the *bearer* of any note by London goldsmiths became part of the money supply. Inevitably, as their greed triumphed, the London goldsmiths began issuing paper receipts to a bearer without the required equivalent gold deposit. The written receipts were soon fraudulently distributed, far above the quantity of gold available to redeem them.[9] The London goldsmiths grew wealthy enough to pay high interest rates for gold deposits, which attracted even more gold deposits. As time progressed and their volume of business increased based on the fraudulent paper notes, they began to issue new goldsmith-banker receipts or notes to redeem notes instead of gold to clear their books. The process fraudulently expanded the money supply with paper money without the required asset backing of gold.

This system was helpful for the expansion of the slave trade as it allowed for the creation of more and more money to finance the trade. Banks could lend out more money than they held in reserve, which led to the expansion of credit and economic growth. However, it also made the economy more vulnerable to bank runs and financial crises.

Historical development of modern banking

13th-century to 1640

Marco Polo	Death penalty issued for refusing to accept increasingly worthless paper notes	The earliest gold-smith-banker receipt was issued—the year banking started in London	King Charles I seizes 200,000 pounds worth of coins deposited in the Tower of London
13th century	**1294**	**1633**	**1640**

(continued)

---

9   AP Faure. *Money Creation: Goldsmith-Bankers and Bank Notes.* SSRN 2244977 Freely accessible.

London Goldsmiths develop modern banking

Mid-17th century

The wealthy no longer trust the government and deposit money in Goldsmith banks.	The restoration of Charles II to the throne—Goldsmith bankers, became debtors in England. Goldsmith's debtors are recorded as assets. Goldsmiths initiate a fractional reserve system.	Goldsmith bankers' power increased dramatically after the state passed legislation to curtail their power had failed.
1640 –	1660	1672

The Enlightenment

Across Europe, as the profits from the slave trade increased, the impoverished European peasant class could no longer suffer the tyranny of monarchical rule—its feudal practices, brutality, excessive taxation, and rising food prices. The modern period began with the 18th-century revolutions that abolished the monarchies' hereditary rule and the Divine Right of Kings. The increasingly challenging conditions of European society initiated The Age of Revolutions. With the second paradigm shift, Enlightenment ideas about human rights and reason shaped the emerging Representative governments based on the bicameral form of government with a balance of power and a written constitution guaranteeing individual rights. The mechanistic and materialist worldview of the Enlightenment further reinforced the idea of man as separate from nature and God. In essence, the idea of God as the source of the law diminished. The church's restriction to its spiritual domain and the empowerment of the state to control civil matters and commerce predominated because of the massive profits from the slave trade.

Despite the humanist ideas of the Enlightenment, the revolutions of the 18th century negated the rights of enslaved Africans and began an era of state-sponsored racial discrimination. France, for example, had successfully challenged slavery in the 1750s when French lawyers sued the sugar manufacturers in court and won freedom for enslaved French Africans. However, in 1786, General Napoleon began to waver from France's anti-slavery directives during the French Revolution. The most highly acclaimed general in the ranks of the revolutionary army was Alexandre Dumas, the black general from Haiti. Although Dumas is renowned for his heroism, Napoleon, with whom he had served in France's invasion of the Marmeuluk Empire in Egypt, refused him his just due as a genuine hero of France and forbade the mention of his name. Napoleon denied the Dumas family their overdue military compensation for his long service to France.

Additionally, he banned blacks from Paris, instituted a pass law that required documentation for their presence, and banished them to the suburbs. Napoleon re-instituted slavery under particular circumstances after it had been abolished by the National Convention in 1794, completely ignoring the human dimension in the problem of slavery where the state could free and arbitrarily re-enslave. The re-enslaved Africans in the Antilles promptly rebelled, and Haiti alone achieved independence in 1805.

The Enlightenment profoundly influenced the leaders of the American Revolution. They based their draft of the U.S. Constitution on the ideas of John Locke, Montesquieu, and other European intellectuals of the Enlightenment. Sadly, after gaining independence from England with African help, the United States Supreme Court stated in its 1854 Dred Scott decision that formerly free Africans in slave states had no rights that the white man was bound to respect. While the Age of Revolutions advanced the cause of liberty, it exposed the latent tendency of a white supremacist sentiment to burden the black-skinned race with a fabricated and racialized view of reality, supported by a belief in God's purposeful enslavement of Africans. In effect, greed triumphed—the human condition had not improved, and it remained moribund in feudal practices and slavery. The European philosophers manufactured their ideas based on the Classics. Still, their hearts remained immune to the highly spiritual messages of Plato, the Hellenistic philosophy of The One, Aristotle's ethics, and the works of Cicero, Rome's plebeian senator—from the ranks of the commoners.

The European Enlightenment championed individual freedoms simultaneously as it tolerated impiety, materialism, exploitation, and chattel slavery, replete with the enormous expenditure of life occurring in Africa, on the seas, and in the colonies. In its wake, the new Western regime distorted revered traditions such as a God-centered pantheist cosmology, a matriarchal- non-racial society, equal protection under the law, and the right to equal participation in the economy. In place of the matriarchy, the foundation of Africa's domestic economy was the rudiments of the whitewashing of reality divorced from the long history of human development to moderate the tendency towards vice and encourage virtue. More profoundly, the Enlightenment maintained the dangerous idea that the tradition of the European slave master was God's will—that their actions against Africans were justifiable through the word of God as written in the bible.

In the 18th century, the broad-based economic and social collapse occurring on the continent of Africa from European greed became statistically measurable as Africa's population growth dramatically lagged the population growth of Asia and Europe. The English abolitionists researching the human cost of slavery discovered the obscured, statistical aberration—the genocide that destroyed the continent's social and economic structure. Their work became the standard used to calculate the deaths occurring during the sea voyages of slave ships and the overall casualties of the trade. As traders and soldiers began operating beyond their native lands and away from scrutiny, their ideas and ethics exhibited a morally bankrupt, utilitarian characteristic. It became prudent to do whatever was necessary to achieve desired profits—the connotation of *sacred*, traditionally attributed to human life, and natural law percepts associated with freemen had vanished entirely.

The drive for profits created the harrowing narratives of the Atlantic Slave Trade. Nevertheless, the allusion to an African brand of barbarity has persisted, based on the smoldering ruins that have become representative of the natural state of all African people. The study of that short, chaotic period of the slave trade and its legacy of racial discrimination routinely takes precedence over the entirety of African people's history, encapsulating all human activity on earth. Slavery has become definitive of African people in modern popular culture and became purposefully confused with their self-identity. However, the growth of the slave trade in Africa has less to do with African people than with the impetus of a European aristocracy that had abandoned their ancient reverence for the virtues and embraced avarice. As Africans adapted to the new reality, they, too, participated in chattel slavery and embraced greed and materialism.

In the Early Modern Era, slavery destroyed Africa's cultural mores and kingship system. Because of avarice and materialism, individual self-interest overcame the needs of the larger society, and African people rejected their evolved cooperative customs. Africa's deep spiritualism, familial cooperation, regional trade links, and prosperity ended, and forced dependence on European-controlled trade in guns, inferior goods, and war for profit ensued. The result was a rapid growth of European chattel slavery. The shift in ethics is understated, although it began a scant 400–500 years ago, including the beginning of our modern era.

Capitalism

Only in the 19th century did European intellects begin to dissect the processes that had brought untold wealth to Europeans and unleashed a deadly force on the world. The process benignly referred to as capitalism came into common usage after Carl Marx's book Capital (1865). The process, rooted in the European use of finance to enable the seizure, transportation, and exploitation of African captives, proved incredibly successful as a means of accumulating wealth against the ethics of the canon law. Modern capitalism, in its rudimentary form revealed by Shakespeare in the late 16th century, equates to exacting a pound of flesh.[10] The phrase from The Merchant of Venice refers to a debt demanded by the Jewish moneylender Shylock, which is difficult to pay and will cause severe pain and death if repaid. The reference is to usury and the severity of the conditions imposed on the borrower. Shylock decides to charge a pound of flesh as collateral to the borrower, the merchant Antonio, who has invested the borrowed money in an overseas venture and has no readily available collateral. Antonio does not condone usury, but he cannot guarantee repayment of the loan until the ships return. After learning that the ships have disappeared, a vengeful Shylock demands Antonio's heart as payment.

The Merchant of Venice references the changing times in Europe as it was transitioning towards a broader acceptance of usury that still had not shed its negative connotations. The play highlights the central role of money in the lives of Christians and the growing bias against Jews in the 16th century. The period was when the Ecclesiastical authorities targeted Muslims, pagans, and all enemies of Christ and restricted Jews to the ghettos, the only place where they could practice their craft of moneylending and usury. Nevertheless, despite usury's negative connotation, the changes in European society favored its widespread use in an expanding European economy and a rapidly expanding need for gold.

German Sociologist Max Weber (1864–1920), in The Protestant Ethic

---

10   Shakespeare. The Merchant of Venice. believed to have been written between 1596 and 1598

and The Spirit of Capitalism, describes the driving force to acquire and accumulate wealth that predated modern capitalism in terms that evoke the obsession of society with accumulating wealth:

> Let us pause a moment to consider this passage, the philosophy of which Kurnberger sums up in the words, "They make tallow out of cattle and money out of men". The peculiarity of this philosophy of avarice appears to be the ideal of the honest man of recognized credit, and above all the idea of a duty of the individual toward the increase of his capital, which is assumed as an end in itself. Truly what is here preached is not simply a means of making one's way in the world, but a particular ethic. The infraction of its rules is treated not as foolishness but as forgetfulness of duty. That is the essence of the matter. It is not mere business astuteness, that sort of thing is common enough, it is an ethos.
>
> —Max Weber, *The Protestant Ethic and the Spirit of Capitalism.* New York: Scribner's Press, 1958, pp. 47 - 78.

Weber attributes capitalism's characteristic accumulation of capital to the ascetic compulsion to save, rooted in Protestantism's prohibition of purchasing luxury goods. When the capitalist refrains from spending on unproductive luxury goods, more profits can create even more. Through this process, the capitalist can consistently look forward to a systemic accumulation of wealth. The roots of modern capitalism are from the staunch Protestant religious ideal that saw labor as godly and the accumulation of money as a religious calling. To Protestants of the 16th century, becoming one of the 166,000 predestined by God equated to hard work and living an ascetic lifestyle. This single-mindedness, motivated by religious fervor, shaped capitalism's hard, cold, ruthless methods. It inevitably made the mortal sin of accumulating money that the Catholic Church had equated to avarice, the preeminent motivation in life that completely replaced salvation. While the Protestants refrained from buying luxury goods, their savings inevitably resulted in investments that propelled the slave trade to more and more profits for investors.

The origins of the Atlantic Slave Trade are from the early modern era beginning in the 15th century. The early Portuguese explorers had a comparatively simple task of bypassing the blockade of The Silk Road, seizing gold and slaves, and returning to Portugal with their booty. The Portuguese monarchy provided the necessary funds to build the first ships and funded the crews. A hundred years later, the accumulation phase of Capitalism occurred not only from usury but, more importantly, from the reinvesting of surplus money into shipbuilding and the enslavement of African people.[11] By 1864, when Weber was born, Europeans had forcibly enslaved more than 15 million Africans in the New World and 10 million more on European plantations in the Arab Slave Trade in Asia.

Nevertheless, the motivation of avarice that enabled genocide on an enormous scale is not the preeminent defining characteristic of capitalism. The compelling arguments that remain of the most destructive era for African people caused by capitalism are the systemic and predictable accumulation of profits, private ownership of the means of production, and private property rights. The glitter of modernism—the stuff that the accumulated money invests in, are the emblems of the process—but nothing of the outlawed motivation that propelled the beneficiaries of chattel slavery towards the ever-increasing cruelty exhibited on the sweltering plantations of the New World. Modernity has come to represent the period of development after World War II that saw the start of the most significant expansion of the middle class and the capitalist economies of the West. When we refer to the term modern, it refers to the glitter of style and the luxury and technological innovation of the Post-Industrial Age created by capitalism. However, if the plight of hundreds of millions of victims of capitalism and The Atlantic Slave Trade could ever acquire meaning in Western society, it would not be representative of an advancement from a backward era.

The regressive nature of the events occurring during the Slave Trade in the modern era, based on its scale, is unparalleled in history. At its peak in the 18th and 19th centuries, The Slave Trade was a massive depopulation of the African Continent that occurred over 400 years. It violated traditional concepts of natural law and just war, as forced migrations occurred to populate the New World to create profits, clear debts and accumulate wealth. Proportionally, the scale of the slave trade, which is normally measured in tens of millions, grossly underestimates Thomas Cooper's casualty estimate of 10 deaths for each captured African.[12] The calamity hardly registers in the social consciousness because the victims are black-skinned. As history is seen linearly in the Western

---

11   Marx, Karl, *Capital, Volume 1*, page 61. Marx explains capital accumulation as the transformation of surplus-value into additional capital, which can produce new increments of surplus-value which leading to new increments of capital.

12   Herbert S. Klein, Stanley L. Engerman, Robin Haines, and Ralph Shlomowitz. Transoceanic Mortality: The Slave Trade in Comparative Perspective, p. 19. Based on (Thomas Cooper, Supplement to Mr. Cooper's Letter on the Slave Trade (Manchester, 1788), 3, 4.)

tradition, it implies a chronological progression from old to new or bad to good. The linear passage of time is associated with progress, and few will dispute that from a historical perspective, the 16th century will appear more backward than the present. However, the escalation of greed that resulted in the near-extinction event in Africa shows an unparalleled deterioration in ethics and quality of life. A drastic change occurred in the ethics of the modern era that, in retrospect, eclipses two of the essential ideas in human history. (1) The establishing of the moral foundation of Homo Sapien Sapiens in the First Cause of Creation or (God) and (2) the ascribing of natural rights of Homo sapiens to natural law emanating from knowledge of the First Cause.

The early modern period was marked by a shift from medieval worldviews to a new paradigm grounded in empiricism, reason, and exploration. This transformation, driven by Renaissance humanism and technological innovation, reshaped Europe's intellectual, cultural, and economic landscape. However, it also entrenched patterns of exploitation, reflecting the persistent feudal mentality of wealth accumulation through conquest and usury. This dual legacy of progress and greed defined the trajectory of European expansion in the centuries that followed.

Chapter 8

Empiricism and the Western Ideological Framework

From its inception in the racial propaganda of French judge, historian, and political philosopher Baron Charles-Louis Montesquieu (1689–1755), the Western racial paradigm was ideologically, anti-Muslim and anti African. While Montesquieu wrote disparagingly about Muslims in *The Persian Letters* written in the 1721, the subjugation of pagans and enslaved persons was ongoing since the 15th century. When the author wrote *The Spirit of the Laws* in 1748, he defined the three main powers in a bicameral government, legislative, executive, and judicial. However, he and other architects of the Western political system were the property owners of noble birth, who showed no genuine love for the democratic principles they championed. Their ideas on liberty did not apply to Africans living under the threat of enslavement on European plantations for more than two hundred years. Montesquieu for example, relies on typical pseudo-scientific climatic and economic excuses prevalent in his time to ironically support enslavement of Africans even as he denounced slavery. To Montesquieu, slavery was bad, but it was good for Africans because it brought them into a civilized state.

Among the early Enlightenment thinkers, Thomas Hobbes, who defined the social contract in *Leviathan* in 1651, recognized the monarchy as the only legitimate form of government. He envisioned the commonwealth as a giant human-like construct with arms representing the diverse functions of the state. The arms and torso are illustrated with tiny individuals that alludes to their function. In one hand is a sword, symbolizing power and authority. In the other is a crosier or staff symbolizing spiritual power and religious authority. Without the sovereign, Hobbes envisions a state of nature that is violent, fearful, and with all against all. He believes that a brutal social order, without a king, forces a bid for peace when all members of society voluntarily give up some of their rights in return for state protection of their remaining rights. Hobbes refers to their pact with the sovereign as the Social Contract.

Other intellectuals in Hobbes's time, who resented the tyranny of the monarchy, could not tolerate a similar monarchical form of government as the outcome of their revolution against the tyranny. They opted for Montesquieu's bicameral government, without an absolute monarch, with power shared by legislative branches in a system of checks and balances. However, in the heyday of the slave trade, neither form of government considered the plight of the enslaved souls toiling to enrich the Western Oligarchy. While these governments based their foundation on social contract theory, which included all members of society, their foremost concerns were upholding the rights of a property-owning Christian oligarchy in a legal document or constitution.

The idea of individual rights existing in the immutable laws of nature were reasoned out of vogue in the Modern Era. Natural law, as a necessary and divine source of law that cannot be impacted by human action was severely hampered by the advance of positive law written by avaricious legislators and empowered by like-minded constituents. Positive law aided the greed of the nobility and ignored the rights of those who were brutally exploited, then ostracized from society according to class, race and sex.

From the inception of the democratic principles of governance, Western intellectuals linked the image of the West with the noble class of Christian property owners. However, the legislative bodies followed the typical example from the Spanish monarchy, Queen Isabella and King Ferdinand, as they arbitrarily canceled land rights, seized wealth, and enslaved freemen in 16th-century Spain. However, the evolved bicameral governments went further to introduce an odious but legal hereditary slavery supported by a pseudo-scientific racial ideology.

After two centuries of slavery in the West, and as Hobbes and other early modern philosophers emphasized reason and experience as the basis of understanding the laws of nature, natural law began to be discounted. The labor of Africans increasingly proved essential to realizing the profit objectives of the monarchy and colonial governments, and their freedom was unthinkable, in secular and religious circles. For example, the profit objectives of the English King, Charles I, in the Virginia colony, coincided with the legislation that fundamentally changed the nature of slavery in the Americas. The King's expectation that gold was on his Virginia property proved wrong, and it became necessary for the colonial administration to plant tobacco to generate the required profits. However, without the labor of the Europeans and Africans, the tobacco plantations would have failed. When the workforce rebelled in the 1676 Bacon's Rebellion as they sought property and voting rights, the inevitable failure of the plantations proved sufficient motivation for the new law that condemned all Africans—those enslaved and indentured servants—as hereditary enslaved people. With their freedom of movement ended and their association with the white race by marriage or birth rescinded, the African population became the legislated, hereditary, and despised slave.

Amid the burgeoning profits of the slave economies trading cotton, sugar, and tobacco, Adam Smith wrote *The Wealth of Nations* in 1776. His famous proclamations about the economic expansion of Western nations rested on words anchored in mathematical abstractions based on supply and demand. He and his contemporaries could not correlate the incredible wealth in the Western European nations with the centuries of sacrifice of African people. As the popular culture had established the inferiority of Africans, even the most capable European intellectuals could not offer a word acknowledging their immense sacrifice. Adam Smith attributed wealth creation to an invisible hand in the market that created an equilibrium between supply and demand. His assumption, a critical premise in modern Classical Economics, begins with individual self-interest operating in a free market. However, the oligarchy and plutocracy had gained generational wealth by plundering the dark-skinned races for centuries.

On the other hand, in the sweltering large plantations of Caribbean islands, including Cuba, San Domingue, Jamaica, Barbados, and the mainland of the United States, the heroes who resisted perceived the importance of natural law. They knew from innate experience the absurdity of the laws against the natural order that kept them enslaved as subhumans were abominations of nature. Justice to them, meant the fulfillment of the natural order where their God given rights were recognized. In his prayer at Bois Cayman, Dutty Boukman, a voodoo priest originally from Senegal, had the insight to know the nature of God was one of incomprehensible goodness, unlike the evil that entrapped his people. He dutifully called for the rejection of the god responsible for their suffering.

Many others who saw the god in themselves took revolutionary action and made the ultimate sacrifice. The many who fought and died had created a counter-trend to the status quo that had negated natural law. The concepts of freedom, fairness, and justice did not come from any European intellectual whose words about equality and freedom are said to have trickled down to the household slave who, in turn, passed it on to the field hands.

The fabrication of the grand culture, like the myths about the enslaved Africans, was produced by intellectuals who were blind to the carnage surrounding them. Montesquieu, for example, elaborated on the popular notion of white supremacy in *The Persian Letters*, which compared his superior Western culture to that of Muslims in the Orient. Montesquieu is more widely known for his book, *The Spirit of the Law*, written in 1748, which is based on the concept of the separation of powers that influenced the authors of the U.S. Constitution. However, the author showed no prior appreciation for universal natural laws in *The Persian Letters*. Instead, he differentiated a homogeneous superior European culture from the East that he portrayed as occupied by a vile Muslim population in the Ottoman Empire. Through sarcasm, innuendo, and fabrication of anti-Christian insults in a series of letters, Montesquieu created an anti-Muslim fervor in Europe.

In the salons of France, where he and Voltaire (1694–1778) discussed new ideas about the natural world, the government, and the human condition, the two men aimed to discern truth and replace the autocratic rule of the monarchy. However, the Enlightenment ideas they had launched spread in a population with a culturally chauvinistic ethic emanating from latent religious zealotry, slavery, and a burgeoning racial pseudo-science. Inevitably, the initial mission of the Enlightenment movement to improve life failed in the Modern Era, as vast swaths of humanity, mainly the enslaved Africans, remained wanting of its promises of liberty and equality.

Western Philosophy and Pseudoscience Reinforce Racial Myths

Two hundred years of profits from the brutal exploitation of African labor had left even the most esteemed scholars with a false view of reality and unable to resolve basic moral questions about the brotherhood of man and the omnipresent, universal consciousness. These fundamental principles of the ancient world established the common origin of human beings in Kemet's Memphis Theology long before the Western acknowledged age of written history began. However, the new scientific method of induction, proposed by Sir Francis Bacon and refined by Descartes and others in the Modern Era, was a boon to those willing to perpetuate deeply ingrained racial biases arising from the social mores and myths of the Slave Trade.

As the science of philosophy advanced during the Industrial Revolution, the framework for a unique Western racial ideology became linked with the newly developed epistemology of empiricism of John Locke who claimed that wisdom is only obtained through experience. However, attributing a metaphysically, historically, and rationally derived subhuman status to African people became an unquestioned reality, not through facts but through the falsified science that sought to establish an experiential reality. Statistical evidence of skull sizes, historical and archaeological evidence of Western civilization's European origin, and other fabricated evidence proliferated while European chattel slavery flourished and Europe grew opulent. Western intellectuals became the primary force allied against the truth that ancient Greeks and others in the Mediterranean region had acknowledged for centuries—that Western civilization stood on the heads of black Africans.

The world had known that the black-skinned African had an unfathomable history of innovation for thousands of years before widespread falsification occurred based on the emerging scientific methodology of inductive reasoning that claimed to rely on empirical data and logic. In the emerging Western empirically based worldview, the status of the black skinned Africans as naturally enslaved people was the only required justification for their inferior and sub-human status.

The profit motive at the core of moral corruption negated humanity's long history of piety from Kemet, the Pre-Socratic and Greek philosophers, and the early Christian Theologians such as Saint Augustine, Saint Thomas Aquinas, and Albertus Magnus. The scholastics such as Thomas Aquinas sought to unify the philosophy of the ancient classical philosophers with Christian theology. As a method of learning based on Socratic dialectical reasoning with a thesis and antithesis, Scholasticism encompassed many studies, including the foundation of modern economics, which pegged the value of goods and services to the cost of labor. European philosophers, such as Hume, Locke, and Hegel, embraced empiricism and were familiar with the dialectic method. They knew of the brutal practices that had facilitated the burgeoning European slave economies, producing enormous wealth and transforming Europe from warring feudal states to industrial capitalist economies.

From the outset of the empiricist movement in the 17th century, scholars who championed a necessary reliance on reason and science demonstrated the potential for fallacy. Locke, for example, lauded his empiricist premise of knowledge derived from sensory experience, which he saw as complementary to the use of reason. While he sees these moral rules as obligatory, at the same time, he sees that humans have the freedom to govern themselves. He reasons that rewards and punishments that produce pleasures and pains are God's incentives to ensure that humans will make correct choices.

In his 1690, *An Essay Concerning Human Understanding*, Locke declared that ideas are not innate and sees experience as the source of wisdom.[1] His declaration reduces all good and evil to specific pleasures and pains that are the rewards and punishments of our choices. To Locke, these are the drivers of morality.[2] Given the European dependence on chattel slavery and the habitual misuse of reason to substantiate the brutal practice, the emergence of a poor ethic—a blindness to the ultimate source of morality in the highest form of the good—became inevitable.

The apparent discrepancy between Locke's two versions of morality exemplifies the entire thrust of the Enlightenment. The pleasures and pains Locke noted can be none but the normative behaviors that produced the wealth accumulation and genocide occurring in Western European society, acquired at the expense of millions of Africans. The contradictions of redefining the innate link to God as individual subjective actions and promoting practical experience as a source of morality deteriorated life's divinely ordained moral purpose in societies dominated by greedy commercial speculators and property owners seeking unlimited profits.

As industrial capitalism took root, a fallacious, White Supremacist ideology emerged free of moral restraints. It prolonged the plight of the enslaved African and sought to make his social status permanent as a non-human destined to fulfill the objectives of the oligarchy. The divergent ethics of the era made the use of unlimited force against the natural moral order a legitimate means of social control that kept the poor and the Africans away from the dining halls of the rich. The old Aristotelian hierarchical model of animal life launched the hierarchical ranking system of Carl Linnaeus, which, in turn, influenced Darwin's Theory of Evolution and then the Eugenics program—a practical way to terminate life through the horrendous torture of the poor. The new ethics led directly to the Nazi holocaust and World War II. While history is replete with evidence of wars and violence, the Modern Era represents the most brutal period in human history, primarily due to the ethics of the Atlantic Slave Trade. Based on calculations from a population study referenced by Walter Rodney in *How Europe Underdeveloped Africa*,[3] Africa's population growth rate dropped to a negative seven percent near the end of the Trade.

---

1   Locke, John. *An Essay Concerning Human Understanding*. 1759. Book 2. chap. 23, p. 37.
2   ———Ibid, pp. 156–161.
3   Rodney, Walter. *How Europe Underdeveloped Africa*, p. 197

As early as the 17th century, the tenor of the times was explicit in European literary forms, tinged with religious, racial, and political themes. In Shakespeare's *Othello*, published in 1603, these themes appear as fully formed stereotypes during the ongoing wars between Venetian Christians and the Ottoman Muslims. In Shakespeare's play, his Moor is an African, a black-skinned Christianized general in the Venetian army, hated by his attendant Lago. As Lago fools him into tragically murdering his beloved Caucasian wife, Shakespeare portrays Othello as easily manipulated, subject to emotionalism, and as someone who reverts quickly to barbarism. European society had coupled these stereotypes with every black-skinned person.

In the 18th century, depictions of European cultural supremacy became more refined and aimed at Islamic culture as Montesquieu exploited the prevailing anti-Muslim sentiment. He depicted a fictitious Persian character, Usbek, as the owner of a harem of slave women and a cruel despot who criticizes the Pope as a magician who can make three appear as one.[4] In his fictitious accounts of life in Persia, Montesquieu betrays a political objective in fabricating a rigid separation between a culturally and politically backward Eastern Islamic world and a superior Western European culture. His negative references to Islamic culture and its contrived antagonism towards The Holy Trinity are innuendos that exploit racial and religious hatred. Author Edward W. Said, in his 1978 publication of *Orientalism*, explains the indoctrination process as follows:

> . . . an enormously systematic discipline by which European culture was able to manage—and even produce—the Orient politically, sociologically, militarily, ideologically, scientifically, and imaginatively.[5]

The xenophobia exhibited in *The Persian Letters* became the dominant mode of expression in the West.[6] Europe's stellar economic success became routinely attributed to European superiority, and the enslaved Africans forcefully deprived of all dignity became living examples that contrasted sharply with a resplendent White Supremacist culture. The empiricist premise driving the racial divide could not reconcile the ancient doctrines espousing equality of all life and the obligation to suppress material

---

4   Charles de Secondat, baron de Montesquieu. *Persian Letters* (1721), Letter XXIV p. 46–47. Athenaeum Publishing Co. 1897.
5   Said, Edward W. 1978. Pub. Random House, Inc., New York. *Orientalism*, p.3.
6   Charles de Secondat, baron de Montesquieu. *Persian Letters*. 1721. ed. Transl. John Davidson. Pup. Gibbings & Company, in London .1899 (3 vols.). Available at Persian Letters Project. http://rbsche.people.wm.edu/teaching/plp/

corruption. European scholars habitually harbored contradictory viewpoints on core beliefs about the soul, equality, and brotherhood settled thousands of years before in Antiquity. Empiricism did nothing for the soul but to insert a void where a yearning for spiritual perfection had existed. Neither the exposure to the Classics nor its ancient and noble idea of civilization as an ideal stemmed the tide of moral decay from avarice and slavery.

Slave societies functioned without moral clarity, and the oligarchy, intellectuals, and scholars found comfort in entertaining contradictory versions of the truth. Consequently, genocide, ameliorated by ideology, occurred at unprecedented levels. The entire thrust of Western ideology focused on the worthlessness of African people while hiding the extent of the carnage during Europe's most prosperous era of the slave trade. Late in the 19th century, the fabrication of *noblesse oblige*, which was the European *civilizing mission* in the Belgian Congo, shrouded the ongoing atrocities until Catholic missionaries revealed photographic evidence.[7] As tens of millions of Africans died and countless others lost limbs for failing to meet rubber production quotas, Leopold's propaganda highlighted the virtues of a Western educational system and modernization program engaged in a civilizing mission in the old African kingdom.

The Empirical Foundation of Ideology

The narrative of the human species as separate races with separate origins did not change even as the selfish motives of the Enlightenment intellectuals became clear. It persisted in deeply embedded social mores, false narratives promoted in educational institutions, fraudulent claims of spontaneous wealth creation, and the inferiority of black-skinned people. The ongoing process of inventing palatable explanations for enslaved Africans' deplorable social and economic conditions found ample support in the work of Destutt de Tracy. He claimed that all ideas have a physiological determinant which is conditioned by the sense organs. Those with stronger sense organs would have an advantage in their judgment and intelligence levels over those with weaker senses. De Tracy recognized the process as a field of study in the 19th century and defined it as ideology.[8] He mimics Locke's empiricist ideas in his making of the new science of ideas by citing the source of all ideas

---

7   The European oligarchy had relied on noblesse oblige to express a Christian obligation to uplift the poor and less fortunate in the moral economy of the Middle Ages.

8   https://www.academia.edu/20176729/Antoine_Louis_Claude_Destutt_de_Tracy_-_Elements_ of_Ideology_Vol._5_Ch._2_-_On_Love

as being in the material world. De Tracy's belief that ideas originate from societal forces that shape people's beliefs aligns with *Lockean* Empiricism. Ideology does not acknowledge nor does it need a divine source of morals. Like Locke, De Tracy premises the origin of ideas in the material world.

Following Locke's empiricist theories, the origins of human action no longer needed a source in God or nature. They emerge from individual whims, occurring from sensations that begin in a mechanical world. As the science of ideology evolved to shape negative public opinion against Africans, it negated the ultimate divine source of natural law that insisted on equality under God. The promise of the Enlightenment to empower the individual served only to legitimize chattel slavery as correct behavior and a blessing to the savage.

The methodology of the scientific method, based on inductive reasoning, is of particular concern because society regards the results of scientific inquiry as conveying the truth. We readily accept the many premises conjured up by the process as certainties. Nevertheless, the empiricist David Hume encapsulated the inductive reasoning premise as one where past occurrences do not necessarily imply any certainty of those occurrences repeating in the future.[9] While conclusions about the natural world based on inductive reasoning may appear logically valid, they may or may not be true depending on circumstances. Thus, the hypothesis is merely a conjecture that does not necessarily have to be a correct assessment but allows a reasonably accurate understanding of the material world.

From the inception of the scientific or induction method in the 17th century, it functioned as a replacement for Aristotelian deductive reasoning. It arrives at conclusions by starting with many empirical observations that end in a hypothesis. The scientific method contrasts with deductive reasoning, which begins with a valid statement and extrapolates into other cases that are also assumed true. In the vanguard of the switch to inductive reasoning was Francis Bacon (1561–1626), who served the English crown during the conflict between Henry VIII and the Roman Catholic Church. Inductive reasoning served as a novel methodology for approximating the truth that could adequately replace the medieval concept of truth based on the word of God in the bible.

While inductive reasoning led to a deeper understanding of the laws of nature, its weakness is in the susceptibility to implicit bias in interpreting data. An example is Darwin's theory of Natural Selection, which posits that within a population, individuals with advantageous

---

9   Hume, David (1711-1776) *Enquiry Concerning Human Understanding*

traits are more likely to survive and reproduce, passing those traits on to the next generation. Over time, this process leads to the accumulation of traits better adapted to the environment, driving the evolutionary process. However, the sociologist and philosopher Herbert Spencer interpreted Darwin's theory to mean "Survival of the fittest," alluding to nature's preservation of the favored races."[10] His error led directly to the Eugenics Movement in the United States, which promoted the superiority of wealthy Caucasians based on a miraculous wealth gene believed to be specific to them which was responsible for their wealth creation. Consequently, Eugenics led to suppression of gene pools that eugenicists believed would contaminate their gene pool. The rudderless, scientific intrusion into nature's mysteries, conditioned by a biased method of inductive reasoning, led to profound deviations from the norm to the genocidal policies of the Nazis during World War II.

An unbiased application of Darwin's Theory of Natural Selection would support the diversity of the gene pool of African people, that allowed the species to survive in the harshest of tropical climates. A profound failure exists in Western culture's standardized and de facto classification of human beings by race. This error continues despite the growing awareness of hundreds of thousands of years of genetic diversification in the human family, which has guaranteed survival.

The Origins and Implications of Materialism in Western Thought

As the foundation which is void of purely spiritual phenomena, the theory of materialism holds that all beings and processes can be explained as manifestations or results of matter.[11] In a universe without matter, materialism cannot account for a universal consciousness. Materialism began in the 5th century B.C.E. with the ancient Greek philosophers Leucippus and Democritus. They believed that reality is made up of atoms that move around in the emptiness of space. These ancient Greek philosophers perceived the universe as empty because they thought it was the only condition where particles could move freely. Their reality consisted of atoms ranging from the densest of the physical plane to the dynamic fire atoms of the Gods.[12] The modern emphasis on the material world and the

---

10 www.smithsonianmag.com/science-nature/herbert-spencer-survival-of-the-fittest-180974756/
11 www.Merriam-Webster.com
12 Popkin, Richard H. The Columbia History of Western Philosophy, pp. 18–20.

diminution of the spiritual enabled widespread contradictions in the logic of empiricist philosophers, who inevitably associated morals with learned experiences acquired in the physical world.

The shortcomings of the empiricist philosophers are evident in their exclusion of a spiritual or non-material reality that shapes behavior. The central idea of God as the unknowable source of everything, visible and invisible, is missing in the empiricist process which is based solely on physical experience. Empiricist thinkers are not required to resolve the universe's origin from nothing. For example, the 1927 Big Bang theory could postulate that the universe exploded outward from a high-density point; however, what existed before the universe's beginning is inconceivable in a material world where the cognitive senses cannot account for infinity.

Kemetic science accounts for the creation from nothing as an act of desire from consciousness or intellect and never as a spontaneous act in the material world that does not require a universal consciousness. The ancient preoccupation with the nature of the creation as an emanation of an unknowable, all-powerful source led to the earliest philosophical subject, *The Study of the First Cause.* The First Philosophy from ancient times and the modern idea of philosophy as an inquiry into what is there and what it is like derives from the ancient Egyptian studies of the first cause of creation.

Materialism and empiricism enabled the personification of a creator, who acquired the proportions of a man inhabiting the creation rather than encompassing it. An ideological indoctrination process based on empiricism and science accompanies the change in perception from the pantheism of the ancients to the mechanical universe of contemporary societies. Empiricist philosophy and the scientific induction methodology have led to a Western concept of history that begins and ends with the empirical world.[13] In effect, empiricism is the primary tool of the contemporary ideology.

The philosophy of German historian Georg W. F. Hegel in the 18th century, described by Karl Marx, reaffirms the materialist premise of modern ideas. In "The German Ideology," addressed to a group of former students of Hegel—The Young Hegelians, Karl Marx, who was associated with the group, but not a member, elaborates on the differences between the traditional Hegelian (German philosophy) and the current mode of thought:[14]

---

13   www.marxists.org/reference/archive/hegel/help/mean09.htm
14   Arthur, C.J. ed. *The German Ideology*, P. 47. Available at: www.marxists.org/archive/marx/works/1845/german-ideology/index.htm

In direct contrast to German philosophy which descends from heaven to earth, here we ascend from earth to heaven. That is to say, we do not set out from what men say, imagine, conceive, nor from men as narrated, thought of, imagined, conceived, in order to arrive at men in the flesh. We set out from real, active men, and on the basis of their real life-process we demonstrate the development of the ideological reflexes and echoes of this life-process. The phantoms formed in the human brain are also, necessarily, sublimates of their material life-process, which is empirically verifiable and bound to material premises. Morality, religion, metaphysics, all the rest of ideology and their corresponding forms of consciousness, thus no longer retain the semblance of independence. They have no history, no development; but men, developing their material production and their material intercourse, alter, along with this their real existence, their thinking and the products of their thinking. Life is not determined by consciousness, but consciousness by life. In the first method of approach the starting-point is consciousness taken as the living individual; in the second method, which conforms to real life, it is the real living individuals themselves, and consciousness is considered solely as their consciousness.

—Karl Marx, *The German Ideology.*

As a significant influence on Marx and regarded as Europe's father of history, Hegel played a key role in Marx's theory of Dialectical Materialism. Based on Hegel's philosophy, the theory posits that historical events, interpreted as the unfolding process of contradictions and solutions, result from conflict among classes. Hegel defines the creation of history as the interaction of opposing forces in society that result in a Hegelian-type dialectic—thesis, antithesis, synthesis. Like the premise of other empiricist Enlightenment philosophers, Hegel's Historical Materialism is grounded in a materialist perception that reality is only the material world. Thus, reality can emanate only from it.

The promotion of materialism is evident in Hegel's philosophy, which is based on the master-slave relationship from serfdom during the Middle Ages. Hegel views the formation of history as emanating from the "rational spirit,"[15] which implies an empiricist perspective—that it is internally derived and dependent on the cognitive senses. The obligation to an ultimate moral authority is not central to Hegel's philosophy of history. His reality is grounded in empirical fact, and he refers to the stages in

---

15   Hegel, Georg Wilhelm Friedrich. *The Philosophy of History.*

the creation of history as an *antagonistic*-creative process that generates complex abstract ideas in man.[16] Hegel associated the formation of history and the evolution of ideas with the simple observation of objects that evolve into complex abstract concepts. He defines history as the unfolding of reality—whether right or wrong, simply as truth or reality—but without moral value.

At the height of the slave trade in the 19th century, men like Hegel knew the deplorable condition of the enslaved African population. Yet, he unabashedly concluded that their impoverished state originated from their deficiencies and that they had not yet evolved sufficiently to be capable of conceiving of God. Hegel's judgment thus begins with the idea of the physical world created by European intellectuals, where the emaciated and enslaved Africans perished in huge numbers from parasitic actions of enslavers. The Empiricist view of reality and the ideology that emanates from it lacks adherence to an eternal or *unchanging* concept of what is good and what ought to be right in the human experience. In Hegel's world, the enslaved chose their fate.

The Legal Foundations of the Western Ideology

The ultimate source of the Church's canon law is God, recognized through natural divine law found in the nature of things, and divine revelation (positive divine law) from tradition. Positive divine law aligns divine revelation with the establishment of specific commandments or legal codes that believers are meant to follow such as the ten commandments. Man in God's image had been presumed to be perfect yet susceptible to spiritual corruption. However, for most of Christianity's history, it was not acceptable to reject the divine revelation and defy the commandments. The racial divide that appears as a permanent feature of Western society is without historical precedent. It did not exist in ancient Rome during the Pelagian-Augustinian debate, when Saint Augustine emphasized the fallen nature of humanity and the necessity of divine grace, and Pelagius, who opposed him, argued that humans are inherently capable of moral perfection and righteousness without the need for divine intervention.[17] The canon laws predating Christianity supported the divine mission. In the Dark Ages, the Christian Church reexamined its mission, reaffirmed its duty to the meek, and reinforced its mission to uplift

---

16 Hegel, Georg W. F. *The Phenomenology of Spirit (The Phenomenology of Mind)*, pp. 11-22.
17 www.veritascatholica.com/grace-sin-and-free-will-the-pelagian-augustinian-debate-unveiled/?-form=MG0AV3

the weakest of the flock to save all souls. The Magna Carter (1215), the Papal Bulls before the 15th century, and the Writ of Habeas Corpus from the early 17th century, all point to the awareness of universal principles of human rights protecting the innocent.

The ethics that placed God at the source of law ended in the American colonies when the status of Africans as hereditary enslaved people became law in the 17th century, when nationalism and scientific racism had not yet emerged in medieval Europe. There was God, the King, the Church and the canon law. However, as labor shortages occurred due to unceasing wars, labor laws to stabilize the workforce made tenant farmer status hereditary and bound peasants to the estates of lords and barons. Class distinctions evolved to distinguish property owners of noble birth from commoners and serfs.

Nevertheless, the influence of the ancient worldview that referred to the sanctity of human life reigned supreme on British soil in 1765, when the English Jurist Sir William Blackstone published the basis in English Common Law for prohibiting slavery on English soil.[18]

> Upon these principles the law of England abhors, and will not endure the existence of, slavery within this nation; so that when an attempt was made to introduce it, by statute 1 Edw. VI. c. 3, which ordained, that all idle vagabonds should be made slaves, and fed upon bread and water, or small drink, and refuse meat; should wear a ring of iron round their necks, arms, or legs; and should be compelled, by beating, chaining, or otherwise, to perform the work assigned them, were it never so vile; the spirit of the nation could not brook this condition, even in the most abandoned rogues; and therefore this statute was repealed in two years afterwards.(d) And now it is laid down,(e) that a slave or negro, the instant he lands in England, becomes a freeman; that is, the law will protect him in the enjoyment of his person, and his property.

> —Sir William Blackstone. *Commentaries on the Laws of England.*
>   1765, p. 326.

English Common Law of that era contained canon law and natural law elements and included precedents for universal human rights. The English law derived from it comprises *Common Law,*[19] which existed up

---

18   Blackstone, William. *Commentaries on the Laws of England.* 1st ed. 1765, p. 423. Available at: http://avalon.law.yale.edu/subject_menus/blackstone.asp (Accessed 11/3/17.)

19   One of three branches of canon law which refers to things. Others are unverasal las which refers

to 1189, and then newer laws were passed by the English Parliament. The most famous example of using English Common Law on behalf of an enslaved African is the case of *Somerset vs. Stewart* (1772). The enslaved Somerset arrived in England from colonial Virginia and sought and won refuge under English Common Law in a case tried by Lord Mansfield. Judges like Mansfield were still free seek legal precedence in the ancient laws that were still part of Common Law. Just nine years later, Lord Mansfield presided in another famous Zong Case where the captain of the Zong threw enslaved Africans overboard and sued to collect the insurance claims. In the case of *Gregson v Gilbert* (the Zong Massacre of 1781), Mansfield eventually ruled against the Slave Ship's owners seeking reparations and for the insurance company, not on humanitarian grounds but because the ship's negligence caused the deaths that created liability for the insurance company.

The initial discrepancy between English Common Law and the laws in the colony of Virginia in the Somerset case occurred because the positive law of the colonies was enacted independently of the old English customs without legal precedence. Somerset's case was decided based on English Common Law, which upheld principles from the older English legal tradition but not on natural law. When enacted in the British colony of Virginia, the law that allowed the enslavement of people of African ancestry into perpetuity occurred because of the profit objectives of the aristocracy. They became empowered by the evolving social mores derived through ideological indoctrination.[20]

The race-based criteria for the permanent enslavement of Africans were legislated into existence by William Berkeley, the British colonial Governor of Virginia.[21] Before the law, the rebels had been united by their cause. All had similar grievances in that they wanted freedom for the enslaved, property rights, and improved living conditions for freemen and bonded laborers. These were all rights ceded to the aristocracy by custom but denied, particularly to the freemen or formerly bonded laborers in Virginia who were of African and European ancestry. Before the rebellion,

---

to territory, and general law which refers to people. www.newadvent.org/cathen/o956a.htm

20   Guild, June Purcell, ed. *Black Laws of Virginia: A Summary of the Legislative Acts of Virginia Concerning Negroes from Earliest Times to the Present* (Afro-American Historical Society of Fauquier County, Virginia: 1996).

21   Allen, Theodore W. *The Invention of the White Race*, V1. 2002 Verso, NY., p. 16–35. &printsec=frontcover&dq=American+Slavery,+American+Freedom:+The+Ordeal+of+Colonial+Virginia&hl=en&sa=X&ei=G84zVaeHHsnYggT_84GAAg#v=onepage&q=bacon%27s%20rebellion&f=false

they had intermarried, lived together, worked and fought side by side, against the oppression of the English land-owning aristocracy.

The decision to criminalize the African-Americans and elevate the European-Americans' status resulted in Virginia's Black Codes, which defined the Negro as anyone with 1/5 African ancestry. Subsequently, people of African origin were prohibited from living and working on an equal stance with Europeans, owning property, voting, and receiving equal treatment under the law. Furthermore, the law prohibited them from becoming Christians, further denying them the right granted to all Christians under English Common Law to be free from slavery.[22]

Erosion of the Ancient Spiritual Basis of the Law

Chattel Slavery and the ensuing race-based social construct that emerged are partially rooted in the customs of merchants and financiers in Europe during the early Modern Era. Positive law opposed the canon law that restricted profiteering. The canon law underwent periodic revisions before the 12th century when it was first reconciled and compiled by the Italian monk and scholar Gratian. It was revised again after the 15th century and again in 1917. However, throughout its many revisions, the function of canon law as a legal code supporting the Church's mission of salvation remained in place. European customs such as usury and the profit motive emerged as the primary drivers of societal change in the Modern Era that defied Canon 1752—the law of salvation.[23]

Although written gloriously as the achievement of brave heroes, the history of Europeans in the New World was the achievement of avaricious men whose objectives of perpetual profits had taken hold in Europe and its colonies. Their haughty profit objectives, often set by the monarchy that owned the land and operated under a feudal mindset, made it inevitable that the oligarchy would criminally seek to control and exploit all forms of labor, particularly African people. With the rise of the plantation system in the Americas, the profit motive drove the heinous policies of colonial governments.

In colonial Virginia, the settlement of Jamestown began with the search for profits to appease shareholders of The London Company. King James I held title to all lands chartered under the London Company, and the inhabitants

---

22 Edmund S. Morgan. American Slavery, American Freedom, p. 332.
23   Canon 1752: . . . the salvation of the soul which must always be the supreme law in the Church, is to be kept before one eyes.

were tenants tasked with producing the King's gold, silver, and copper.[24] Virginia's settlers were desperate for wealth from its founding because there were no precious metals where they settled, and the only viable alternative was tobacco. The desire to maintain the only source of profit enjoyed by the London Company featured prominently in the decision to criminalize the African American population to maintain control of their labor on Virginia's tobacco plantations. In Virginia's absence of precious metals, tobacco was the sole means of profit in the colony, and slavery made it feasible.

Ideological Deception

The earliest example of obscuration that served to protect the profit objectives of the oligarchy in the 16th century is the suppression of Bartolomé de las Casas's report of the genocide of the Native American population. When he published the report titled, *A Short Account of the Destruction of the Indies* in 1542, false claims of the racial and cultural inferiority of Native Americans were widely circulated by slave traders seeking to protect their profits. Author Eric Williams in *Capitalism and Slavery* points out that Liverpool slave traders in England also resorted to secrecy and fabrication to hide their heinous practices from public scrutiny.

After the abolition of the slave trade, the Belgian King Leopold went on to perfect the methodology of Colonialism. He presented a noble façade to his enslavement and mutilation torture of the population of Congo. The Belgian King built the administrative and cultural centers of Western civilization, which he claimed to have bestowed to the native population in the Belgian Congo. But the schools, roads, and railroads he built with slave labor were designed to facilitate rubber extraction and other natural resources. He successfully hid the extermination of 90% of the Congolese population under his reign in his quest for profits.

The economic dependence on slavery fostered a racial ideology that saddled future generations with a race-based ethic supporting segregation and historical and scientific fabrication to support white supremacy. At the start of the American Civil War, southerners who seceded from the Union fought to keep slavery and their white supremacist ideology that functioned to procure cotton for the world markets.

Decades after the war, and while under the victorious flag of the United States, many of the southern states still sought undue state's rights through

---

24   See The First Charter of Virginia. Available at: http://avalon.law.yale.edu/17th_century/va01.asp

Amendment X[25] of the U.S. Constitution to restrict African Americans' freedom by eliminating their voting rights and political power. More than a hundred years after the Civil War, southern states opted to reintroduce the symbol of slavery on public buildings and to erect statues of Confederate soldiers. The goals of those promoting their racial ideology were based on money and attaining or keeping political power. Their appeal to the base instincts of their White segregationist constituents would allow these politicians to maintain political power in their respective states.

The bloody history of racial oppression associated with the Confederate flag as an emblem of racial hatred and slavery became purposefully twisted to represent an expression of Amendment X, which is more popularly known as *states' rights*. The consequences were profoundly felt on June 17, 2015, when the flag again became a contentious issue in South Carolina. A twenty-one-year-old white supremacist, Dylann Roof, who had exhibited images of himself holding the flag in Internet posts while parroting racist language, stalked and then killed nine churchgoers, including Democratic State Senator Clementa Pinckney of South Carolina. His manifesto claimed to be influenced by the separatist group, the Council of Conservative Citizens. The group had connections to the White Citizens' Councils formed as a response to the advances of the Civil Rights Movement in the 1960s. The White Citizens' Council was implicated in the racist murder of civil rights leader Medgar Evers by Klansman Byron de la Beckwith, who was convicted in 1963. Several of the Republican Party's top members and presidential candidates were found to have received money from the Council of Conservative Citizens.[26] On June 21, 2015, the Republican governor Nikki Halley of South Carolina (January 12, 2011 – January 24, 2017) called for the removal of the flag from the Confederate memorial in front of the Capitol, but only after public pressure erupted after the murders. The South Carolina Legislature, also bowing to public pressure, complied with the order on July 10, 2015.

In the contemporary period, the Confederate flag as the adopted symbol of advocates of *southern states' rights* nevertheless promoted the ideas of the defunct Confederacy—slavery, racism, and violence against African Americans. It is the latest example of the deception that goes hand in hand with White Supremacist ideology. While pretending to advocate for constitutionally guaranteed rights, white supremacist

---

25   The tenth Amendment is the rights not ceded by the constitution to the Federal Government, but belong to the states or the people.
26   Michael Wines and Lizette Alvarezjune, "Council of Conservative Citizens Promotes White Primacy, and G.O.P. Ties." New York Times: June 22, 2015.

advocates seek to whitewash the symbol and disassociate it from the recent past. Deception has worked to realize profit objectives and has been a vital component of racism from the earliest years of the slave trade. Consequently, the history of racism is punctuated by efforts to obscure the humanity of non-European people to legitimize, revitalize, or perpetuate their economic oppression.

The Illusion of Progress

The term modernity commonly encapsulates an unceasing aim to be at the cusp of Western civilization's progressive cultural and technological thrust. The term was initially used by the 19th-century French poet Charles Baudelaire as a description of the urban setting, and it alluded to the responsibility of art to capture that experience.[27] However, the popular idea of modernity is beset by xenophobia, which is reflected in the opinion of many European American conservatives who routinely portray Western civilization as the most outstanding achievement in the history of the world. Almost simultaneously, the African Slave Trade is made prominent as an example of how Africans have enjoyed and benefited from access to this xenophobic idea of civilization. However, the view of a progressive Western society in modern times discounts a defining characteristic of the Modern Era: its shameful history of avarice and regressive ethics. The façade of progressiveness masks ingrained customs based on self-interest, opposing the idea of the larger community. The biases built into the Modern Era conveniently disparage the past and promote the status quo, where men are preoccupied with their immediate self-interest of attaining wealth while at the same time destroying the means to peace and prosperity.

The Linear view of progress—from Bad to Good

The First Transition

The tendency to think of history as a linear progression that unfolds from inferior to superior, occurs early in European history. In 2,500 years of

---

27 Baudelaire: "By modernity I mean the transitory, the fugitive, the contingent which make up one half of art, the other being the eternal and the immutable." Charles Baudelaire, "The Painter of Modern Life" in *The Painter of Modern Life and Other Essays*, edited and translated by Jonathan Mayne. London: Phaidon Press, 13.

history, modern academia's major historical transitions, **Antiquity**, the **Middle Ages**, and the **Modern Era**, are each viewed as an advancement from the previous era in the linear recounting of history. The first transition proposed by modern historians from a prehistoric period begins with Antiquity (3000 B.C.E.–500 C.E.) A century after Rome had converted to Christianity in the 5th century, the Roman writer and statesman Cassiodorus first used the term *modern* to glorify the status quo after Constantine's brutal suppression of religious freedom in the previous century.[28] However, despite Cassiodorus's allusion to the progress of the times, the transition was characterized by state terror, when Constantine enforced the Nicene Creed. In doing so, the Roman Emperor sacrificed the ancient worldview that had upheld the very foundation of the Roman Empire, based on social cooperation and religious tolerance. Constantine's adoption of Christianity as Rome's state religion marked the end of Roman polytheism and religious freedom. In Cassiodorus's lifetime, the Classical Age of the Western Roman Empire ended, and the Middle Ages began. Still, his reference was not to the plight of the vanquished ancient religions, and the Christian Orthodoxy who were exiled or executed. On the contrary, he glorifies Constantine's enforced social order that had become the status quo.

Religion and National Aspirations

While Roman civilization is shown to triumph historically, less attention is paid to the more essential fissures created between East and West when the Eastern Christian Orthodoxy was destroyed and fled the Roman Empire for the safety of Ethiopia. The split has played a significant role in cordoning the Christian West from the Eastern Orthodoxy, and setting the stage for developing a distinct European Christian identity, intolerant of non-European religious views. Before Christianity, Rome thrived by assimilating the religions of its conquered peoples and allowing them to practice their faiths.[29] However, a latent ideological layer bordering on fanatical zeal and nationalism developed that initiates violent resistance to change along the borders where the three religions converge in the Near East, Russia and Ukraine.

The differences between Western Christianity, Orthodox Christianity,

---

28   Hodgkin, Thomas. *The Letters of Cassidarious. Being a Condensed Translation of the Varia Epis-tolae of Magnus Aurelius Cassadiorus Senator* , pp. 1–2.
29   Koch, John T. *Celtic Culture: A Historical Encyclopedia* (ABC-Clio, 2006), p. 974.

Islam and Judaism remain active as determinants of the relations between the various peoples. In the Near East the fissures created by the partitioning of the Ottoman Empire and the creation of the state of Israel has led to violent confrontation since the 1916 Sykes Picot secret agreement between the United Kingdom and France. The post World War I agreement was a prelude to the breakup of the Ottoman Empire which was on the loosing side of the war. The idea of separate boundaries for different peoples led to promises of homelands for Arabs and Jews that has resulted in continuous friction and wars between Arabs and Jews, and Western and Eastern nations.

In areas such as modern Ukraine, the split between religions is easily exploited as a political rift between Russia to the East and Ukraine in the Western sphere. From 2014 to the present, the Christian Orthodox East Ukraine and the Christian West experienced an ongoing civil war delineated along the ancient boundary between the two types of Christianity, the Russian Christian Orthodoxy, and Ukrainian Western Christianity. There is also a language difference between the two nations and peoples that further complicated relations. When the war started, Ukraine had passed laws in 2012 and 2014 that aimed to promote the Ukrainian language and limit the use of Russian in official settings. It also sought religious independence from the Russian Orthodox church. These changes led to a rebellion by the Russian speaking population. More than 14,000 Ukrainian civilians, mostly Russian speaking civilians, were killed during eight years of the Ukrainian Civil War before the Russian Special Military Operation (SMO) began on March 5, 2022.

From the Middle Ages to the Modern Era

The Second Transition

The second transition in Western history is from feudalism in the Middle Ages (9th–15th century) to capitalism in the early Modern Era. Feudalism is represented as a necessary adaptation to socio-political conditions of the medieval period after Rome's collapse. However, Europe's formerly autonomous peoples—the Goths, the conglomeration of the Franks, the Lombards, the Anglo-Saxons, and the Vikings did not benefit from feudalism but lost their social cohesion and became landless serfs. Their institution of *vassalage,* which once benefited the fighting members of their societies, was adopted by the emerging monarchies of The Holy

Roman Empire and used to reward Emperor Charlemagne's new guard—the very forces who oppressed them.[30]

In his study of the early laws and institutions of the Franks, Heinrich Brunner credits Charlemagne's adoption of the militaristic tribal practice of *vassalage* with the formation of feudalism in Europe. The Franks were known to invest military power in their men for their loyalty to the higher order of obligation to the tribe.[31] This traditional tribal institution of rewarding fighters with vassalage—land (fiefdom), booty from war, and other rewards for their loyalty—was adopted as Charlemagne's conquest of European lands extended to include the Germanic tribal regions. As his need for a larger fighting force to maintain order grew, Charlemagne's system of vassalage also expanded. The original use of vassalage by the Germanic tribes had been in effect more than one thousand years before the start of the Holy Roman Empire (800 C.E.) and was described by Roman writer Gaius Cornelius Tacitus in the 2nd century in *Germania*[32] (a history of Germany). The custom was based on an investment in the men of the tribe as warriors, and it was based on war and its rewards of wealth and social advancement, which the chief bestowed.

The adoption of this system of vassalage foreshadows the European oligarchy's system of patronage, which benefited a minority of the nobility and their armies, who organized into manors allied with the monarchy. The larger community of peasants was forced into slavery as tenant farmers by these private armies seeking wealth (land). Still, more importantly, European society lost its cooperative communal character, which is typical of communal societies. Even as feudalism was a destructive force in Europe, its successor, capitalism, is a more destructive appropriative force that operated most efficiently in Africa and the Americas and, to a lesser extent, in Europe.

Modernity

Modernity has come to represent the period of development after World War II that saw the start of the greatest expansion of the middle class and the capitalist economies of the West. When we refer to the term modern, it refers to the glitter and sparkle of style and the luxury and technological

---

30   Stephenson, Carl. 2007. Medieval Feudalism, pp.3–10.
31   ———Ibid. pp. 11–12.
32   Thomas Gordon ed. "Internet Medieval Sourcebook." 18th-century translation by Thomas Gordon. Available at https://fordham.edu/halsall/source/tacitus1.html

innovation of the post-industrial age. But if the plight of hundreds of millions of victims of capitalism and The Atlantic Slave Trade could ever acquire meaning in Western society, it would not represent advancement from a backward era.

The Age of Enlightenment, glorified as the Age of Reason and the foundation of the Modern Era, is contradictory. The 100-year span from the 17th to 18th century saw the most significant expansion of European chattel slavery and genocide of African and American populations in history. Even as the English Parliamentarian Sir William Wilberforce wrote of the economic power of the slave traders that controlled every facet of the society,[33] and as he quantified the genocide of the early Modern Era, an additional period of genocide associated with colonialism occurred in the nineteenth and twentieth centuries. Africans fared only slightly better as resources were plundered with additional millions of casualties. The pace of war and slaughter spread, and quickened, in the aftermath of the Slave Trade. World War I had a total casualty listing of 37 million; in WWII, there were 60 million casualties. These statistics are unprecedented and cannot be evaluated as advancements in the human condition particularly when the underlying causes, the mechanism operating insidiously towards an extinction level disaster, are continually reformulated.

The Profit Motive Remains Fabulously, Triumphant

More than ever, in the 21st century, the ability of the profit motive to create massive economic distortions and social imbalance globally are ignored despite the apparent disastrous results. One example is the rescinding of the Glass Steagall Act of 1933, written to prevent criminal abuse of the unwary and poor by preventing excessive risk-taking in the banking sector. The Act had functioned effectively since the Great Depression of 1929. However, it was quickly replaced by the 1999 Gramm-Leach-Bliley Act that allowed banks to commingle personal and commercial funds and to put customer funds at risk in highly leveraged, and dangerous derivative instruments.

The flawed derivative instruments based on mortgage contracts, were restructured to obscure the risk posed by financially weak mortgage holders to the investors who routinely bought mortgage instruments. Their

---

33   Wilberforce, William. *A Letter on the Abolition of the Slave Trade: Addressed to the Freeholders and other Inhabitants of Yorkshire. Volume 1* . Luke Hansard & Sons. 1807. pp. 12–14

mortgages were bundled with those of the more financially sound mortgage holders. The bundled mortgages, with the strong and weak mortgage holders were fraudulently labeled as AAA. In the 2007 sub-prime financial crisis, as weak hands defaulted on their mortgages, the ripple affect on the highly leveraged loans caused the loss of trillions of dollars in real-estate value and nearly collapsed the economies of the United States and the world during the 2007 crisis.

The profit motive remains obscured as a primary source of crime and, on the contrary, receives support from the government. At the core of the sub-prime economic collapse, the financial instruments and structured derivatives, engineered by international financial corporations, received massive support from the U.S. Federal Government, making more cash available to these banks to replenish their coffers. The moral failure in these situations that violate the public trust erodes Western ethics. The message from the Age of Reason—that the pursuit of profits at any cost is beyond reproach corrupts the foundations of Western society as reason and science are habitually misused to avariciously increase profits.

Many modern-day social ills stem from the historically restricted vice of avarice and its manifestations, such as usury. Throughout history and up to the Middle Ages, usury was outlawed or suppressed. Nevertheless, under the control of merchants and the oligarchy, it rose to fuel European chattel slavery and colonial expansion. It now exists as a legal foundation of Western society. The manufactured image of Western society is of the most advanced and equitable society in history. We bask in the light of modernity—the bustling and opulent façade of a just, democratic society, living in freedom, equality, and prosperity in a democratic and capitalist system. However, the more representative face of the Western world is the glaring disparities built in the system and sustained since the 17–19th century during the Atlantic Slave Trade.

Chapter 9

The Door of No Return
Perpetuating Ignorance

The Door of no Return is the famous disembarkation point on Gorée Island, in Senegal, West Africa, for the unfortunate victims of the Atlantic Slave Trade. The doorway was the last view the captives would ever have of African soil as they were forcibly transported across the Atlantic Ocean to slavery in the New World. The term here has acquired symbolic significance, representing the paradigm shift for Europeans and enslaved Africans torn from families and land to a status of non-human. As the world became mired in the Slave Trade, The Door of No Return symbolically applies to the profound changes in ethics that created an unnatural socio-economic condition for a once free and proud people. As the slave trading nations adapted to total dependence on slavery, common sense gave way to xenophobia parading as reason and science that simultaneously created and obscured the unimaginable genocide occurring in plain sight. Where divine love and compassion had stood as a guide, the profit motive became the driving force of insatiable greed. The idea of The Good became like an unremarkable threshold, easily overcome by evil. Humanity, straining to justify the incredible carnage of the slave trade occurring on the seas and plantations, saw it as a duty to discard these noble ideals of the past that stood in the way of the profit motive.

As profits of the Slave Trade increased, immorality no longer mattered because the need to validate it by comparison to the highest standard of good, had passed. Elements of the ancient worldview that had survived in Africa's longstanding traditions, in Greek Mystery Schools, Stoicism, and early Christianity, the admonition to be free of material corruption, which was the ethical foundation of the past, became the unnecessary burdens of the slave trader. The Christianized concept of salvation by grace, stood in place of virtuous living. Christians evolved to believe that God's unmerited favor, bestowed on humanity despite our sinful nature, was a gift that could not be earned through human effort. This concept was especially significant in the context of the early Christian Church, as it provided a means of salvation for believers who could not fulfill the strict religious requirements. God's grace is a central tenet of Christian doctrine, with its roots in the teachings of Jesus Christ and the writings of the apostle Paul, which became the preferred Christian doctrine that gained prominence in the fourth century with theologian Augustine of Hippo. Augustine's teachings emphasized original sin and the need for God's grace to save humanity from eternal damnation.

During the Protestant Reformation, the religious reformers, including Martin Luther and John Calvin, revived in the doctrine of *sola gratia*, or salvation by grace alone, and challenged the Catholic Church's belief in the necessity of good works and sacraments for salvation. The traditional requirement of virtue as a prerequisite for everlasting life became contingent on faith alone, with each denomination interpreting it differently. Catholics, for example, believe in ritualistic grace by sacraments, while Protestants believe in grace based on the believer's faith in God. Calvinists believe in grace bestowed to a reawakened Christian, predetermined by God for salvation. The ancient Egyptian idea of the Amit monster, waiting at the judgment to devour the impure heart-soul weighed against the feather of Ma'at, had succumbed to earthly rationalization as Christians evolved to believe that God grants everlasting life to the sinner who has faith.

The fundamental idea brought forth by the ancients had rested on understanding the material world as the primary source of spiritual corruption. In the earthly sphere, that corruption could be prevented, only through obeying the laws of Ma'at. However, in the theist tradition of the Christian religion, the ancient pantheist idea of God as an unknowable Father of Creation, existing everywhere and in everything, became a personified image that granted material favors only to the faithful. As the theism of Christian theology increasingly appropriated and reformed the pantheistic views of the ancient religions, such as the first known trinity of Osiris, Isis and Horus, the Church declared these ancient ideas as heretical although it had appropriated the same idea. Philosophers further nullified pantheism in the Enlightenment era by insisting on physical evidence for all presuppositions. The English empiricist philosopher John Locke proffered that morals came from subjective feelings created by impressions in the mind. His argument held that truth was internally derived. Consequently, there could be more than one version of an ultimate truth.

The one eternal and universal truth of the ancients that all life is created in the image of the first cause of creation gave way to a subjective and relativistic truth emanating from individual whims. After the Enlightenment had established a scientific explanation for human understanding and the origins of law, it placed the omnipotence of God in question, and it was a simple exercise to use inductive reasoning as the new barometer of truth to impose a newly fabricated standard for reality. Natural law from God became associated with physical sensations of the body. Vice, which could be perceived as having no moral foundation, no longer featured prominently as the impediment to everlasting life. The changes coincided with the accrual of money from chattel slavery, which increased the tendency to normalize avarice and usury in contradiction to canon law forbidding the vices.

The point at which the European ruling class and intellectuals opted to discard the ethics of the Ancient and Classic worlds is not as important a question as to why they did so. During The Enlightenment, they had created an energetic but speculative body of work supported primarily by pseudo-scientific, racial classification of the human family to defend chattel slavery. However, arguments based on religion that supported the European enslavement of Africans also occurred in the 15th century. The common thread between the two eras is the uncontrollable desire to accumulate wealth, which drove the ethical divergences from previous eras. Still, the idea of enslaving human beings is not solely a European practice. Aristotle believed that slavery was a natural occurrence, and in the 5th century C.E., St. Augustine rationalized slavery in the Roman Empire as a function of the natural interactions between peoples during war and peace. St. Augustine, who was born in North Africa, concluded that slavery was the result of the fall of man (sin). He points to war as the sin of passion, which resulted in the enslavement of defeated peoples, but he also believed that slavery resulted from personal sins such as incurring debt.[1] Islam condones slavery and sees it as a religious duty authorized by the prophet. However, the reliance on *chattel slavery* in the early modern era was motivated by an outlawed profit motive contrary to natural law. It relied on unprecedented, unprovoked wars that violated the legal definition of a Christian concept of just war consistent throughout the Classical period. Most importantly, it became contingent on a racial policy that led to the African genocide.

Unbridled greed of the oligarchy drove the capture and sale of a specific group of innocent human beings strictly for profit. The normalizing of avarice sustained usury and chattel slavery. The growing tolerance of vice in the early modern era defied the ancient natural order that criminalized avarice and denied everlasting life to the sinner. While the an-

---

1   John Martin Littlejohn. *The Political Theory of the Schoolmen and Grotius*

cients had sought to actively repress avarice, the European aristocracy turned a blind eye and encouraged it in the flourishing financial centers of Medieval Europe. Business customs became based on debt with usurious charges in Florence, Venice, Amsterdam, Paris, and London. The tradition of issuing credit and charging exorbitant interest became a normalized practice and the primary tool of an aristocracy that had grown extremely wealthy through debt, compound interest, and chattel slavery.

At the beginning of the 15th century, remnants of the ancient and classical periods were still vibrant in intellectual and theological circles. Ideas on protecting the weakest members of society existed alongside the new trend that embraced avarice. The theologians, known as the Schoolmen at the University of Salamanca, still adhered to the old beliefs that the Bible, the Church Fathers, and the canon law were the ultimate arbiters in all moral state and religious issues. Based on their ethical principles, the idea of justice as fairness prevailed. However, two centuries later, even the Schoolmen had loosened their objections to usury and rejected medieval price controls that had the objectives of helping the poor and saving their souls. Instead, they focused on economics and profit schemes that had increased in European society since the beginning of the Atlantic Slave Trade.[2] The loosening of canonical restrictions on usury increased investment in the slave trade to the disastrous levels reached in the 18th and 19th centuries. An accommodation occurred, not only with chattel slavery but with the forbidden vice of compound usury, the practice of money making money that Aristotle had condemned, which enabled the vicious cycle.

The European aristocracy had grown enormously wealthy from usury at its point of refinement in Europe in the 14th century with the Medici Banking innovations. With their increasing wealth, the oligarchy increasingly exploited the poor in Europe, denying them access to the natural resources traditionally shared by all members of the close-knit societies. The increasing hordes of idle peasants forced off the land and into the cities were further penalized for their idleness. For example, in 16th-century England, the Vagrancy Act of 1547 forced increasing numbers of poor and displaced peasants into the labor force as enslaved persons. The law outlawed vagrancy and punished offenders with mutilation, enslavement, or death.[3] The European aristocracy gathered thousands of enslaved Europeans and indentured

---

2   R.H. Tawney. *Religion and the Rise of Capitalism, p. 16.*
3   R. O. Bucholz, Newton Key, Early Modern England, 1485–1714, p186

The Gleaners. Oil on Canvas by Jean-Francois Millet, 1857. Museum d'Orsay, Paris. A remnant practice of the moral economy where European peasants were allowed to collect excess grain from the commons.

servants to work plantations as far away as Southeast Asia, where the Dutch East India Company used them to replace the massacred local inhabitants of the Banda Islands to gain control of the nutmeg trade.[4]

Morality was central in day-to-day social interactions throughout the Classical Era and the Middle Ages. Conducting commerce was thus intrinsically linked to moral principles. The results of canon laws that regulated prices and promoted a Christian worldview protecting the poor came to be defined as the moral economy.[5] Theologians at the School of Salamanca read many of these proclamations and laws of the moral economy as sermons. Their work, based on natural law, influenced the development of international law principles, including protecting the human rights of the indigenous inhabitants of the Americas, whom the Schoolmen viewed as equals under God with land rights that could not be usurped. Their work also led to debates on the legality and morality of the conquest and colonization of the Americas. Nevertheless, the Portuguese and Spanish oligarchies remained undeterred in exploiting, killing, or enslaving the native populations in the Americas. The Jesuit priest Bartolomé de Las Casas's eyewitness account of the atrocities committed by the

---

4   See the history of Jan Pieterszoon Coen.
5   Thompson, Edward P. (1991). *Customs in Common.* New York: New Press, pp. 185–258.

Spanish in South America, failed to slow the genocide. Although de Las Casas advocated on behalf of the Indigenous South American population, he advocated for the use of Africans in their place. Inevitably, the book was banned in Europe and suppressed for 300 years by the slave trading aristocracy.

The School of Salamanca had one influence from natural law and another from the Roman law of Justinian, which was revived in the Holy Roman Empire. Justinian Law emphasized civil law but also accepted the rights of people under natural law. Natural law permits the use of the commons or free land not farmed by the lord of the manor as part of the natural right of all human beings. Thus, in their sermons, the Schoolmen of Salamanca advocated on behalf of the poor. They granted them the right to glean the fields of excess grain after the harvest, to hunt in the forests, and to graze cattle on their ancestral lands known as the commons. Before the advent of chattel slavery and agrarian capitalism on the Portuguese colony of Madeira Island, Europeans had been insistent on applying market prices based on the moral economy so that the poorest member of society could afford to buy grain. However, as Europe experienced rapid economic growth from slavery, even the School of Salamanca began reconciling the classical era ethics with the changing times by adopting the theory of supply and demand. The new economic reality of capitalism had replaced the moral economy's just price theory that had set standards of fairness in commerce based on the needs of the poor.

Despite the laws of the moral economy, from the 5th to the 15th century, the aristocracy gradually claimed the land legally and through force. The poor in Europe became trapped in involuntary slavery as their available land resources dwindled and prices increased. The Schoolmen's theories at The School of Salamanca changed from protecting these poor to demanding adherence to the natural order, such that no person in the feudal system could move out of his class to impinge on the rights of another. Even in the throes of the moral economy, the aristocracy's right to usurp power was upheld and led to the revoking of price controls. The price controls of the moral economy rested on what the poorest in society could afford, placing emphasis on the Church's overarching aim of saving souls. By the 18th century, as landless peasants crowded the cities or were enslaved in the manor or on plantations overseas, the aristocracy formalized the right to set prices based on the newfound economic laws of supply and demand. Understandably, the poor, landless peasants began to riot as their means to a livelihood were destroyed by the ongoing seizure of the commons and dismantling of the moral economy. As grain prices rose, the poor resorted to rioting out of sheer necessity.[6] Peasant rebellions against the aristocracy's encroachment on the commons remain obscured by the mislabeling of the legitimate peasant protests as riots by unruly mobs. The elite saw rebellions against enclosure laws occurring in 18th-century England as a menace and not as a necessary opposition to their encroachment.

The father of modern economics, Adam Smith, further developed the Schoolmen's reformed, free-market economic theory of supply and demand. In his 1776 book, *An Inquiry into the Wealth of Nations*[7], Smith is familiar with St. Aquinas's definition of just price, which covers the cost of labor. In his use of *natural price*, he alludes to the lowest price a commodity can fetch in the marketplace, reflecting all production costs. However, when Smith wrote *The Wealth of Nations*, the European men in the marketplace he refers to, with their private interests and passions, seeking to better their life, had been conducting trade across the seas for more than 200 years. As their greed had been unbridled in the prior centuries, Africans had witnessed the most significant decline in their history due to the Atlantic Slave Trade. The success of the aristocracy coincided with a decidedly occult process—a covert accommodation with vice. Whether by force or by fraudulently printing notes, the avarice proceeded unimpaired as long as a steady supply of expendable human beings produced the coveted wealth in the final leg of the scheme in the plantations of the New World and Asia. The slave traders acknowledged their reliance on slavery, and they lived in fear of public scrutiny of their ghastly business and the denial of their presumed right to enslave others. The flurry of legal formulations and economic and social theories that worked to legitimize the theft is exemplified by a slate of new Papal Bulls, a rejection of the premise of natural law, and the use of positive law such as Vagrancy and Enclosure Laws to privatize the commons, and dismantling the moral economy.

> ...the first private bill of enclosure ever passed" came up to parliament in February 1710. It concerned Ropley Commons and the old disparked park of Farnham, within the bishopric of Winchester.
>
> —Thompson, Edward *Customs in Common*. (1991) New York: New Press, p. 109.

---

6   Thompson, Edward P. (1991). *Customs in Common*. New York: New Press, (They relied on the Book of Orders from King Charles, I, or on the custom law itself for moral direction. Thompson, Edward P. (1991). *Customs in Common*. New York: New Press.)
7   Smith, Adams. *Wealth of Nations*. Available at: www.econlib.org/library/Smith/smWN.html. Accessed 8/31/2016.

Many social, philosophical, and economic theories during the 17th and 19th centuries favored the aristocracy's avaricious ethics. Works of intellectuals such as Thomas Hobbs mandated obedience to the sovereign, John Locke redefined truth as whatever an individual believed, and Adam Smith retired the just economy of the old Christian Theocracy with his formalized theories of supply and demand. The revolutionary ideas of these intellectuals served to obscure the innate perception of the divine moral principle that had helped to protect the poor. Adam Smith's Theory of Supply and Demand defined the equilibrium point of unit price levels to the number of goods or services. However, it ignored the fundamental causes of inflation from the seizure of the commons and its agricultural resources, the plundering of the wealth of Africa and the Americas, and the fraudulently printed banknotes as the drivers of increasing prices.

Europeans, in practice, lived in two different universes, one that evoked the word of God in the Bible and another that opposed it. Science's inductive reasoning and formulation of truth were devoid of divine moral value and relied on an empirical basis for all truth. The cultivated belief in science granted greater individual freedom to rely on personal whims as valid truths. Empiricism and moral relativism that establish excuses for ethical actions helped justify the immorality inherent in ongoing atrocities such as the enclosure of the commons, the Atlantic Slave Trade, and the racial ostracizing of people of African ancestry. The justification for the gross immorality sprung up after Europeans had solidly established African slavery as the economic foundation of their new society. Just as earlier customs such as serfdom had given rise to rigid class distinctions and economic and social Darwinism, The Atlantic Slave Trade gave rise to a new way of perceiving reality from a deterministic vantage point. Before capitalism and slavery could be sanitized, its history of corruption propelled by usury and investing for profit in human chattel though widely known had to be erased from the historical record. New theories arose that provided logical and unrelated explanations for capitalism's brutal impact on society. From its normalized and unbridled greed and cruelty came the ranks of its white supremacist supporters who insisted on the righteousness of their cruelty based on the intellectual efforts affirming white supremacy and black inferiority. Their only recourse was to continually seek vindication through reason and falsifying the truth.

The relentless drive to substantiate white supremacy in the modern era continues to validate the status quo that portrays African people as undeserving of God's grace. It links directly to the behaviors that arose in defense of chattel slavery that occurred to protect the slave-trading nations' burgeoning economies. The normalizing of chattel slavery, which required violating the Christian canon protecting the poor, followed the same pattern of guile and obfuscation that occurred in Europe's post-feudal era when the aristocracy derived new theories to support the privatization of the commons.[8]

The overarching result of white supremacist ideology is the obfuscation of humanity's foundation in an original African cosmogony and its ultimate meaning to humanity. No other civilization after Kemet had denied the ancient concepts upon which civilization rests, except that of Europe from the 18th century to the present. Even as Greece became a significant world power, Alexander the Great, who coveted the mantle of a divine ruler, honored the Kemetic goddess Aset as the source of his divine authority. His capital city, Alexandria, was built in the land he named Agyptos two thousand years before nationalism and racism defiled the concept of humanity in the 18th century. In the ancient Roman Empire, where Stoicism predominated, Roman society accepted the basic premise of unity in all creation. In the fourth century, despite Constantine's brutal enforcement of the Nicene Creed, Rome never claimed ownership of ancient knowledge or the reasoning process. The most profound concepts of civilization—cosmogony and the concept of the divine man, balanced between intellect, imagination, and intuition—have an origin in the mysteries of ancient Africa.

The Wages of Immorality

Humanity has not escaped the consequences of the Atlantic Slave Trade and the normalization of vice. If these consequences have slipped from memory, it is due to the well-established pattern of obfuscation occurring repeatedly since the Oligarchy privatized land ownership and enslaved the peasant and menial laborers in Europe. Obfuscation, however, cannot hide the consequences of the historically unmatched chaos of slave trading activities in Africa and the Americas occurring from the 16th century up to abolition. Most of the enslaved people from Africa disembarked in the European colonies in the 17th and 19th centuries. In 1875, the total number of embarkations was approximately 12.5 million total which is 93,601 percent larger than the first quarter of the 16th century.[9] The table on page 174 shows

---

8   See the 1833 essay by the Victorian economist William Forster Lloyd, where he attributes the hypothetical destruction of the commons to unregulated grazing. https://archive.org/details/twolec-turesonch00lloygoog

9   The general methodology used in deriving estimates is described in David Eltis and Paul

Contemporary Estimates of Embarked and Disembarked Enslaved Africans

Dates	Embarked	Disembarked
1501-1525	13,363	9,376
1526-1550	50,762	35,534
1551-1575	61,007	43,132
1576-1600	152,373	111,244
1601-1625	352,844	274,830
1626-1650	315,050	252,876
1651-1675	488,065	400,281
1676-1700	719,675	594,689
1701-1725	1,088,909	924,567
1726-1750	1,471,725	1,244,321
1751-1775	1,925,315	1,644,353
1776-1800	2,008,670	1,796,628
1801-1825	1,876,992	1,667,172
1826-1850	1,770,978	1,514,396
1851-1875	225,609	189,257
Totals	**12,521,337**	**10,702,656**

Source: www.slavevoyages.org/assessment/estimates. Accessed 1/21/2023.
    See Appendix on page 243 for additional information.

that the 13.3 thousand embarkations of enslaved Africans in the first quarter cumulatively equaled more than 12.5 million by the end of 1875. Nineteenth-century abolitionists and scholars such as Sir William Wilberforce and Thomas Cooper shed some light on the ramifications of the slave trade on Africa's population growth rate using the logs of slave ships. However, the severity of the assault on Africa's people, particularly its near-extinction-level implication, is rarely noted and has virtually disappeared from memory in discussions of the slave trade. The use of ship logs during Wilberforce's time, and those discovered in the contemporary era, show four hundred years of a casualty rate that, by any measure, is a shocking indictment of the moral corruption and racism that permeates modern society.

The genocide that took place from the Age of Discovery to the 19th century was not limited in scope like the more widely studied genocides of the 20th century. It is far more ominous because its intensity and duration precipitated a noticeable extinction of human life in the Americas and Africa. In West Africa, the Congo, and Angola, up to 90 percent of the population was reported

---

Lachance, "Estimates of the Size and the Direction of the Transatlantic Slave Trade." Available at: www.slavevoyages.org/estimates/aGkJSUeO   Accessed 1/14/2023.

killed.[10,11] The trend of genocide subsided, but only after the alternative profit mechanism of industrialization had developed that would allow avarice, the root cause of the disaster, to propagate. It again resurged after the scramble for Africa's mineral wealth began after the Berlin Conference of 1865.

Wilberforce revealed the magnitude of the genocide associated with the slave trade in his 1789 speech to Parliament. He details the total shipboard mortality rate of Africans during the Middle Passage to be 12.5%. One to two weeks before the sale, 4.5% of the survivors of the voyages died, and during seasoning, 33% of the remaining African victims died. Overall, Wilberforce estimates a 50% mortality rate.[12] While Wilberforce's analysis does not deal with the mortality rate of Africans on the continent, author Thomas Fowell Buxton, also a British Parliamentarian, wrote of the overall casualty rate of the slave trade in his 1839 book *The African Slave Trade and Its Remedy*.[13] As an abolitionist, Buxton is careful to attribute the causes of the wars occurring in Africa to European demand for slaves and to African complicity in the trade as he alludes to the total breakdown of civilization in Africa. He gives first-hand accounts of slave raids where the old were killed and the young were captured, and he describes attacks on towns that were followed by brutal retribution.[14] These eyewitness accounts shed light on the overall number of people killed during the capture of slaves.

Thomas Cooper, a contemporary of Thomas Jefferson, is the source of the estimates of 10 deaths on African soil for each survivor. He further lists a 20% casualty rate during the middle passage and a 33% casualty rate during seasoning in the New World as shown in the excerpt:[15]

> Seymour Drescher, in correspondence with the authors, points out estimates made by Thomas Cooper, Supplement to Mr. Cooper's Letter on the Slave Trade (Manchester, 1788), 3, 4, who argued that, for each slave taken, 10 were lost due to warfare in Africa, 1/5 died in passage, and another 1/3 died during seasoning. Using estimates of slaves arrived during the period of the slave trade, the 10 million slaves arrived in the New World meant a cost of 180 million

---

10   Walter Rodney.
11   Adam Hochschild. *King Leopold's Ghost.*
12   *William Wilberforce's 1789 Abolition Speech.* From 'Debate on Mr. Wilberforce's Resolutions respecting the Slave Trade' in William Cobbett, The Parliamentary History of England. From the Norman Conquest in 1066 to the year 1803, 36 vols (London: T. Curson Hansard, 1806-1820), 28 (1789-91), cols 42-68.
13   Buxton, *The African Slave Trade and Its Remedy* (London, 1967; orig. pub. 1839, 1840), 73.
14   Ibid. Buxton, pp. 61–62.
15   Herbert S. Klein, Stanley L. Engerman, Robin Haines, and Ralph Shlomowitz. *Transoceanic Mortality: The Slave Trade in Comparative Perspective, p. 19.* Based on (Thomas Cooper, Supplement to Mr. Cooper's Letter on the Slave Trade (Manchester, 1788), 3, 4.)

lives. This would mean that Middle Passage deaths were equal to about 2% of all the deaths attributed to the slave trade. In making his estimates in this and in subsequent presentations of the same numbers, Cooper drew on the work of numerous contemporaries, including Thomas Clarkson, *An Essay on the Slavery and Commerce of the Human Species, particularly the African* (Dublin, 1786).[16]

The Trans-Atlantic and Intra-American slave trade databases of independent scholars using data in libraries around the world presented in the new SlaveVoyages website hosted at Rice University sheds a modern viewpoint on the scope of the slave voyages. The total embarkations figure from the database of 12,521,337, as shown in the table on page 174, also indicates a disembarked or surviving population of 10,702,656.

Figure 4: **Comparison of Population Growth by Region** (in millions)

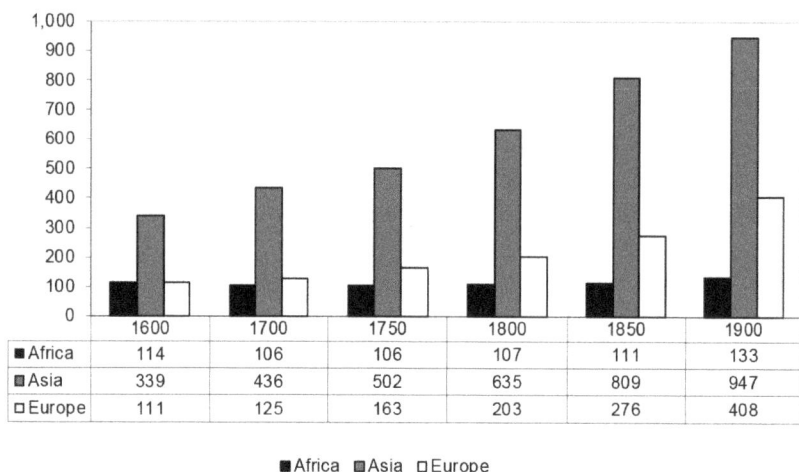

	1600	1700	1750	1800	1850	1900
■ Africa	114	106	106	107	111	133
■ Asia	339	436	502	635	809	947
▢ Europe	111	125	163	203	276	408

■Africa ■Asia ▢Europe

Source: World Population Prospects (United Nations). 2008 Revision Population Database. http://esa.un.org/wpp/unpp/panel_population.htm

Besides the work of the English Parliamentarians in the 19th century, more was done in the 20th century by African American scholar W.E.B. Dubois, who continued collecting data from ship logs while conducting his study. Although the truth of the effects on Africa's population is difficult to fathom, the United Nations Population Fund (UNPF) studied the subject. The analyses in Figure 4 above, which is supported by the table on page 177, show

---

16 Herbert S. Klein, Stanley L. Engerman, Robin Haines, and Ralph Shlomowitz. *Transoceanic Mortality: The Slave Trade in Comparative Perspective, p. 19.* Based on (Thomas Cooper, Supplement to Mr. Cooper's Letter on the Slave Trade (Manchester, 1788), 3, 4.)

Table of Comparison of Population Growth by Region — Cont'd (in millions)
(1600 and 1900)

| Region | Years | | Gain in population (%) |
	1600	1900	
Europe	111	408	267.57%
Asia	339	947	179.35%
Africa	114	133	16.67%

Source: United Nations Population Fund (UNPF)

Figure 5: **Comparison of Population Growth Rate by Region** (YOY in percent)

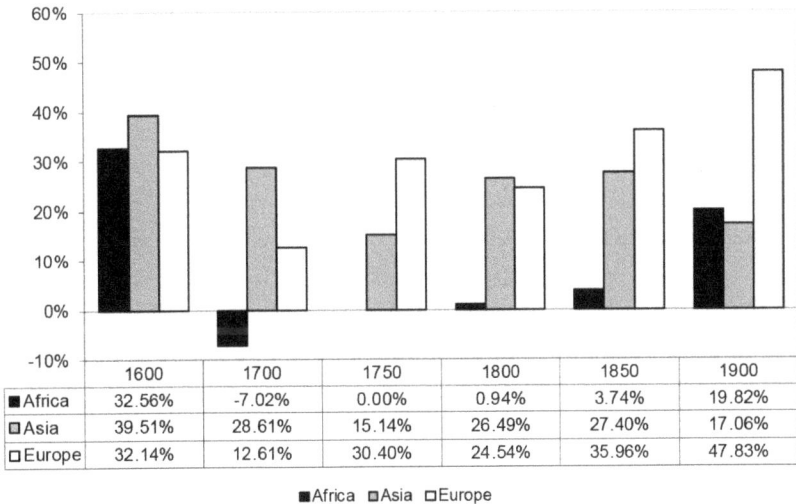

	1600	1700	1750	1800	1850	1900
■Africa	32.56%	-7.02%	0.00%	0.94%	3.74%	19.82%
□Asia	39.51%	28.61%	15.14%	26.49%	27.40%	17.06%
□Europe	32.14%	12.61%	30.40%	24.54%	35.96%	47.83%

■Africa □Asia □Europe

that in 1600 Africa's population was approximately 114 million. In that year, it compares favorably to the populations of Europe and Asia in terms of the natural growth rate. However, in 1900 Europe's population was 267 percent larger, and Asia's grew by 179.35 percent. But Africa's population growth stagnated. In contrast to the normal population increases in Europe and Asia, Africa's population growth was 17 percent. From 1700 up to the point that the wars for slavery had ended late in the 19th century, Africa's population growth remained below its original level in 1600. Population growth was negative seven percent in 1700 (*see figure 5, above*).

Population growth models developed since Malthus's 18th-century theory of population are used to estimate population growth rates. The growing database of up to 35,000 logs of ships involved in the slave trade is another valuable tool that helped uncover the mortality rates of captured Africans and European sailors on slave ships—the database of logs of slave ships maintained by W. E. B. Du Bois Institute for Afro-American Research at Harvard University makes the failure to account for the genocide of the African population a cause for concern because it highlights an ongoing catastrophe coinciding with the divergence from the orthodox ethical foundation of the human species.

In percentage terms in the chart on page 177, the comparison of populations of Africa, Europe, and Asia becomes more comprehensive. In 1700, for example, Africa's population fell precipitously by a negative seven percent, while the maximum population growth in Asia was 29% that same year. The numbers of overall casualties vary, and they become readily dissociated from the events on the ground in Africa—the narratives of victims who died from wars fomented by European demands for slaves, from the forced marches stretching for miles, famine, and disease, and the transatlantic crossing into slavery. The carnage was such that deaths outpaced births in several regions of Africa where nature had begun the process of extinction as insect-borne epidemics overpowered the human capacity to innovate and survive.[17]

The path to the extinction of Africa's population, while it played a vital part in the abolitionist movement, did not end with abolition. The fundamental drive for profits firmly established since Europe's feudal era, mushroomed after the Portuguese and Spanish seizure of land and the wealth of Muslims and Jews. The confiscated wealth was instrumental in building new technologies for naval warfare. When the Portuguese arrived in Africa, they had a complete methodology to subjugate, plunder, and enslave the local populations they encountered. Their military objectives and achievements in the newly discovered lands were driven by irrepressible greed and the need for money to service debts. Their reliance on borrowed money and usury set the precedent that succeeding empires emulated.[18] The Papal Bull, Romanus Pontifex ("The Roman pontiff"), issued on behalf of the Portuguese King Alfonso V by Pope Nicholas V in 1455, documents some of the military activities of the King's forces in Africa under the command of Henry the Navigator.

Romanus Pontifex commemorates the military victories of Portuguese Christian armies against the Muslims in Ceuta in North Africa. Apart from

---

17   Walter Rodney states that enslavement was causing people to loose their battle to tame and harness nature—a battle which is at the basis of development. HEUA-P. 98

18   the **Middle Ages**, or **Medieval period**, lasted from the 5th to the 15th century. It began with the collapse of the Western Roman Empire and merged into the early modern period.

the Papal claim to spiritual ownership of the world, the document works in concert with Portuguese military objectives and legalizes its activities in Africa and anywhere in the world. The Pope discloses that the Portuguese waged a protracted war lasting several years. Fifteen hundred nautical miles to the south, on the coast of Guinea, they captured and also purchased an undisclosed number of Africans who were promptly enslaved on plantations in the islands off the coast of Africa that the Portuguese had seized. Their slave enterprise on the island of Madeira marks the first instance of agrarian capitalism, where the slave plantation system first occurred. Pope Nicholas admires these exploits despite their violation of the preexisting Christian code of just war.

In 44 B.C.E., the earliest record of a discussion of the principles of just war in the ancient Western world was written in *De Officiis*, the letter on official duties, by Roman Politician and historian Cicero to his son. Cicero's just war principles were reinterpreted and elaborated on by St. Augustine and finally codified by St. Thomas Aquinas in *Summa Theologica*. St. Augustine lists three main points of his Just War Theory.[19] First, the proper authority to wage war belongs to the Sovereign, not an individual. Second, a just cause must exist, such as a war to right a wrong or to punish those who refuse to make amends for wrongs. Third, an honorable intention should exist to advance good and avoid evil.

> The passion for inflicting harm, the cruel thirst for vengeance, an unpacific and relentless spirit, the fever of revolt, the lust of power, and such like things, all these are rightly condemned in war.
> —Source: Suma Theologica

The terms under which a just war could be waged did not feature prominently in Pope Nicholas's 1452 Papal Bull, *Dum Diversas*. The bull granted the monarchies of Europe the divine authority to reduce Muslims, pagans, and other unbelievers to perpetual slavery based solely on their differing religious beliefs, which made them enemies of Christ. Following *Dum Diversas*, the actions of Europeans in Africa and the Americas are conspicuous as exhibitions of the newfound commercial ethics of the Middle Ages. Ethics of commerce evolved from rudimentary origins in the Roman Empire, where the corporation's legal rights were first established.[20]

---

19 *Summa Theologica; The New Adventist Encyclopedia/* Available at: http://www.newadvent.org/summa/3040.htm
20 Harold Joseph Berman, *Law and Revolution* (vol. 1): *The Formation of the Western Legal Tradi-*

After the fall of Rome, the corporation's legal rights arose simultaneously with a new form of commerce and finance that had flowered in Europe with the rise of the Venetian Empire (800 C.E.). Venice's banking system and corporate structure facilitated the issuance of shares to its members. Finance had evolved from carrying gold by pack mule to elaborate credit mechanisms based on the profit motive and undergirded by usury.

In practice, the corporation is a monopoly of shareholders that operates with the state's authority. The Ancient Roman Empire used the principle which recognized guilds, religious cults, municipalities, and the state as corporations. While Rome appropriated resources and material wealth on behalf of Roman generals, senators, and the emperor, Europeans organized the corporation using the most abstract financial methods to *project* its destructive power worldwide.

> From Italy, came manual exchange transactions and the use of bills of exchange for transferring funds, as well as the credit operations which developed in connection with those operations, deposits, credit transfers and various investments.[21]

The history of the devastating global impact of corporations in Africa, the Americas, and Asia began with the search for profit to appease shareholders and creditors. The European Age of Discovery had gone awry from the outset, as it started an era of historically unparalleled brutality in line with a corrupted moral philosophy.

In their drive for profits, the European oligarchy unleashed a ruthless army of privateers empowered to wage war and establish colonies worldwide. The largest of these, the Dutch East India Company (Verenigde Oostindische Compagnie or VOC), 1602, sent more than one million Europeans to work in Asia from 1602–1796. The VOC alone operated 4,785 sailing ships and controlled over 2.5 million tons of Asian trade goods, while the English East India Company (EIC), founded in 1600, operated an additional 2,690 ships.[22] These corporations and privateers operated without the traditional legal and moral constraints on commerce and war that ancient customs had imposed. The Dutch

---

tion, Cambridge: Harvard University Press, 1983, pp. 215–16.

21   Handbook on the History of European Banks. Edited by Manfred Pohl, Sabine Freitag, European Association for Banking History,p 185. Available at: http://books.google.com/books?id=eXvfNDHp-fWwC&dq=the+lombard+bankers&q=lombards#v=snippet&q=lombards&f=false

22   Van Boven, M. W.. "Towards A New Age of Partnership (TANAP): An Ambitious World Heritage Project (UNESCO Memory of the World – reg.form, 2002)". *VOC Archives Appendix 2, p.14.* Available at: www.tanap.net/content/voc/organization/organization_intro.htm

East India Company (VOC) enslaved entire populations in Asia. It exterminated and replaced those who did not comply with its profit objective to establish a monopoly on the spice trade in the Banda islands. The British East India Company, founded in 1600 under a charter from Queen Elizabeth, grew even more significant and devastating as it operated under the authority of the British monarchy and Parliament with financing from the Bank of England.

The profit demands of traders and bankers that had wreaked havoc in Africa and the Americas fueled four hundred years of slavery. However, their greed did not end with the abolition, and it resurfaced in a more organized form, as devised at the Berlin Conference of 1884–1885. The ultimate objective of the conference was to divide the spoils of the African continent among the European nations. The impoverished Africans were yet again conscripted to provide the immense labor needed to extract the raw materials for an expanding Western industrialized economy. A vicious form of European political economy thrived in areas such as the Congo, South Africa, and Rhodesia that, once again, as in slavery, was defined by a complete negation of humanity's most basic ethical standards. The pattern for the behavior of European capitalists such as King Leopold II (1835–1909) and Cecil Rhodes (1853–1902) is from the original model established by the Venetians in the 11th century. Cecil Rhodes, for instance, patterned the British South Africa Company after the Dutch East India Company from the Venetian empire and ruthlessly used its autonomous military power against the indigenous Africans.

These corporations, forming the point of exposure to the world, demonstrated an entrenched view of dark-skinned peoples as disposable objects to be exploited and subjugated as efficiently as possible in line with the profit objectives of European empires. To that end, the methodology developed to achieve this goal is an exploitation of the fundamental weakness in human nature as part of a psychological war against humanity—a reliance on moral corruption—the debasement of the intricate nature of the soul.

Zimbabwe (1652–1961)

With the abolishment of slavery in the late 19th century, European ideology persisted as the driver of Africa's mechanism of social transformation. Among the suppressed facts are those of the British Empire, relating to the colonial system in Southern Africa, recounted in an interview on April 12, 2008, by the Zimbabwean Ambassador to the United States, Machivenyika Mapuranga:

"In areas such as South Africa, one half-century after the Dutch established the colony of Cape Town in 1652, the ratio of settler to native African was 1 to 19,000, today, that ratio is 1 to 10. In Zimbabwe, in 1894, four years after the British South Africa Company colonized the country the ratio of settler to Native African was 1 to 17,000. By 1961, at the height of the Federation of Rhodesia and Nyasaland, that ratio was 1 to 13."[23]

Congo (1877–1908)

During the 1877–1908 genocide in the Belgian Congo, King Leopold II (1835–1909) more effectively destroyed the evidence of his genocidal activities in the Congo Free State, which he operated as his personal property. These atrocities claimed the lives of 10 million[24] people, who died extracting rubber for use in the newly developed automotive industry begun by the American industrialist Henry Ford. Leopold's atrocities in Congo were publicly exposed by photographic evidence compiled by the Reverend John Harris and his wife, Alice. The Catholic missionaries revealed images of the maiming of men and the women and the children of farmers who failed to meet rubber quotas established by Leopold. These atrocities were published in Mark Twain's 1905 *King Leopold's Soliloquy*.[25] Before relinquishing control to the Belgian Parliament in 1908, Leopold burned the evidence of his crimes in furnaces in the Congo over several weeks.

The atrocities in the Congo were first revealed by an African American politician and historian, George Washington Williams (October 16, 1849–August 2, 1891). Williams was a Bedford Springs, Pennsylvania native and author of *A History of Negro Troops in the War of Rebellion* and *The History of the Negro Race in America 1619–1880*. He spent a year traveling around the continent and six months in the Congo, where he witnessed atrocities firsthand that led to his public outrage in an open letter to King Leopold. Williams details the horrific nature of the slave trade conducted by the Belgian King, which was still occurring within Congo in the rubber industry. He exposed the very nature of slavery and colonialism, from the severe disruption of local African trade to the theft of land and the exploitation of labor and resources Leopold practiced in the Congo.[26]

---

23   From an interview with the Zimbabwean Ambassador Mapuranga to the U.S. "The LaRouche Show available at: http://youtube.com/watch?v=chUpfOYZI5A. Accessed 2008/ (Start at min. 19:25)
24   King Leopold's Ghost.
25   Available at: http://msuweb.montclair.edu/~furrg/i2l/kls.html
26   As Adam Hochschild details in *King Leopold's Ghost.*

From the beginning of the atrocities such as the forced labor and genocide occurring in the Congo, The Royal Museum for Central Africa obscured these activities. King Leopold founded the museum to portray a falsified and gentile face of his empire. In the 21st century, it continued to function as originally intended.[27]

Kenya (1952–1960)

In Kenya, under British rule, the genocide occurring there was punctuated by the seizure of the most fertile land for use exclusively by British capitalists to grow cash crops for export to Europe. The native Kenyan population was reduced through forced relocation to barren native reserves and by mass killing of the Agikuyu, Abagusii, Nandi, Ababukusu, and Giriama peoples who resisted colonialism.[28] In 2002, five[29] remaining Kikuyu who fought against British imperialism in 1952–1960 in the so-called Mau Mau uprisings to reclaim seized land and to end colonial rule filed suit in a British Court for compensation for the tortures they endured.[30] The British government chose to settle as 300 boxes of evidence were uncovered in early 2011. In June 2013, Britain's High Commissioner William Hauge issued a formal apology and laid out plans to compensate 5,000 elderly Kikuyu who suffered torture and coercion under the British colonial administration. The payments totaling £19.9m in costs and compensation have opened the door to Britain's recent activities in its vast global empire, particularly in the West Indies, where there is a resurgent reparations movement.[31]

Rwanda (1994)

More recently, in 1994, the conflict in Rwanda between the Tutsis and Hutus cost approximately 800,000 lives. The genocide that Western

---

27 See the Afterword, in the second publication of *King Leopold's Ghost*. Accessed 5/19/2013. Available at. www.houghtonmifflinbooks.com/readers_guides/hochschild_king_leo.shtml#
28 Peter O Nedge, Colonialism and Its Legacies, p. 3. Lecture delivered during Fulbright – Hays Group project abroad program: July 5th to August 6th 2009 at the Moi University Main Campus
29 The number given by William Hague, Britain's High Commissioner, reported in the Guardian. Available at: www.guardian.co.uk/world/2013/jun/06/uk-compensate-kenya-mau-mau-torture. Accessed: July 6, 2013.
30 Plaut, Martin (31 August 2003), "Kenya lifts ban on Ma Mau." BBC News. Retrieved 12-22-2012) and Mike Pflanz (11 October 2006) "Mau Mau veterans issue writ deadline." *The Daily Telegraph*, retrieved 12-20-2012
31 *The Guardian*

governments largely ignored has a causal link to the colonial class structure first established by the Germans, who divided the population into the superior cattle-owning Tutsis and inferior Hutu farmers. The Germans empowered the pastoral Tutsi minority over the majority Hutu farmers and established the first division they exploited for material gain. The Belgians racialized the two interrelated groups by redefining their racial classification. The Tutsis became the long-nosed and privileged Caucasian types, and the Hutu the broad-nosed, lesser types. Before the arrival of the Europeans, these groups, who were relatives and allies, had kept their peace through intermarrying and cooperation in a communal civil society. In 1994, during the Tutsi genocide, France had a colonial interest in Rwanda. It exploited this old division, as they militarily supported the Hutu militias with training in using ordinary garden implements for warfare and with French troops and air power. In 2008, the President of Rwanda, Paul Kagame, reported French complicity in the Tutsi genocide in a 500-page report.[32]

Democratic Republic of Congo (DRC) (1998–Present)

The war in the Democratic Republic of the Congo (DRC), referred to as Africa's First World War, surpassed 5.4 million casualties since the start of the war in 1998.[33] That war also has deep roots in the ethnic divisions between the cattle herders and farmers, which the Belgians exploited. Today, neither of these Congolese groups seems interested in their traditional cooperative life patterns. Instead, organized gangs are focused on fighting over the vast rare earth mineral resources in the Eastern Congo on behalf of international corporations that profit 400-fold from the raw materials they acquire for pennies. Resources such as Coltan, which is radioactive, but widely mined in a cottage industry, is a vital material used in cell phone communications technologies and defense industries of the west. Although there was a peace accord in 1999, the latest flare-up lasted until a formal peace accord was signed in Kenya in December 2013. The United Nations has revealed that Uganda and Rwanda, which both border the Eastern Congo, orchestrated the last stage of the war. The United States and Britain were traditional allies of Rwanda and Uganda in the first

---

32 *Rwanda: Government report documents French role in 1994 genocide*. By Kumaran Ira and Alex Lantier. 14 August 2008..www.wsws.org/en/articles/2008/08/rwan-a14.html
33 Global Issues: "The Democratic Republic of Congo, by by Anup Shah. Available at: (acc. 11-29-2012) www.globalissues.org/article/87/the-democratic-republic-of-congo

war against the senior Congo President, Kabila. United Nations Security Council (UNSC) documents released in 2012 show evidence of weapons as well as captured Rwandan military personnel in the DRC captured in 2012 that substantiate the U.N. claims of Rwandan complicity in Congo's ongoing genocide.[34]

United States (1776–Present)

Early in the United States, history, the land was cleared of its indigenous population in 100 years. However, there is a widespread effort to obscure the facts of the apparent genocidal policies highlighted in a 1763 letter from the British Commander-in-Chief of British forces in North America to Colonel Henry Bouquet. In his letter, Amherst requested that smallpox germ warfare be conducted against the Indians. The communications of Colonel Henry Bouquet and Sir Jeffery Amherst are rife with contemptuous references to the Native American population with suggestions such as hunting them with English dogs as the Spanish do. However, although there is more reason to believe that this deliberate policy of genocide existed in the Americas, the persistent opposition and obscuration of the facts continue unabated.[35] For example, the University of Colorado fired Professor Ward Churchill for claiming that germ warfare was used against the Indian population by the United States Army.[36]

Evidence of a Statistical Aberration in the United States

Since the 17th century, the effects of legislated racial segregation have haunted African descendants. Its effects linger, although slavery legally ended in the 19th century. For example, the United States has the largest prison population in the world, and the National Registry of Exonerations revealed that approximately 3,372 prisoners had been exonerated since 1989, when DNA evidence was first used.[37] Five hundred seventy of these exonerations were based on DNA, and 2,802

---

34   U.N. Report Alleges Rwanda Aids Rebels in Congo, By Christopher Rhoads. www.online.wsj. com/article/SB10000872396390443749204578050973460153196.html .
35   www.nativeamericannetroots.net/diary/2521 Accessed 9/7/2016.
36   www.quod.lib.umich.edu/p/plag/5240451.0001.009/--did-the-us-army-distribute-smallpox-blankets-to-indians?rgn=main;view=fulltext Accessed 9/7/2016.
37   Exonerations by year: DNA and Non-DNA. National Registry of Exonerations. Current as of: 2/8/2023. Available at: www.law.umich.edu/special/exoneration/Pages/Exoneration-by-Year.aspx

on non-DNA evidence. Due to the persistent bias in applying the law, most of the exonerations in the U.S. are people of African ancestry. Racially discriminatory laws have led to a vastly disproportional incarceration rate for African Americans. Racial profiling and mandatory sentencing drug laws have worked together to continually criminalize the African American population for minor offenses such as marijuana possession. Biased public policy or ingrained racism established a precedent where police officers routinely violated the 4th amendment[38] of the U.S. Constitution against unlawful search and seizure, acting with impunity among the black population in major urban centers such as New York City and throughout the United States. These conditions of inequity in administering the law that primarily affects people of African ancestry are indications of a persistent ethical failure in society. The evidence substantiating some of these trends is consistent in delineating a statistical aberration since records on race were first kept in the U.S. in 1947. The decennial census for 2020 lists the African American population as 49.6 million, but despite being only 14.9% of the population, that group historically has shared an unequal burden in U.S. society, as most statistical categories show.

Median Household Income

The data provided by the U.S. Census Bureau shown in the chart on page 187, measures median household income from 1947–2001. Analysis of the data using a 5-year mean is shown on page 188. The household income for African Americans from 1947 to 2001 hovered approximately 7-standard deviations below the 5-year mean, while White median household income hovered approximately 3-standard deviations above.

The median household income for all families in 1947 was $3,031, while that of the White household income was $3,157.[39] For African American households, the data shows $1,614. Throughout the five decades the data represents, the percentage lag of black median incomes was between 47% and 35% below that for all families. In 2001, for

---

38   Article IV.: The right of the people to be secure in their persons, houses, papers, and effects, against unreasonable searches and seizures, shall not be violated, and no Warrants shall issue, but upon probable cause, supported by Oath or affirmation, and particularly describing the place to be searched, and the persons or things to be seized.
39   U.S. Census Bureau. No. HS—25. Money Income of Families—Median Income in Current and Constant (2001) Dollars. Accessed 1/15/2007. Available at: www.census.gov/prod/2002pubs/tp63rv.pdf

Median household income: 1947–2001 (2001 inflation-adjusted dollars)

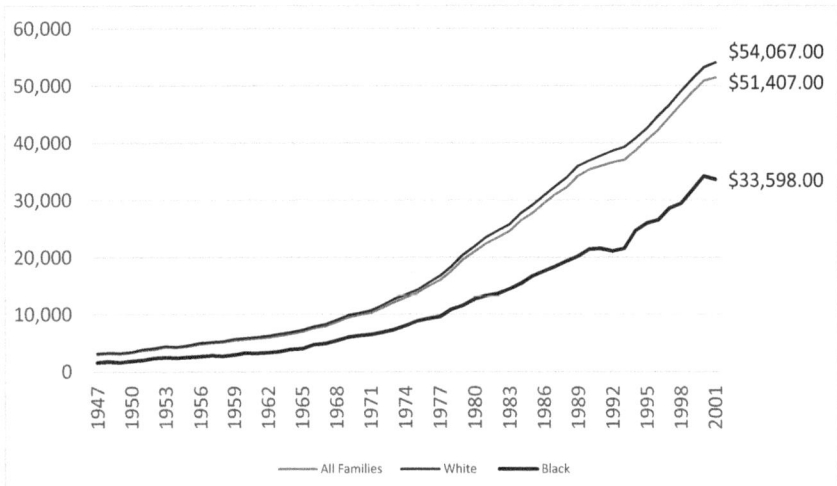

$54,067.00
$51,407.00
$33,598.00

Source: Compiled from data from the U.S. Bureau of the Census, Population Reports.

Households by total money income, race: 1967 and 2021 (2021 inflation-adjusted dollars)

Year	All families	Whites	Hispanics	Blacks
2021	$70,784	$74,262*	$57,981	$45,208
1994	$58,515	$61,714	$42,447	$38,135
1967	$50,803	$52,980	NA	$30,761

*Whites alone

Source: U.S. Census Bureau. Accessed: 1/11/2023. Available at: www2.census.gov/programs-surveys/cps/techdocs/cpsmar22.pdf

example, all families median income was $51,407; For White families, it was $54,067, while Black families had a $33,598 median income. The disparity ratio for African American households averaged minus 43% below all families (see appendix on pages 246 and 247).

Recent figures from 2021 in the table above, show household income 2021 inflaton-adjusted for all families from 1967 to 2021 is 70,784. It is $74,262 for White families, and Black households, $45,208. African Americans' median income is consistently and abnormally 5 to 7 standard deviations below the all families average. As earnings increases from year to year do not keep pace with inflation, economic conditions can only worsen for low-income families, as the overall population in the U.S. increases, and economic conditions fluctuate with frequent re-

Standard Deviation From the 5-year Mean For All Household Income:
1947–2001 (2001 inflation-adjusted dollars)

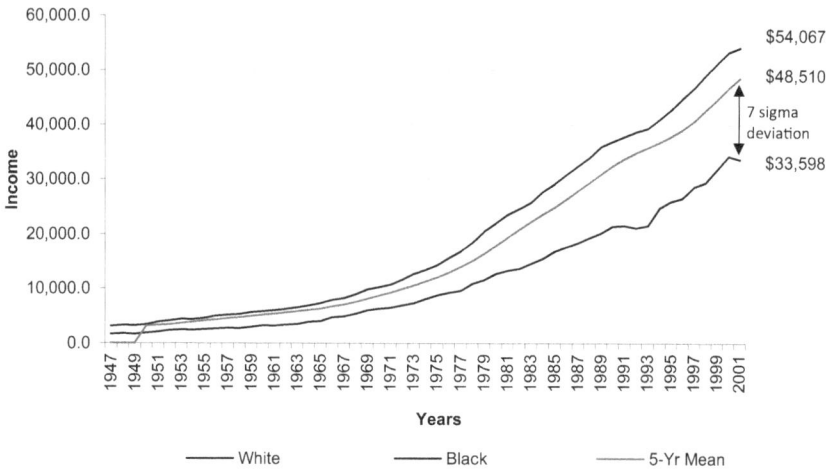

Source: Compiled from data from the U.S. Bureau of the Census, Current Population Reports, P60-
218. See appendix for available data from 1947 to 2001.

cessions, such as the 2008 financial collapse caused by the real estate subprime crisis.

Statistically, variations in the data should hover around parity in normal samples. However, over a 5-year average, White family income hovers consistently at 3-sigma above the 5-year mean for all families, while the Black family income is consistently around 7-sigma below, as shown in the Standard Deviation from the 5-year Mean for All Household Income. *(see figure above).*

Incarceration Rate

A disproportional incarceration rate that negatively impacts economic advancement further burdens African Americans. In 2019, the federal and state prison systems combined had an incarceration rate of 655 per 100,000 population. The incarceration rate of African Americans relative to the population varies widely among the states.

Blacks are incarcerated five times more than Whites, and Hispanics are nearly twice as likely to be incarcerated as Whites:

Race / Ethnicity	% of U.S. population	% of U.S. incarcerated population	National incarceration rate (per 100,000)
White (non-Hispanic)	64%	39%	450
Hispanic	16%	19%	831
Black	12%	40%	2,306

Source: www.prisonpolicy.org/reports/rates.html

African Americans are disproportionately represented in the criminal justice system across the United States. The skewed statistics are due to various factors, including poverty, lack of access to education and job opportunities, racial profiling, and bias in the criminal justice system. However, the counter-narrative routinely cites inborn criminality of people of African ancestry as the main cause for disparities in incarceration rates.

Racial Discrimination, an Unnatural Phenomenon

The statistical disparities occur across many other categories, making it doubtful that such a consistency can happen without a correlation to the one significant and common factor of race. Nevertheless, illogical and deterministic popular opinion attributes these discrepancies in black communities to a lack of cultural cohesion, absent fathers, and other social ills, alluding to the character flaws of people of color. Still, in each of the statistics listed, race is the one common denominator linking those who experience multi-generational disadvantages.

Ideological indoctrination nurtures the prevailing belief that the issue before the world is not injustice but the inability of African descendants to aspire to the challenges of civilization. The consequences of racially discriminatory policies—the symptomatic poverty among people of color, racism, genocide, colonialism, and imperialism—are shown maliciously to originate from character flaws and genetic and intelligence deficits. Racial discrimination and the ambivalence it generates towards the plight of Africans in the Diaspora originated from the legacy of slavery. However, vast swaths of society believe the demands for reparations should be cast aside, and the descendants of enslaved African people should assume full responsibility for their condition of social and economic degradation. The dismissive attitudes towards the lingering injustice of racial discrimination highlight a profoundly flawed national psyche, particularly in nations that benefited from Africa's ruin. In these nations, an unnatural lack of compassion exists in the face of the incomprehensible injustice.

An ongoing example of the duplicitious natue of the Western political and ideological doctrine occurred in December 2012 when French president François Hollande visited the former colony of Algeria, where he acknowledged the brutal system of colonialism imposed by France but stated that he would not apologize on behalf of his nation. The president again visited Haiti in 2016 and repeated the same policy. France's imperialist stance, historically based on its divine civilizing mission, "La mission civilisatrice," precipitated the atrocities that claimed more than 1.5 million lives in the war for Algerian independence.[40] After several centuries of fabricating Africa's history and demonizing its people, some truth can be brazenly expressed, as the French president did. Still, it is with a contemptuous attitude lacking in spiritual grace.[41] It is, in effect, the face of secularism with a focus on power and ambition but void of absolute morality.

Despite the needless deaths that occurred from their actions, the French and the other waning imperialist powers maintained their missions in Africa. The North Atlantic Treaty Organization (NATO)'s brutal war in Libya (2009–present), labeled as a humanitarian action, is a reminder of an old imperialist tradition that targets natural resources. The Libya war destroyed a prosperous nation and expanded the boundaries of NATO's war into the Sahel nations of Mali, Burkina Faso, Niger and Chad. In Northern Nigeria, the Islamic fundamentalist group Boko Haram received weapons captured from the Gadhafi government to wage war against the Nigerian people. At the same time, the ISIS forces gained access to weapons to conduct their war against the populations in the Sahal region, displacing millions and seizing their land.

---

40   LA Times. "French president says Algeria suffered under 'brutal' colonialism." By Emily Alpert. Dec 20, 2012)
41   (The spiritual Law of Grace tells us that grace is a Divine dispensation of mercy.)

Chapter 10

Turning a Blind Eye

In the contemporary period, *turning a blind eye* is a phrase that started with the English Admiral Horatio Nelson who was blind in one eye. However, in this context, it more aptly applies to deliberately ignoring natural law, civil and international norms, and legal conventions that protect societal ideals. The societal norms that emerged during the European Enlightenment promoted reason over superstition, individual rights, civil liberties, property rights, and government by the consent of the governed. These values are rooted in the liberal ideal, which originated in the Classical Greek and Roman traditions and is grounded in the Latin word *liber* or freedom.

The Western Democratic principles we associate with the liberal philosophy are traced to ancient Athenian citizens, who exercised direct control over their government's decisions through voting. Given this heritage of classical works from ancient Greece, Rome, and European philosophy, any breach of the social contract between a state and its citizens is considered especially egregious in the contemporary period. Based on philosophical or ideological differences, such breaches have often resulted in war.

Regardless of the well-meaning aims of social contract theorists, efforts to maintain a civil society have often, ironically, ended in the subversion of the rules-based, liberal foundations of many modern societies. The values of the Enlightenment liberal philosophy based on freedom and democracy have failed to end destructive wars and exploitation of weaker and poorer nations. Routine violations of the rights of the most vulnerable populations continue, driven by greed, political ambition, and economic gain. Historically, many of these violations have resulted in repeated genocides that society habitually and willfully ignores.

Towards the peak of the Atlantic Slave Trade in the 18th century, as Enlightenment ideas about freedom and democracy thrived, the plight of the enslaved populations was not important. From the inception of the 400-year Atlantic Slave Trade, avarice and the resulting search for profits freely developed into the most brutal period in history. Racial theories based on falsified data thrived and seeped into all branches of the sciences only to ensure that the slave trade and profits would grow. Moral corruption ensured that the ruthless behavioral standards during the slave trade would persist in the laws and philosophical outlook of the modern era. The latent methodologies enabled multiple wars of opportunity. The greed of imperial European powers, which had become re-imagined as mercantilism, empowered the strong to plunder the weak. Mercantilism casually sought to fill the treasuries of the European nations through piracy or trade.

In the post-slavery era, the more economically advanced nations, the beneficiaries of the Atlantic Slave Trade and the Berlin Conference, and those seeking to improve their economic base, such as Germany, the Austro-Hungarian, and the Ottoman Empires, were a portent for disaster. The competition between these nations, made worse by tariffs and trade barriers, erupted into warfare. Inevitably, as violence erupted, the assassination of Archduke Franz Ferdinand of Austria and his wife on 28 June 1914 led to declarations of war and the beginning of World War I (28 July 1914 – 11 November 1918).

The debilitating societal mores that emerged from the 17th to the 19th centuries have repeated in the contemporary period. These include routine violations of European Just War concepts and the bond financing based on unsecured fiat and usury that had previously funded the slave trade. The most distasteful of these behaviors carried forward was the parasitic economic exploitation of weak and defenseless nations and peoples who became the fodder for the economic model of the emerging capitalist economic system. These behaviors sustaining contemporary economies are the same ones that created the impoverishment of vast swaths of land and the displacement of hundreds of millions of people in Africa.

In the contemporary period, society remained steeped in the culture of the slave trade. However, there has been no attempt to grapple with the world's habituation to the grand deception and immorality that began the extinction-level depopulation event in Africa. The mind-boggling toll on the African population is calculated at 10 times the size of the enslaved population at the peak of the trade. Consequently, the world continues similarly, seeking unlimited wealth while discounting the consequences of death and destruction by commercial and political interests seeking to increase profits.

The *ignoring of immorality* occurred definitively about halfway through the slave trade during the Protestant Reformation. The slave trade became acceptable to devout Christians when the religious reformers turned to the bible to justify the evil in their midst. They evoked the philosophical concept of determinism that Aristotle, the source of Christian philosophy and theology, had rejected in his time. As a philosophical theory, determinism holds that all events, including moral choices, are predetermined.[1] In the 16th century, Martin Luther established faith as the only factor necessary to receive God's grace and salvation. It was apparent then that God punished only those without faith. John Calvin extrapolated further on determinism, proclaiming that God had already chosen *the elect* ones, who were the saved, and *the reprobates,* who were dammed. The understanding brought about by the Protestant Reformation had profound implications that left a lasting impact on religious thought and practice. Christians, who thought of themselves as *the elect*, looked upon the miserable kidnapped and enslaved Africans as *the reprobates*. Determinism allowed god-fearing Christians who were prohibited from indulging in luxury goods to turn away from the horrific crimes occurring in their midst and allow their investments in the slave trade to grow.

Determinism, a white supremacist social structure, and a falsified history inform the present. Fabricated, racially biased misrepresentations in scientific and historical literature assure a continuance of ignorance among a population continually brainwashed by the social mores arising from the last 400 years of exploitation of Africa. After centuries of ravaging defenseless populations, a Machiavellian philosophy, which legitimizes all actions of the state and is the basis of the unrelenting struggle for supremacy, makes the lust for more wealth, territory, and power at any cost a recurring phenomenon in modern society.

In the aftermath of the devastation of the African continent, with hundreds of millions of casualties and the destruction of African civilizations and cultural norms, European nations could only accelerate their genocidal, land-grabbing policies by secretly crafting the 1865 Berlin Conference designed to partition Africa and further plunder its resources. At the height of territorial seizures and mass displacement of the local populations in the English colony of Nyasaland in Southern Africa, the English capitalist Cecil Rhodes affirms the philosophy of the European elites:

> "Africa is still lying ready for us; it is our duty to take it. It is our duty to seize every opportunity of acquiring more territory, and we should keep this one idea steadily be-fore our eyes: that more territory simply means more of the Anglo-Saxon race, more of the best, the most human, most honorable race the world possesses."

> —Cicil Rhodes, "Confession of Faith" from 1872

1   www.Britannica.com
2   Available at: www.pages.uoregon.edu/kimball/Rhodes-Confession.htm

The appropriation of Africa's resources and the destruction of its cultures are the manifestations of uncontrolled greed, deliberately disguised as a benefit to society. The vice had seeped into the core of the world's nations that prospered from slavery and increasingly complicated finance schemes based on monopolized production of unsecured paper money. The greed that showed in the territorial ambitions of European Imperial nations and their control of trade led inevitably to World War I. The war began amid growing mutual suspicion and covetous territorial, economic, and political objectives of the world's foremost Imperial powers that had spent more than a century pillaging the natural resources of the African cultures. As the war began, these imperial powers fought worldwide, along the boundaries acquired through the Berlin Conference and in Europe. World War I ended with the Versailles Treaty, signed in 1919, and the creation of the League of Nations, dedicated to avoiding other catastrophes like the Great War.

However, The League of Nations, created to prevent a repeat of the devastating World War I, appeared to be a monument to ineptitude. It could do nothing to suppress the fundamental flaw in the human psyche, which is at the root of repeated conflicts. It stood as the self-serving proof of unfathomable corruption as it championed more of the unjust partitioning of the world into spheres of influence that generated much more conflict and violence. The winners of World War I seized more than they should have and deprived the losers of what they needed to survive. One of the foremost economists, Lord Meynard Keynes, who founded the school of Keynesian Economics, stated that the surrender terms of the Western powers would destroy not only the economy of the losing side but also that of Europe. Consequently, as the Axis powers of Germany, Italy, and Japan suffered from crushing economic burdens, they aggressively pursued their vital national interests, and the even greater tragedy of World War II occurred.

Realism

Despite the grandiose liberal objectives of the Enlightenment philosophers, the reign of never-ending imperialist wars of opportunity comes from a philosophy of realism. Realism assesses international relations based on the worst elements of human character. It defiantly supplants the idealism of the liberal world order and leads to power politics and wars. Barely 26 years had passed after World War I before the losing countries of Japan, Italy, and Germany violated the liberal world order imposed on them. However, their territorial expansion and war reflected their determination to fulfill their vital national interests to survive. Consequently, the more deadly and significant World War II emerged because of the policy of ignoring the natural rights of those on the losing side.

Italy, a nation committing the first of the offenses, violently overthrew its liberal government using an ideology of fascism that borrowed from socialism and far-right politics. The fascists, led by Benito Mussolini, relied on violence as their brand, confronted and disrupted the status quo, and took power. Mussolini also used violent methodologies to eradicate opponents, and his fascism became the new face of rebellion and exploitation emulated by Germany. His array of methods included the use of mustard gas in Ethiopia, a traditional enemy of Italy since Ethiopia won the 1896 Battle of Adwa. Mussolini's fascism became the template for Hitler's Nazi movement in Germany and for other states seeking national liberation.

Realism in international relations is a concept developed by British political scientist and historian E.H. Carr, who critiqued what he perceived as a deluded idealism of liberalism.[3] His Theory of Realism, which emerged in the mid-20th century, is a theory of how the world works. It emphasizes the role of power, national interest, and the perception of the unruly nature of a global system without rules or principles to give it order. Under this scenario, the self-interested, modern state will readily resort to force to procure their vital national interests. While the theory discounts the global legal system, it is the deliberate and willful ignoring of these rules that creates the appearance of a lawless society.

Although realism is a 20th-century theory, it is identifiable in practice throughout Europe's colonization and pacification of Africa in the late 19th century after the Berlin Conference. The Imperial European nations resorted to genocide to seize and control territory and natural resources in Africa to further their industrialization projects. The continent's impoverishment through collective European action is a case of realism in practice, which is historically misrepresented as heroic exploits of Europeans on a civilizing mission in a barbaric Africa. Following the Berlin Conference invasion and pillaging of Africa, the First World War, which occurred primarily in Europe, is not widely regarded as an Imperialist war but one that happened incidentally after the assassination of Archduke Franz Ferdinand and the series of treaty violations that followed. However, it was part of an ongoing war for territory and raw materials among like-minded nations

---

3   Britannica.com

that had become habituated to the concept of imperialism and exploitation of the weaker countries around the world. The European losers of the war ceded land, paid reparations, and agreed to the global world order under the League of Nations.

In the years leading to World War II, Japan followed the European imperialist model when it invaded Manchuria in 1939, seeking raw materials for its economic and military expansion. In Italy, Mussolini's fascist dictatorship re-invaded Ethiopia even as Emperor Haile Selassie unsuccessfully sought aid from the League of Nations while warning them that Europe would be next. Germany followed with a series of land seizures with a grand plan to conquer Europe to provide living space for the German people. The military aggression of the Axis powers led to World War II, which saw approximately 50 million deaths, and, once again, the creation of an organization of states under the United Nations Charter tasked with maintaining international peace and security, upholding international law, promoting higher standards of living and human rights without discrimination.

In contrast to the practice of realism in contemporary international relations, liberalism became associated with The United Nations Charter in 1945. The Liberal philosophy of the Western Alliance encouraged global cooperation while abhorring the reliance on war that causes economic damage and civilian deaths that far outweigh the gains. The United Nations is the most potent outcome of the Liberal establishment and rules-based order with a systematic approach to achieving justice. Nevertheless, multiple wars flared as the world powers and members of the United Nations fought to dominate weaker nations. Again, powerful nations revisited past sins for present-day gains to acquire wealth and power through coercion, trickery or the latest fads. The results are measurable in the plight of the poor in the exploited lands.

Willful Ignorance in Economic Practices and Policies

The effects of the racialized Western economic system are most evident in Africa, where the Human Development Index (HDI)[4] calculated by the United Nations shows almost all African countries at the lowest rung. The index measures life expectancy, educational level, and per capita income, and it ranks countries into four tiers of human development. Despite all

---

4   https://hdr.undp.org/data-center/human-development-index#/indicies/HDI

the fanfare and modern architectural towers in Africa's large cities that boast of material success, the per capita incomes of these economically segregated countries have not come close to the global average for several generations. In 2022, even with the vast stores of natural resources in Africa's 54 countries, 19 with the highest black populations have a per capita income ranging from $240 to $990. That equates to $.65 to $2.63 per individual per day. Of the remaining 35 nations, only two, Seychelles, with $14,340, and Mauritius, with $10,760, have a per capita income above the $10,000 threshold.[5] On the other hand, the world's top 18 earners are all Western nations. The top three are Iceland – $79,473; Luxembourg – $78,310; and the United States – $77,463.

Ironically, a comparable income disparity is notable in the United States, where there is a considerable income gap between the majority of white and black Americans. Despite living in one of the wealthiest countries in the world, people of African ancestry had had incomes at least five standard deviations below the mean since the 1950s when record-keeping began. In Africa, violations of international law by powerful militarist democratic governments with racially discriminatory policies that have been in existence since the 1865 Berlin Conference have kept Africans at subsistence levels. France, for example, maintained business interests in Africa, extracting trillions of dollars of wealth from its colonial territories. More notably, throughout Africa, the seizure of vast areas of fertile or mineral-rich lands has driven the expulsion of large populations into some of the world's largest slums. These occurrences contrast sharply with the luxury of Western business conglomerates that preach the advantages of private ownership to the poorest populations living on subsistence wages. The policies of land, wage, natural resource theft, and financial chicanery have left the majority of people in these lands subsisting on less than $2.63 per day for at least 150 years. In the United States, where slavery was the economy, the incomes of blacks continued to lag far below the mean for all families.

Most corporations and governments in Africa function as they were initially designed at the Berlin Conference and, consequently, have created some of the wealthiest business conglomerates in the history of the West and the poorest people in the world concentrated in Africa. The public often obscures and ignores the techniques and scale of these appropriative

---

5   Available   at: www.statista.com/statistics/1290903/gross-national-income-per-capita-in-afri-ca-by-country/. Accessed 10/7/2023.

mechanisms. The political assassinations, coups, wars, material destruction, and genocide, occurring for generations with impunity, are barely noticed despite their brutality. The policies of contemporary democracies to control the poor and dispossessed populations are informed by a Machiavellian political philosophy that diverges radically from the selfless idealism implied by the United Nations charter.

Machiavelli focused on the material sphere and catered to the worst impulses in human beings, particularly their lust for money and power. His political economy emerged in the 16th century as he sought to advise the Florentine ruling class on the best methods for keeping their power by controlling the people. In his book, *The Prince*, written in 1513, Machiavelli's pragmatism opposes the Classical Era's idealism, described in *Plato's Republic,* where Plato balances the three parts of the soul that work together to enable justice to exist. Plato identifies these as the mind, the will, and the emotions. Machiavelli worked to activate only one-third part of the soul, which Plato described as controlling the emotions. In doing so, Machiavelli guaranteed that an unjust human being and society would prevail and reward the prince.

In the modern era, it has been more than 510 years since the publication of Machiavelli's *The Prince*. The world has thoroughly adopted his view that reality is only about what men do in their daily lives and not about the right things they should do, as Liberal philosophy advocates. Pursuing money and power has become the species' primary purpose in the modern era. When nations in the contemporary period mimic Machiavelli, they assert the right to rule the weak—to control their natural resources and lives by force, cunning, or betrayal. If the victims protest, they will be the example used to discourage other groups or nations.

Following Machiavelli's playbook, the Africans, who were dispossessed of their ancestral land, became the newly impoverished masses. They worked for starvation wages, often clawing with their bare hands in mines for dangerous, toxic minerals deep in the ground. As favorable laws and military power exist solely to perpetuate the mechanism of confiscation and profiteering, the abysmal history of inequality and the lack of a viable concept of justice in modern society perseveres. The Machiavellian philosophy thrived in the Congo, where King Leopold enslaved the population of the vast territory and controlled rubber production through the barbarous tortures of men, women, and children.

While the stern ideologues no longer cut off the hands of Congolese children as incentives for increasing production, they nonetheless use financial sanctions and threats of war. The sanctions against Zimbabwe, for example, were imposed by Western democracies after President Mugabe began seizing White-owned farmland in retaliation for British Prime Minister Tony Blair's cancellation of the Lancaster Treaty with Zimbabwe. The treaty was an agreement to legally transfer the White-owned land to their lawful owners in an agreement described as a willing seller and willing buyer agreement. The sanctions against Zimbabwe was a ploy by the Western nations to keep the appropriated land and their vast mineral deposits in the hands of the English aristocracy. The land's original owners, whom the government of the apartheid state, Rhodesia, segregated from society, became the newly exploited labor force working to produce cash crops such as tobacco and corn for export or mining gold, rare metals, and precious gems for absentee owners at subsistence wages.

With an estimated 24 trillion dollars of natural resources in Congo, military-style gangs working in concert with international corporations acquire rare metals such as coltan, gold, precious gems, and labor from artisan miners working on unclaimed land for starvation wages. The raw materials sell for hundreds of times the acquisition cost in international markets. The beneficiaries are the mega-corporations of the military-industrial complex. In the Sahel region in North Africa, up until its 2023 coup, Niger had supplied 18% of France's uranium in the Sahel region to power France's uranium needs. However, the French Corporations that acquired the mineral fetched €200 / kg on the international market for surpluses until the coup leaders in Niger expelled the French and canceled their mining contracts in July 2023. Until the cancellation of France's contracts, Niger received a minuscule €.80 per kg.

Restoring Justice to a World at War

From the end of the Roman Empire to the contemporary period, approximately 25 significant wars occurred over either territory or religion. However, the constant state of war in history does not imply that it is innate to humans. On the contrary, wars often begin with a breakdown in observance of natural law that seeks to protect and preserve life. Over time, a near-constant state of war with indiscriminate killing has become the preferred mode of resolving conflicts. However, nature provides the best model for human coexistence in the family unit, where survival depends on cooperation and mutual respect. As populations increased and technology provided military advantages, war increased as human resources depleted and territorial boundary violations occurred. The motivation for revoking natural law begins with a condemnable vice—the selfish pursuit of wealth and power that denies natural rights to others and threatens survival.

The idea of using lethal force dates to the deep recesses of time when organized hunting scenes with bows and arrows appeared on cave walls as humans transitioned from nomadic to settled life around 10,000 years ago in the Neolithic era. Settled life and innovations such as plant and animal domestication led to food and wealth surpluses and increased populations, leading to long-distance trade and conflict. The need to protect food surpluses, settlements, and people from raids led to innovations in warfare and prolonged conflicts over territory. In ancient economies and modern lesser-developed ones, tensions that end in violence routinely develop between agriculturalists seeking to protect land and herders seeking to exploit it. As herders destroy grasses and crops, the agriculturalists are at risk of starvation, and conversely, herders deprived of available land will lose their herds.

Efforts at establishing an ethical society appeared in ancient civilizations in North East Africa when laws governing behavior were first written around 2680 to 2190 B.C.E. in the Old Kingdom. The Code of Hammurabi, from 1750 B.C.E., consists of 282 laws covering daily life, trade, property, family, and crime. Ethics specific to Kemet and the early Greco-Egyptian civilization focused on education as the key to behavior modification, rejecting vices that corrupt the spirit and encouraging a virtuous path leading to everlasting life. In Kemet, the laws of Ma'at were a behavioral control that guided human aspirations toward good and the highest reward of everlasting life. In Greece, Plato's philosophy warned about the spiritual flaws that lead humans to destruction and stressed reliance on an educated class— the philosopher-kings— as rulers with the knowledge to build flourishing civilizations. Aristotle taught Greeks to seek happiness through virtue as life's paramount goal. However, the Roman Empire focused on natural and civil laws controlling behavior locally and internationally but elevated its civil laws of the state over natural laws protecting the population. The consequence was an immense expansion of militarism, slavery, and war.

The vices condemned by the ancients, particularly avarice, resurfaced with devastating consequences. The Roman Empire is the best example of a state with an ideology that promoted avarice through war, wealth and territorial acquisition, and slavery. Although the empire had an array of administrative policies to run smoothly, it inevitably collapsed from internal strife resulting from the crippling effects of greed—inflation and bankruptcy. Rome's inevitable collapse left it unable to pay the Visigoth King Alaric and his army, who had been conquered and absorbed into the Roman Empire. Another example of the decline and collapse of empires is The Abbasid Caliphate (752–1258 C.E.), which stretched from its capital in Baghdad to the Arabian peninsula, Northern Africa, and far to the North and East. The empire was weakened by unchecked internal divisions, corruption, and exploitation of slave labor.[6] The Ming Dynasty (1368–1644) collapsed from the internal pressures of maintaining a wealthy, stratified society.[7]

Rome's decline left a feudal society in Europe without money and reliant on a system of land barter that plundered the peasants' resources, enslaving them in the manor. In the Middle Ages, the monarchy and Church's insatiable greed accelerated the pace of war and territorial acquisition throughout Europe, leading to peasant revolts. An exhausted Europe inevitably looked to the lands beyond its borders. More than two hundred years of Crusades against Muslims branded as the enemies of Christ led to a Christian reliance on pillage and plunder of Muslim territories. The escalating wars for wealth resulted in Europe's rapid economic growth, which sparked the Renaissance. Inevitably, European advances in navigation and warfare acquired during the Renaissance led to the catastrophic collapse and colonization of the continent of Africa and the Americas as European armies destroyed and plundered the peaceful kingdoms they encountered. The cycle of greed, war, and conquest comes to a new beginning as some of the most impoverished people on Earth, such as in Africa's Sahel, which is dominated by a French neocolonialist system, finally grasp their perilous plight and initiate change. However, attempts at overturning the progress of the Sahel states, Mali, Niger, Burkina Faso, and Chad, are accelerating with increasing assassination attempts against the leadership.

A just and lasting peace has not occurred through centuries of wars from the medieval to the modern eras. A litany of opulent empires, with vast wealth acquired through war, has never pacified the uncontrolled acquisitive appetites of the wealthy. The vanquished are, instead, molded into positions benefiting the wealthy that impoverish the colonized. They operate in nations with artificial borders that have split families, destroyed trade routes, and repurposed the nations' economic production to benefit the wealthier nations. It is not uncommon to find child labor exploitation on a massive scale in dangerous and toxic mines. The borders created during the

---

6   www.britannica.com
7   ———. Ibid.

Berlin Conference continue to fuel conflicts in Africa today, even as it has set the stage for the economic disparities and military conflicts that persist in Northern Nigeria, across the Sahel, in eastern Congo, Cameroon, Sudan, and South Sudan.

This is not to say that Europeans have not proposed ideas to bring peace. Philosopher Emanuel Kant, for example, wrote essays about his political philosophy of perpetual peace, where he suggested that reason could improve the human condition and control how humans should act according to a Categorical Imperative. In Groundwork of the Metaphysics of Morals (1785), Kant defines his Categorical Imperative by suggesting that humans should act unconditionally and based on *a priori* acquired by reason, independent from any experience, and universally applicable to everyone without contradiction. A second European philosopher, Rousseau, critiqued inequality as the root of conflict. Unquestionably, if applied unconditionally, the Golden Rule would produce a highly moral society that applies equally to everyone. However, the underlying fault in the human condition is the susceptibility to vice and spiritual corruption that inevitably leads to conflict and war.

Justice in The Moral Economy

Privatization of the commons and rent obligations began to replace the communal property rights of Africans after the Berlin Conference land reorganization and seizure scheme had become fully established. Privatization grew to absurd proportions as it decimated the social structure and the inter-Africa trade links that had sustained Africans for thousands of years. It created a massive displacement of populations that flocked to makeshift slums on the outskirts of growing cities. The poor peasants in Europe's feudal economy had experienced similar privatization long before Europeans built the first trading and transmission forts in Africa. The European peasant's reactions to natural law violations were violent, as they experienced rising grain prices and low-quality bread, leading them to perceive the threat to their lives from dwindling resources. The European peasants' resistance, like that of Africa's displaced peoples, rested on the directives of the moral economy to evoke an innately perceived customary law that recognizes the right to be treated fairly—to be afforded life.

The Moral Economy is a contemporary concept developed by British social historian E. P. Thompson, who looks back in history to find the patterns of direct popular action that occur with clear objectives.[8] The violent resistance by the poorest members of European society was against the grain dealers who manipulated food prices, resulting in life-threatening conditions of hunger and starvation. The results were the peasant rebellions against the unfair price increases that denied the penniless masses their sustainability— their right to life. The moral economy is the automatically and naturally derived method opposing societal inequity that aims to achieve a fair society that protects human rights to ensure societal harmony.[9]

A Moral Economy for the Contemporary Period

In the contemporary period, the profit motive and positive law enforcing a legal obligation to a profit-seeking aristocracy have crushed the natural predisposition to move towards a moral economy. The charging of rents in the midst of falling or non-existent wages has thrived, putting most of the world's poorest populations at risk. The social upheavals that have occurred since the global revolutions against the capitalist order in Africa, South America, and Asia occurred as life giving resources dwindled. However, they were often attributed to socialist agitation when the revolutions were in reaction to violations of natural law.

The reaction from the Western nations was to fight to defend democracy and stem communism. However, noticeably lacking in the repurposed economies of colonized nations is the expectation of reciprocity that ancient cultures had revered in The Golden Rule—do unto others as you would have them do unto you. While the capitalist economy boasts of affording a fair share of the wealth to those who trade their labor for money, an obscenely high proportion of that wealth has consistently gone to the ownership class, the top .01% of the population. Corporate greed has created a two-tiered system of wealthy owners exploiting the labor of a class of impoverished workers who create the wealth but do not adequately benefit from their labor and production. The growing slums in major cities built with scraps of metal and wood in poor nations and others in the wealthiest nations that are the brightly colored tents that line the streets, are testaments to the growing crisis. The gap between rich and poor has never been greater than in the 21st century. The reactions from the poor are mass migrations, or descending into underground spaces for

---

8   Thompson. E. P. "The Moral Economy of the English Crows in the Eighteenth Century", p.50
9   ———. Ibid.

shelter, building shanty towns or tent cities. However, and inevitably, nature will dictate survival by any means with the growing perception of threats to life.

Justice in The Golden Rule

When confronting injustice, the ancients had an elementary rule that they believed would lead to fairness. One example is the Golden Rule, which appeared in the ancient Egyptian literature, *The Eloquent Peasant*, in the Middle Kingdom (2050 to 1710 B.C.E.). It is an ethical system that teaches reciprocity and promotes the individual initiative to avoid harming others. Plato emphasized reason and education as the best means to cultivate the moral inclination to act correctly rather than relying on rules and punishment. The Golden Rule sets the conditions for seeking reparations in the same way that the moral economy concept establishes a social norm in line with natural law.

In the Roman Christian Theocracy in the 5th-century C.E., philosopher and theologian Saint Augustine's arguments about justice in his work of Christian philosophy, *The City of God,* imply that it is better to look to God rather than seek an equitable solution to injustice. Augustine's political theory deals with justice in a profoundly new way that set the stage for its adoption in Western civilization. Augustine highlights reason as the way to learn about God. However, his idea of harmony acquires a uniquely Christian vantage point that explains the evil in the world as the result of free will. His acceptance of slavery, for example, rests on its origins in sin or war in the world. He did not believe slavery was natural and worthy of human beings, nor did he believe that God intended for humans to enslave each other. However, while Plato advocated for education to instill a sense of justice, Saint Augustine did not seek a direct means to remedy injustice except by placing faith in God. As Rome approached its collapse from the Visigoth's assault, Saint Augustine found the earthly city (Rome) and its impending destruction meaningless compared to the profundity of God's kingdom.

In the medieval period, natural law was the pinnacle of the law, and it adhered to a divine principle in line with the nature of the divine as beneficent and compassionate. It is the basis of the moral economy which is based on moral and ethical principles that equitably govern economic interactions and societal relations. The term refers to the economy of pre-modern societies, where economic activity was closely connected to the Christian Church's social and moral obligations of fulfilling God's work on Earth to save souls. Participants in the economy, such as merchants, farmers, or workers, justified their actions in terms of the moral and ethical teachings of the bible and not the profit objectives of commercial traders and the secular authorities.

Separation from the Self-Administration of Natural Law

Early in pre-history in Kemetic civilization, there was a separation between Ma'at and the civil law in Kemet when the first written attempt to explain the law occurred.[10] Reciprocity, or cooperative interchange, is one of the earliest rule-based systems that emerged to explain how to live peacefully within society. Extending kindness to another and expecting kindness is the basis of reciprocity. However, a rules-based system evolved from the need to administer the law that systemized how a person could remain virtuous and achieve happiness. However, laws written during the administration of law introduced punishments as a form of justice, and Law diverged from a concept of self-administration to policing and punishment.

Over time, a rigid separation developed between the natural laws that empower the population and the civil laws that oppress them. In the contemporary period, the powerless majority have had little to do with writing laws, unlike in ancient Rome, where citizens participated in deriving the laws through an interrogative process that considered their local circumstances. Without full participation of the public, the oligarchy's control of the legal system in the modern era has caused irreparable harm over several generations. In the late 17th century, during the Atlantic Slave Trade, the proponents of positive law in the English colonies of Virginia and Barbados abandoned the obligation to the divine source of the law that protected the weakest members of the society. The indentured workers and enslaved people of African ancestry in Virginia became the first legislated hereditary slaves by order of the Governor of Virginia. His motivation was to protect the King's tobacco profits by permanently enslaving and debasing the humanity of African people to create a permanent labor force. The traditional commitment to The Good became more of a hindrance to the special interests seeking financial gain at any cost rather than a pathway toward justice.

Advocates for positive law proclaimed that there is no proof of a divine source of the law and that natural law is unnecessary. Under a positive law scenario, the state effectively replaces a divine entity as the ultimate judge, and

---

10 www.ancient.eu/Egyptian_Law/

consequently, it can become the best ally of the tyrant. The powerful state and monarch, enforcing unjust laws and obscuring the meaning of justice, were the tyrants seeking to materialize every carnal desire of an avaricious, powerful elite while obscuring the perception of justice as a natural phenomenon perceived universally and attributable to a divine power.

The idea of justice as punishment derives from the philosophy of European scholars during the era when European commercial interests fabricated their justification for the barbarism of chattel slavery. Slavery, for the profiteer and their supporting institutions, was a legal means of correcting those whose ethics, religious, and behavioral norms were unacceptable to Europeans. These societies of slave traders and power-hungry monarchical governments erected a bureaucracy to legitimize their unjust laws at the beginning of the European Slave Trade. Initially, they relied on the legal authority of Pope Nicholas V, acting as God's representative on Earth. He assumed the right to establish the confiscatory laws that condemned the majority of the Earth's population to slavery. The Pope, with a misguided understanding of salvation, proclaimed slavery as a benefit to godless savages—their only means of salvation. The law, as expressed through the Dum Diversis Papal Bull, which claims to be based on divine authority, favored profiteers seeking gold and slaves, who sought the legal means to violate the early Christian traditions of compassion and theological rules controlling the declarations of war.

The Theory of Legal Positivism

Jeremy Bentham and John Austin

Towards the end of the 18th century, English philosophers devised theories that negated the link of the law to natural law. English philosopher Jeremy Bentham proposed that laws are created by the sovereign and enforced through power and authority. Bentham's ideas were a departure from traditional Natural Law theory, emphasizing that legal systems are human-made and should be judged by their utility and effectiveness. At the peak of the Slave Trade in the 19th century, the English jurist John Austin posited the Theory of Legal Positivism, which holds that law and morality are separate.[11] In doing so, the theory supported social mores based on the prevalent empiricism of David Hume and John Locke, whose empiricism had rejected

---

11   www.plato.stanford.edu/entries/legal-positivism/

Natural Law links of divine morality to behavior. Locke, for instance, could find no connection between facts and a supernatural source of morals. These morals, he claimed, originated from the individual's subjective feelings. The ethics of the modern era thus succeeded in its ongoing, extremely profitable process of denying African people their natural rights and enslaving them based on Positive Law and rampant racial speculation.

Even as the proponents of Positive Law acknowledged it as separate from morality, its introduction and adoption occurred when slavery was at its height and had mostly changed the ethics of the time to one where the brutal enslavement of innocent human beings was seen as a civilizing process necessary to bring the savages into the civilized world. The law merely reflected the precedence established by the black codes or other legal remedies, which reflected the profit objectives of the ruling elites and their hatred for the Africans and other lower classes. Today, this concept of Legal Positivism is so widely accepted that the letter of the law often supplants fairness. Positive law enshrined in the legal system, while purporting to be fair, targets people of color predominantly. Usually, it wrongly imprisons and executes many of these innocent people in far greater proportions than they represent in the population. The victims of the biased legal process are often powerless and surrender their rights to fair trials to this administrative body that defines the concept of the law based on many legal precedences founded during the slave trade.

Justice as Fairness, Retribution, and Restoration

In the post-slavery era, Africans and their descendants lived in extreme poverty within a system bolstered by laws legitimizing racial discrimination established during slavery. The two-tiered class system persisted until the U.S. Civil Rights Movement successfully challenged the prevailing public opinion supporting legal segregation in the United States. Thurgood Marshall, who served as an Associate Justice of the United States Supreme Court from 1967 to 1991, was instrumental in the fight for civil rights and the end of school segregation. This struggle was necessary because the U.S. Supreme Court had previously refused to recognize the rights of African Americans. In the 1857 *Dred Scott v. Sandford* case, the court ruled that people of African descent, whether free or enslaved, could not be regarded as United States citizens and had no right to sue in federal court. Moreover, the court upheld the Fifth Amendment rights of enslavers over their enslaved individuals.

Despite the abolition of slavery and the 1868 ratification of the 14th Amendment, which guaranteed citizenship rights, entrenched cultural norms continued to support the notion of America as a functioning slave society. The 1896 *Plessy v. Ferguson* decision upheld legal segregation, disregarding the rights of African Americans in favor of established legal precedents that deemed them less than human. This unjust stance persisted until the Civil Rights Movement, led by NAACP lawyer Thurgood Marshall, successfully challenged *Plessy v. Ferguson*. In the landmark 1954 case of *Brown v. Board of Education*, the Supreme Court, under Chief Justice Earl Warren, unanimously ruled that state laws supporting segregation in public schools were unconstitutional and violated the Equal Protection Clause of the Fourteenth Amendment. However, the court did not provide an immediate remedy to end racial segregation in schools, leading to further societal conflicts and the implementation of measures like busing to address the issue.

The slow and long overdue implementation of fairness in the law to address historical racial discrimination, as incremental and as long overdue as it was, has led to charges of reverse discrimination from a disenchanted white population. Their challenge to affirmative action has drawn Asian Americans to the cause of the white supremacists. Inevitably, with the combined challenge of white Americans and Asians, the conservative Roberts Court overturned Affirmation Action in education. However, the court ignored the reparations claims for injustice against generations of people of African ancestry in the United States, where they were denied education and other financial benefits and suffered from confiscation and destruction of property, which generated decades-long disparities in income, health, incarceration rates, and in every other category measured by the U.S. government.

The groundless challenges to the reparative justice agenda of the aggrieved black community are part of an agenda for generating sympathetic public opinion in the quest to maintain the semblance of white power. The insincere charges of injustice against Whites find their expression primarily in the politics of the Republican Party, which stands against the erosion of white privilege and power. To white supremacists and those who aspire to their cause, the deliberate misperception of people of color as usurpers of undue rights is seen as a correct assessment of their demands for equality. So entrenched is this opinion that issues of charity where the state feeds the hungry, affirmative action that attempted to bridge the gaps in education, income, and other metrics, limitations of hate speech, gun control, crime, and the election of the first black president are rallying cries to oppose power grabs by black Americans. These rallying cries occur on the public airwaves, from person to person via e-mail, and through politically incorrect vocalization in the workplace and public places.

The issues of the white supremacists are being forced onto the mainstream consciousness as harmless prognostications from an injured party under the banner of free speech. The aim is to influence public policy by insinuating that a favorable prevailing popular opinion of the white supremacist cause exists. In our recent history, white supremacism permeated society and nearly destroyed the continent of Africa. When allowed to surface again, it decimated Europe. Today, desperate gun-wielding proponents of racial hatred are in a make-believe do-or-die war generated from the depths of their self-generated fear of black-skinned people.

Racial discrimination, whether expressed through neocolonialism, a corrupt criminal justice system, job discrimination, or violence, is permitted to destabilize African communities and play a part in destroying the psyche of the African child despite the abolition of slavery and the civil rights laws enacted in the 1954 School Desegregation Act and the 1965 Voting Rights Act. The most compelling argument against racial discrimination is that it forestalls humanity's reckoning of past moral indiscretions that have established and perpetuated social inequities among African and African American communities today. In the United States, the persistence of racial discrimination is perhaps due to the unwillingness of the Supreme Court to allow re-distributive laws and the failure of the Civil Rights Movement itself to establish the needed political and social structures on the local level. As a professor from Chicago in 2001, President Barack Obama expressed that sentiment:

> . . . generally, the Constitution, a charter of negative liberties, says what the states can't do to you, says what the Federal can't do to you, but it doesn't say what the Federal Government or the State Government must do on your behalf. And, that hasn't shifted, and one of the, I think, the tragedies of the Civil Rights Movement was because the Civil Rights ovement became so focused, I think there was a tendency to lose track of the political and community organizing and activities on the ground that are able to put together the actual coalitions of power through which you bring about re-distributive change and in some ways, we still suffer from that. [12]

---

12 2001 Obama Chicago Pulic Radio Inverview WBEZ..FM. Accessed March 21, 2009. Available at: www.wbez.org/audio_library/od_rajan01.asp#010102

The failure to address racial and economic inequality enables repressive conditions to persist and evolve into permanent behaviors aimed at exploiting the victims. Their racial inequality is defined as emanating from the failure of African Americans to rectify their self-inflicted inequality. Consequently, a day-to-day personal struggle must take place for African Americans to advance beyond the constraints of imposed inequality and social degradation. In myriad ways, we can note the daily barrage of assaults on the sensibilities of people singled out simply because of their skin color. However, despite these debilitating conditions, political and community organizing has not proved effective in erasing the effects of the legacy of slavery.

The inability to restore racial equality is not rooted in the lack of initiative on the part of African Americans but is mandated by the system of white supremacy. The *Black Panther Party* took the initiative to organize minority communities during the 1960s through locally derived peaceful programs. They focused on feeding hungry children and providing badly needed services to black communities ostracized by the United States Government. Their efforts were widely lauded by the communities they served and were successful until the U.S. Government decided to wipe out the Black Panthers through its COINTEL program of spying, public executions, and imprisonment of the Panther leadership. The government effectively silenced the Black Panthers' work in impoverished communities. The policy of assassinations and intimidation has been used frequently to silence the individual initiative among African Americans. Through the murder of civil rights activist Medgar Evers in 1963, the Birmingham Church bombing in that same year, Dr. Martin Luther King's murder in 1968, and countless other acts of violence instigated by the Klu Klux Klan, as well as U.S. law enforcement, the African American organized mass resistance is silenced.

The individual search for understanding the brutality of chattel slavery on such a colossal scale leveled against Africans from the Sub-Saharan region of Africa and the solution to its debilitating effects becomes a necessary part of a self-generating process of healing. The need for such healing is partly due to a phenomenon termed "genetic memory." They are horrors that each of us carries in a personal way. Additionally, these horrific memories are constantly revitalized in a society where racist rants or hate crimes occur regularly and are magnified through the public media.

The search for understanding is a personal effort to put to rest the demons that haunt us. Understanding encompasses redemption and atonement and is the final step in moving past the hurdle of inhumanity towards one of reconstruction and reconciliation. However, the quest for understanding is being fulfilled alone by African descendants who are burdened with an imposed psychological trauma and shock that continues to cause alienation, resentment, and anger and blocks the reestablishing of a broken lineage of humanity. The larger dominant society plays a vital role in fostering this alienation through racial discrimination, and the lack of the gesture of long-denied reparations indicates that society has still not arrived at an understanding, nor has it attained a willingness to assume responsibility for the continuous damage.

The Search for the Understanding

The search for understanding by African descendants has led to a Pandora's box of negative consequences for the inhuman practice of the most brutal form of slavery from 1444, when the first cargo of 235 Africans left Africa, to emancipation in the U.S. in 1865, more than 421 years. Contemplating the nature of the enslavement of Africans from an African perspective leads to assertions of the moral composition of human beings and whether Mankind is deserving of his status in the world. The descendants of enslaved Africans knew little of the Europeans at the earliest encounter. They were not traditional enemies, nor did they express any hostility towards him, yet there was the long-drawn-out pillage, plunder, and enslavement of these Africans. The rejection of a divine purpose posed by such immorality stares at us daily and stands as a misapplication of justice that has continued to corrupt society. We can note the consequences of the drift towards self-serving individualism, where one's selfish interests are held to be greater than the self-evident objectives of a Divine Creator and His creation. The symptoms of the sickness are abundant, ranging from a rapid extinction of life forms to a reliance on dishonesty and deceit. Moral corruption, selfishness, materialism, and a disregard for life originate from developing a mechanism for extracting the wealth that the individual covets most. These symptoms prove that the human species is adrift and incapable of effecting sustainable peace, spiritual evolution, and aligning a rebellious spirit with the immortal soul. Instead, humanity continues in the same fractious and fallacious direction established in the heyday of slavery and capitalism.

Human beings are perceived as possessing the qualities of humility and compassion. Nevertheless, we differentiate humans from animals because we speculate that only those defined as humans can reason, bury the dead, and seek a successful transition to the afterworld. However, being human has ancient connotations, implying that we are bound to a Divine

Creator who can modify our behavior. Nevertheless, we fail to apply such an internal moral arbiter when confronted with systemic immorality. Our artificial conventions of religion, law, philosophy, and ethics that purport to guide our morality have become tools of power brokers or oligarchies working to achieve selfish objectives. The individual, dependent on the same system and imbued with free will, participates in the grand deception, choosing not to surrender to a higher morality.

In the U.S. and the African Diaspora, the descendants of Africans are left with an ostracized self-identity, to cope and to do the needed work of correcting the ramifications of an imposed system of racial discrimination. Without the cooperation of the larger society to engage in earnest pursuit of the truth and subsequent redemption, the descendants of Africans have only their appeals to the Divine for answers. We can find commonality between ourselves and all others, even those who would violate our moral code. Through this understanding, we can move toward redemption. At the core of this understanding is that power brokers whose motive is greed are deliberately suppressing the soul's role. When our spirit becomes confused with the soul, we are left at the mercy of those who would exploit us by claiming to provide the path to spiritual unity or denying us knowledge of that path.

Comparison of God vs. Reason as a Moral Anchor

Aspect	Modern Philosophy (Empiricism/ Rationalism)	Ancient Greeks and Romans	Ancient Kemet (Egypt)
Source of Morality	Human reason, experience, or sentiment	Metaphysical principles or divine order	Divine cosmic principles (Ma'at) are upheld by human actions.
Role of God	Often absent, secular frameworks prevail	The divine (polytheistic or monotheistic) serves as a moral backdrop.	Central. Gods like Ra, Osiris, and Ma'at personify moral order.
Moral Absolutes	Generally absent. morality is contextual	Present, often tied to the Good, Nature, or God.	Present. Ma'at represents an absolute cosmic balance that humans must maintain.
Definition of Evil	Relative, psychological, or social dysfunction	Ignorance of the Good (Plato) or failure to fulfill one's purpose (Aristotle).	Isfet (chaos, falsehood, disorder), the antithesis of Ma'at, disrupting divine harmony.
Goal of Ethics	Human well-being, social harmony	Virtue, flourishing, or divine alignment.	Preservation of Ma'at through righteous living, ensuring cosmic balance and harmony.

Chapter 11

Towards a New Reality in The New Economy

Overview of the New Economy Paradigm

The new economy refers to the modern system of production and consumption, which is subject to central bank control through manipulating interest rates. The U.S. Federal Reserve and its central bank counterparts worldwide all maintain fiat currency and interest rate mechanisms to stabilize their economies. As the dominant global economic power, the U.S. Congress created the Federal Open Market Committee (FOMC) in 1933. However, it was not until 1935 that it was formalized under the Federal Reserve Act as its policy-making arm to achieve full employment and price stability.

The FOMC uses three tools to influence the economy.[1] It conducts Open Market Operations by buying and selling government securities. It sets The Discount Rate, the interest rate charged to commercial banks and other institutions on loans from their regional Federal Reserve Bank. Until 2020, when reserve requirements were set at zero, the FOMC also determined the funds banks must hold in reserve and cannot loan out. These tools collectively help regulate the federal funds rate, the interest rate at which banks lend and borrow funds overnight from each other.[2]

Since its founding, the FOMC and central banks worldwide have managed the new economy, including its credit-driven economic expansions. During such expansions, when the federal government's revenue generation through taxes, tariffs, fees, and public-private partnerships is inadequate, the Federal Reserve may purchase Treasury securities to add money to the economy. Government funding requirements and private sector cash needs can influence the federal funds rate. During such cash crunches, when the

---

1   www.federalreservehistory.org/essays/federal-open-market-committee.
2   www.investopedia.com.

government needs to borrow more money, it issues Treasury securities, which can reduce the available funds in the market, leading to higher overnight rates as banks compete for limited funds. Shortages of short-term money force short-term yields above those of longer duration and signal an inverted yield curve, a precursor to recession. The yield curve inverted in the 4th quarter of 2022 as the Federal Reserve raised interest rates in 2022 and 2023. It remained inverted until December 2024, when the Fed lowered rates. However, it is uncertain when or if a recession will manifest in U.S. history's most extended yield-curve inversion.

The profit motive drives speculation on future asset price movements through hedging market exposure using highly leveraged derivative financial instruments made feasible by low interest rates. Financial threats to these derivative positions can result in their rapid collapse, bankruptcies, recessions, or depressions. The most recent collapse was the 2007 Subprime Crisis, which saw the bankruptcies of Lehman Brothers, Bear Stearns, Washington Mutual, Countrywide Financial, and AIG due to the reverberating collapse of derivative schemes in the mortgage industry. Additionally, thousands of homeowners defaulted on their loans and lost their homes as adjustable mortgage rates increased.

The crisis began with the risky mortgage-backed securities created by bundling mortgages with low credit ratings with those with higher credit ratings. Excessive lending in the mortgage industry and in the expanding economy led to the housing market bubble and to the Subprime Crisis. Risky mortgages with the lowest BB ratings for borrowers with 300-579 credit scores were bundled with AAA-rated mortgages with the highest credit scores of 800-850 and resold as safe. Despite the inherent risk, these mortgages were sold as highly valued, sound investments. However, as interest rates increased, the weaker borrowers defaulted on their mortgages, collapsing the derivatives markets. The derivative-driven collapse shows that while the Chicago Board of Trade (CBOT) used derivative instruments in 1848 to stabilize grain prices and help farmers lock in future crop prices, they more often serve as tools for speculation and financial risk-taking that significantly impact financial stability. The global derivatives market is valued at over $1 quadrillion, or a thousand trillion dollars. This figure includes many positions that offset each other, making the net market value significantly lower, around 12.4 trillion.[3]

The partnership between business and government perpetuates the accommodative Federal Reserve's interest rate policy, which keeps debts affordable to large businesses. By adjusting interest rates the Fed impacts

---

3   www.investopedia.com

the unemployment rate, a key factor in controlling inflation by reducing demand. However, the tendency has been to keep rates low, for as long as possible despite the negative consequences, in order to avoid collapsing the economy. On January 17, 1961, President Eisenhower warned about the initial and growing partnership between the U.S. government and defense contractors that began during World War II and continued to the Cold War. He referred to the heavy allocation of funds, technological advancements, and sustained production by defense contractors as The Military-Industrial Complex. As the government became dependent on arms manufacturers, the defense sector became fully integrated into the national economy, making reductions in military budgets difficult.[4] Eisenhower understood that massive expenditures on inefficient, redundant military systems and foreign wars would severely strain the U.S. economy.

The focus has shifted to the more lucrative information technology sector, which focuses on artificial intelligence. In his farewell speech on January 15, 2025, the outgoing U.S. President Joe Biden, like his counterpart in 1961, elaborated on the latest ongoing threats to democracy from greed and the oligarchic control of the technology sector of the United States:

> "Today, an oligarchy is taking shape in America of extreme wealth, power, and influence that literally threatens our entire democracy, our basic rights and freedoms, and a fair shot for everyone to get ahead.
>
> Americans are being buried under an avalanche of misinformation and disinformation, enabling the abuse of power. The free press is crumbling. Editors are disappearing. Social media is giving up on fact-checking. The truth is smothered by lies told for power and for profit." [5]

—President Joe Biden, January 15, 2025 Farewell Address

The problem of unsustainable increases in the national debt surfaced in 1971 during the Vietnam War when the U.S. could no longer support the dollar with its gold reserves. President Nixon responded to the crisis by ending the dollar's convertibility to gold at a fixed rate. During the war, increasing federal budget deficits had consistently surpassed the value of U.S. gold reserves when President Nixon ended the gold standard and

4   www.history.com
5   *The Associated Press, MSN*. Available at: Five things to know about Biden's farewell address that also served as a warning to the country

implemented wage and price controls to curb inflation.[6] That year, the National Debt was $398 billion, with gold reserves of 261.6 million troy ounces worth $10.4 billion. By 2023, the debt had surged to $34 trillion. The gold reserves were now worth $507.5 billion, impacted by inflation. As inflationary spending continues in 2023, unrestrained by the gold supply, the interest payments on the debt have grown into a $1.2 trillion, non-producing liability that surpasses the 2023 military budget of $820 billion.

The underlying cause of the demand for money begins with uncontrolled spending enabled by excessive printing of fiat currency and the ensuing increases in debt and usury. As early as the 1st century, unsecured loans by Roman banking houses led to the financial crisis of 33 c.e. In the recent past (c. 17th –19th century), excessive borrowing of fiat money enabled speculative ventures such as the European colonial expansions, the Thirty Year's War, the Slave Trade, and national and private debt, leading to multiple cycles of financial booms and inflationary depressions. The over-issuing of money-like credit instruments without gold backing inevitably spurred profit-driven, large-scale investments and borrowing from companies like the Dutch East India Company (VOC) and the British East India Company established to pool resources, spread financial risk, and create debt while spreading war and destruction worldwide. Usury became more widespread during this period, and Europe's financial centers, Venice, Amsterdam, and London, expanded into global finance centers.

Integrating Traditional and Modern Economic Principles

In the contemporary period, as the debt crisis worsens and income inequality and war increases, finding a solution to economic injustice requires a hardened resolve, primarily as the interest rates have remained extremely low during the COVID-19 pandemic and the U.S. 2024 elections. The unusually high level of fiat-driven credit expansion by the Fed during the pandemic ended in 2022, with rate hikes going from .08% to 4.33% in 2023. However, as the U.S. 2024 election campaign began, the Fed again lowered rates from 5.33% to 4.48%. The extended period of low interest rates from 2008–2015, with monetary policies such as quantitative easing and low borrowing costs, enabled international entrepreneurs to reap trillions of dollars in profits and to bid up asset prices.

---

6   Nixon Ends Convertibility of U.S. Dollars to Gold and Announces Wage/Price Controls | Federal Reserve History. Available at: www.federalreservehistory.org/essays/gold-convertibility-ends. Accessed 11/28/2024.

In 2024, as housing prices reached a national average of $510,000, food prices increase weekly, and the Fed was forced to increase interest rates to cool inflation. However, the lesson of the Subprime Crisis remains as the vast global operations built on cheap debt, face collapse should the slightest financial threat to their ability to manage that debt occur. Increasing workers' wages or increasing interest rates, which make debt more expensive, are not feasible options. Nevertheless, the borrowing continues, and investing in assets, such as real estate, increases the prices of farmland, food, housing, and mortgage-related products, making them too expensive for the middle class and poor, whose decreasing wages do not keep up with inflation. Additionally, as a nationalistic trend has taken root in the U.S., the mechanism established during the Nixon Administration to import cheap goods to offset inflation is crumbling under U.S. tariffs and sanctions war, particularly against Russia, China, Canada and Mexico.

Currently, there is no clear solution short of placing faith in human ingenuity to solve the debt driven problems of modern economies. A spiritual approach, like that proposed during the medieval period, will likely have results like those of that era. Considering the historical tensions between the secular state and the church, spiritually inspired efforts are difficult to implement, as the failure of the Papal revolution in 1045–1257 shows. Medieval economic concepts originated in unique social settings, alien to the modern era when the separation between religion and the secular state became recognized after 212 years of hostilities, and despite the terms of the 1122 *Concordat of Worms*. The same type of divisions carried forward to the 17th century when the influential church witnessed divisions among its members and the secular society seeking profits, which affirmed that no common moral standard could be enforced. There were stark differences between Catholicism that stuck to religious tradition, and the combination of the Protestantism of Luther and Calvin and the secular authorities that rejected the established canon.[7] The result of centuries of conflict was the realization of the overbearing power of secular authorities we see today, that are empowered to do whatever is necessary to realize increasing profits.

However, the linear thinking prevalent in the modern era, that aids the rampant abuse of power through the monopolization of fiat currency is not an historical norm. The solutions many propose that consistently enable human character flaws, particularly greed are traditionally outlawed vices. Lower

---

7   Tawney, R.H. *Religion and the Rise of Capitalism*, p. 17.

interest rates make borrowing cheap for the billionaire class while making education, gasoline, food, and other necessities unaffordable for the poor and middle class. As budget deficits increase exponentially, the wealthy clamor for lower and lower interest rates while the poor and middle class descend into increasing poverty from inflation. The fear of losing access to fiat currency drives the behavior of the wealthy to rely on mass layoffs of the workforce and reliance on robotics. Their actions or policies exist to thwart any effort to solve the unceasing pursuit of accumulating and monopolizing wealth.

The Positive Law of the modern state, supported by immense military and political power, coupled with actions of Non-Governmental Organizations (NGOs) or think tanks, devise and impose their self-prescribed public policies on an unwary public. Across the various market sectors, such as Automobile, Healthcare, Energy, and Consumer Staples, lobbying organizations give massive amounts of dark money to politicians in return for the government's adoption of their self-serving policies. Many of these corporations that have become reliant on cheap money and borrow more and more money to pay off their debts are known as zombie corporations. However, cutting off the flow of cheap money will inevitably end in an economic downturn.

The further we go back, the more evidence there is of the determined efforts to achieve justice that failed due to opposition from the alliances of the secular society of merchants and governments. Attempts to run medieval society based on Christian moral values and tradition occurred among the Scholastics, such as Anselm of Canterbury, credited with founding Scholasticism. Saint Thomas Aquinas and William of Ockham's reconciling of reason defined in Greek philosophy with Christian faith and theology was an early attempt at a comprehensive analysis of Christian thought. Scholastic economics focused on just prices based on what the poorest members of society could afford. It abhorred slavery as unjust and banned any charging of interest as unjust and contrary to natural law.

In *Religion and the Rise of Capitalism*, by R.H. Tawney, the author summarizes the thrust of the time accordingly:

> Morality was a central issue in Medieval Europe. Economic interests are subordinate to the real business of life, which is salvation, and that economic conduct is one aspect of personal conduct, upon which, as on other parts of it, the rules of morality are binding.

—R.H. Tawney. *Religion and the Rise of Capitalism. P. 34.*

Up to the 16th century, usury in Europe was so maligned that anyone seeking a profit was avaricious and a usurer. Nevertheless, the longstanding medieval efforts at a spiritual solution to economic injustice ended in compromises with the secular state. The split between church and state, resulting from the wars for papal rights against the monarchy or *The Indenture Controversy*, carried the societal divisions and failures forward. At the same time that the theologians intended to live in the light of God, their theology lacked sufficient force to restrain the commercial sector from seeking illegal profits.

The interest-rate mechanism of the new economy only marginally differs from the classical economic, free-market principles outlined by Adam Smith in 1776. In his two-volume work, *An Inquiry into the Nature and Causes of the Wealth of Nations,* Smith attributes economic growth to free markets, division of labor, innovation, and capital accumulation. His free-market economic principles emphasized the economic benefits of individuals freely pursuing their self-interests in the marketplace. Smith found it convenient to refrain from identifying the role of the unsecured fiat currency with interest, as the main drivers of the modern economic system. Unsecured credit and usury provided an unwarranted advantage to the slave traders and the network of financiers in Smith's time. He and the classical economists did not account for the slave labor funded with paper IOUs, secured with a promise to pay, as the driver of Western economic growth, except to say that slavery was not as profitable as free labor.

The compelling point about the new economy in the contemporary period is its reliance on mechanisms, traditionally considered fraudulent, to control prices and supply and demand initiatives from consumers. By adjusting the money supply, central banks influence interest rates, making debt too expensive or more affordable for businesses and individuals. Increasing the money supply, which equates to decreasing interest rates, can boost spending and economic growth while increasing it can help control inflation.[8] Fiat currency provides a stable medium of exchange, which is essential for economic transactions. However, its usage rests on the unnatural manipulation of the economy that favors the wealthy and politically connected in ways that increase the income gap between rich and poor. Like in the past, when the definition of usury was guided by Christian morals that

---

8   www.accountinginsights.org.

condemned avarice, the beneficiaries of unsecured credit were still overwhelmingly the wealthiest and politically connected.

Empiricism and the Birth of Inductive Reasoning

Foundations of Empiricism

By the 17th century, the empiricist philosophical revolution found truth in the material world, rejecting the connection of morals to God. Francis Bacon and John Locke led the empiricist movement, which held that knowledge is based on sensory experience and material evidence instead of unsubstantiated speculation. Their empiricist philosophy called for experimentation and data gathering using inductive reasoning, which was restricted solely to facts in the material world.

Empiricism triumphed as the efforts of the Scholastics failed to embed Christian moral principles in society to ensure the welfare of all its members. The scholastics favored economic principles such as just pricing, which covered the cost of production to keep prices affordable to the poorest members of society. However, after the Papal revolution of 1045, the split between civil law and the Church cannon favored the church only in its spiritual domain, where its property could not be taxed, and it maintained complete control over its bishops. On the other hand, the state insisted that the church abstains from interference in state matters. While the earliest economic and social theories from the School of Salamanca argued for the rights of everyone, including the New World's indigenous peoples, the Schoolmen's medieval sermons could not prevent the brutal exploitation of those in Spain's South American colonies, as De Las Casas divulged in *A Short Account of the Destruction of the Indies*. The school's principled adherence to the revered tradition of Aristotelean and the medieval Just Price legal doctrine failed to protect the neediest from exploitation. The doctrine gave the neediest members of society the right to determine the prices of goods and services based on their needs. However, the vast stores of Inca gold acquired by the European explorers easily swayed the Papacy into an accommodation with avaricious merchants seeking unrestricted wealth.

The state's growing power predominated, and as it ignored the church's moral principles, the 17th-century empiricist philosophy sprang up with the means to legitimize the changes in morality. Empiricism popularized sensory experience as the source of morals and diminished God's role. The

Schoolmen's medieval Christian theology quickly relinquished control of the narrative to the empiricists who reasoned away its restrictive morals. Inevitably, with the amassing of wealth in the economy, even the esteemed School of Salamanca embraced the system of fiat and usury as a vital part of the economy.

Empiricism led to science and technology as the foundations of modern society. Science led to a deeper understanding of the natural world and inventions that propelled economic growth based on increased industrial production. However, while empiricism triumphed, it created an inverted deterministic logic and a faux science to shift responsibility for the Slave Trade and obscure the brutal truth amid the intellectual advances of the Enlightenment. The empiricist looked no further than the emaciated slave for evidence of inferiority. On the other hand, the Protestants accepted the plight of the enslaved as examples of God's punishment for their unfaithfulness. The European imperial powers expanded their empires through chattel slavery, which was driven by usury and fiat currency until it became critical to their slave-based economies. The contrast between the intellectual progress of the Enlightenment and the growing immorality of the slave trade that remained obscured reveals a disturbing inversion of the truth that questions the validity of the morals of a secular society seeking truth in the material sphere.

Diminishing the necessity for a first mover in creation as the source of morals allowed society to veer unchecked toward chaos without a divine measure of what is good. An unrestrained spirit had become engrossed in greed, financial chicanery, or *usury* at historic levels. The use of fiat currency with no intrinsic value, under the control of the London Goldsmiths and the Bank of England, was the catalyst in the expansion of the slave trade to near extinction-level population declines in Africa. Fraudulent printing of IOUs without backing in silver or gold allowed the expansion of the vast slave enterprise conducted by the English monarchy to flourish. The use of fiat currency to finance the Slave Trade coincides with the beginning of the Bank of England in 1694. The bank offered loans with usurious fees to the Royal African Company and the South Sea Company, the key players in the Slave Trade. It also provided the British government with fiat currency to fund colonial wars and to expand the British Empire. The use of limitless fiat currency could only return the massive profits of the English banks because of the enforced labor and production of enslaved Africans.

After the abolition of the Slave Trade in England, the profits of the debt-fueled growth went towards reparations for the enslavers. Some of whom were directors at the bank. The enslaved were freed but left penniless, without reparations or means to survive in an economy where the wealthy aimed to become even more wealthy by becoming landlords and collecting rents in the industrialization phase of capitalism. A growing body of evidence shows the debilitating effect of fiat currency from the early years of Agrarian Capitalism when traditionally forbidden, usurious, and avaricious morals conspired to sacrifice countless nameless African people for profit. They were the primary means of production but could never lay claim to their immense production or their innovations.

Nevertheless, there is a reluctance among a cross-section of the global population to engage in meaningful dialogue on repairing the ramifications of a base crime that continues to reverberate. On the contrary, the abhorrent social mores have been forced into a position of normalcy and portrayed as progress, a better way, which is more beneficial to society. At the same time, some of the most significant wealth disparities expand, and the corporative basis of civilization is demolished in favor of competition, rivalry, and war.

The Atlantic Slave Trade: Context and Consequences

Historical Overview

The patterns of economic and social inequality established during the slave trade continue to shape the race-based socioeconomic structure and its modes of social control. The premise of the conflict, which preserves the supremacy of the controlling class, is from the social mores of a system of racial oppression or hegemonic social constructs intentionally designed to dehumanize enslaved people and justify the exploitation of labor for economic gain. As it opposes the noble ideals of ancient tradition based on divine unity, the resulting social construct of a racial hierarchy based on the Atlantic Slave Trade can be referred to as a pseudo-culture. It represents a thoroughly obscured reality that redefines the nature of divine unity or universal justice as a force that discriminates and abuses the weak and vulnerable. In the fundamental way that the ancient Egyptians saw injustice as the ultimate destructive force named *Isfet,* the pseudo-culture perpetuates a racial hierarchy that threatens the foundations of human society.

The broadcast media, educational, and other cultural institutions work to perpetuate inequality automatically by amplifying the social mores of the pseudo-culture, which is rooted in xenophobia, greed, and racism. Rewarding harmful behaviors destroys the more vital cultural patterns based on cooperation developed over hundreds of thousands of years of human activity. Historical fabrication taught in educational institutions worldwide continues unabated at present. In myriad ways, modern societies vehemently and routinely deny any pioneering and meaningful cultural traditions in Africa and wrongly attribute their notable contributions to fictitious populations outside of Africa. Over several centuries, the sustained denigration of African culture designed to shatter the model of cooperation as the foundation of civilization has sustained the pseudo-culture that emerged from the social mores of chattel slavery.

Contrary to the prevalent narrative, African civilization contributed significantly to the foundations of global culture and innovation. Emerging after approximately 140,000 years of isolation on the continent, humans in Africa developed crucial cultural mores that ensured survival and prosperity. These cultural traditions have been embedded in Africa's languages and cultures since prehistoric times. Innovations spread over vast distances on the continent and beyond and have continued to influence human activity as archetypical developments. Far from being non-productive, humans in Africa have consistently innovated new technologies necessary for survival, often under extreme climatic conditions that the worldwide monoculture, which is based on the racial hierarchy, has never experienced.

Economic and Moral Implications of the Atlantic Slave Trade

The Foundations of the Pseudo-Culture

The pseudo-culture of the modern era, based on a fabricated racial hierarchy, is the set of behaviors adopted by a group or forced upon other groups that promote monetary gain as the primary objective over society's moral or cultural aspirations. African cultures, which evolved gradually over thousands of years, were thoroughly transformed into accommodative and submissive modes of interaction with the Portuguese early during the slave trade, approximately 100 years after they began the wars in Congo. Chattel Slavery expanded throughout Africa to become the primary economic mode Africans relied upon as their traditional, inter-Africa trade routes were destroyed. By the beginning of the 18th century, the redefinition of reality from a strict biblical representation to an empiricist philosophy and ideological indoctrination based on the pseudo-science of the racial hierarchy had embedded the social mores of the pseudo-culture in Europe and its colonies. It focused solely on attaining the avaricious goals of a controlling class seeking wealth by exploiting the most vulnerable of human beings. In the heyday of the Slave Trade, most of the Western world, the Near East, and Africa became engrossed in the exploitation of African slave labor. From the Arabs and Africans who fought and captured other Africans to the European commercial traders with debt obligations seeking new trade routes, they all participated in the genocide occurring in Africa and on plantations in the Americas and Asia.

By the 17th century, financiers, slave traders, and pseudo-scientists had firmly established the pseudo-culture in European society. As greed triumphed throughout the Age of Discovery, the natural rights of all human beings based on the bible no longer extended to Muslims, pagans, and Africans based on the Papal Bull Dum Diversas in 1452. Across the New World, where the enslavers ruled, they established a new reality void of adherence to what the world had once accepted as just according to the universal divine moral principle of reciprocity.

The hunt for gold to establish trade surpluses turned Europeans into ruthless marauders empowered by their sovereign kings to wage war and establish colonies in newly confiscated lands of the New World. From Mercantilism's inception in the 16th century to its culmination in the 18th century, they waged war amongst themselves only to fill their treasuries with gold. The violence was turned against the native European populations and those in the Americas, and, finally, against Africans. The defining characteristic of the evolving pseudo-culture of slavery was mindless and insatiable greed. It was the same greed St. Augustine of Hippo from the Scholastic period had warned needed to be restrained through controls placed upon usury, land-grabbing, and the infringing by one class on another. These were the mechanisms he identified that corrupt the spirit and debase humanity.

Moral and Cultural Impacts

The transition from a genuine European culture to the chaos of the modern era occurred gradually due to the Medieval wars of the Papal Revolution between the church and the state. The wars for the indenture of bishops resulted in a separation of the church and the state. The divisions allowed the development of two moral foundations, one based on the Church canon and another driven by the ambitions of the monarchy or state. Neither could impinge on the other's right to operate in their domain.

Despite the oppressive nature of Medieval feudalism, an implicit recognition of the rights of human beings under natural law still existed in Europe, based on the moral economy of the Middle Ages from the School of Salamanca. It recognized the inherent rights of all human beings as freedom, land rights, and dignity based on traditional Christian values that cared for the least of the Christian folk.

However, as European bankers adopted usury to compound money contrary to the church's moral proclamations, international traders' greed for wealth compromised the church's dedication to saving souls. Usury became the means of corrupting society, making it dependent on borrowed money with compound interest rates. The fraudulent use of paper money in unsecured credit schemes flourished from the mid-seventeenth century. It featured prominently in the rapid expansion of the Slave Trade and the arbitrary debasing of the sanctity of life contrary to Christian ideals of salvation.

The moral degeneration from slavery legitimized greed, xenophobia, and injustice in a pseudo-culture without the moral foundation that has traditionally characterized a legitimate culture. For example, Plato's examination of the soul provides a clear example of the best way to rule society by drawing parallels between the greater society and the soul. Nevertheless, the elites of the modern era spent excessive time and effort suppressing ancient culture while creating a New World culture with an implied legitimacy based on haughty philosophical proclamations. During the Enlightenment, scholars pledged to create a just society that respected human rights but excluded those with black skin. For the enslavers, the contradictions of slavery as an ethnically based practice had corrupted the basis of civilization and culture, redefining it and separating it from its source in the universal divine principle.

Europeans living in the New World spent large sums of money to create a semblance of culture that rivaled that of Europe. American artists emulated the Salons of Europe, founded fine arts schools and theaters, and built monumental architecture to legitimize their intellectual foundations. In Virginia, President Thomas Jefferson, in his mountaintop mansion, which was a model of classical architecture, was based on the plans of the Italian architect Adrea Palladio in the 16th century. Jefferson sought to be equated to the classical culture of ancient Greece and appear as sophisticated as the Europeans in his historical outlook. However, he could not imagine relinquishing his six hundred enslaved people operating his mansion and estate at Monticello in Virginia. Instead, Jefferson kept their presence invisible to the occupants of the main house. He restricted those who worked in the main mansion to the underground kitchen facilities by using the dumb waiter, operated from the underground quarters, and had food hoisted to the main dining room without the enslaved people ever being seen. The semblance of legitimacy was in obscuring the problem of slavery or presenting it positively.

Modern Consequences

Historical practices of mythmaking generated by the Western slave-based economic system from centuries ago set a standard that many in the present seek to revisit. The values of the new culture generated by the racial myths from centuries past have led to massive financial gain for a select group that prospers financially and politically from the engineered chaos. The unseen reality, however, is the unprecedented increase in inequality encouraged by the race-based value system, which is revealed in the 10% proportion of the wealthiest members of society that own most of the wealth despite the extreme poverty of the majority, primarily dark-skinned people. After the Great Depression of 1930, the skewed distribution of wealth persisted and grew larger and larger. Data for 2010, for example, show that the 10% share of wealth surpassed the levels attained during the Gilded Age in the late 19th century, formerly the benchmark for measuring opulence in the United States.

Below is a table showing the wealth inequality in the United States by decade from the 1890s to the 2010s based on data from economist Emmanuel Saez's database:

Decade	Top 10% Wealth Share	Top 1% Wealth Share	Top 0.1% Wealth Share
1890s	73.10%	45.60%	20.70%
1900s	72.80%	44.20%	18.40%
1910s	71.70%	39.30%	13.60%
1920s	84.40%	44.20%	16.40%
1930s	67.10%	29.80%	8.60%
1940s	67.20%	29.80%	9.10%
1950s	69.20%	33.00%	10.90%
1960s	68.20%	32.40%	10.30%
1970s	67.20%	31.10%	9.30%
1980s	73.10%	37.40%	12.80%
1990s	67.70%	34.60%	11.40%
2000s	70.40%	35.60%	12.20%
2010s	76.00%	39.70%	14.00%

Source: data from Emmanuel Saez database. Available at: lecture_saez_chicago14.pdf

The disparities in the wealth of 10% of the population since the 1809s appear to be a permanent feature of the Western economic system. They are related to the misappropriation of funds diverted to a few capitalists. The majority of the population is fooled into confusion, fighting with limited resources, low-paying jobs, lack of adequate housing, or extreme poverty. An economy based strictly on scientifically verified economic principles designed to control supply or demand cannot effect the needed change in poverty levels without a determined effort to elevate people experiencing poverty to create a more equal society.

The American Counter Strategy to Emancipation and the Civil Rights Movement

The persistence of the socioeconomic patterns rooted in slavery led to a counter strategy against emancipation and efforts to rectify past injustices. Although the Civil War and the Emancipation Proclamation formally ended slavery, systematic resistance emerged to maintain the pseudo-culture founded on racial supremacy and economic exploitation. This resistance took shape during the Reconstruction period (1865–1877), with violent retribution against newly freed African Americans, beginning with the assassination of President Abraham Lincoln in 1865. As Reconstruction ended, Southern states swiftly enacted Jim Crow laws (1876 to 1965), legally codifying racial segregation and disenfranchisement. These laws ensured the continued suppression of African Americans by restricting economic opportunities, enforcing voter suppression tactics, and upholding social norms that reinforced the ideology of white superiority.

In the post-emancipation era, though African Americans were legally free, they were still restricted by the remnants of the "Slave Codes." The laws dictated their movement and behavior under severe penalties, including whipping, amputation, and lynching. The dominant narrative defining African Americans shifted from enslaved laborer to that of the rapacious, drunken buffoon in widespread attempts to suppress cultural aspirations and terrorize.

The counter strategy has persisted despite the 1964 Civil Rights Act outlawing racial discrimination and the Voting Rights Act of 1965 that granted African Americans full citizenship rights. The strategy to suppress freedom for African Americans continued through the assassinations of the '60s in the war against poor people. It was an unabashedly physical assault against the poor and working-class people of color and poor whites who, unknown to them, were also deprived of their fair share of the economic pie.

On the streets of America's major cities, an outraged population resorted to marching for equal rights against an inflexible system that sought to maintain the status quo through massive force. Given such resistance, the FBI, under Herbert Hoover, employed a Counterintelligence Program that targeted members of the African American community who were declared to be a threat to national security in 1968 and assassinated or threatened with death.

The opposition to Dr. Martin Luther King, Jr. and the Civil Rights Movement, with its millions of supporters, grew increasingly violent and showed the underlying determination to oppose racial equality percolating in society. His poor people's campaign severely challenged the elite and the system of White Supremacism and capitalism. The counterstrategy against racial justice turned mo7re violent with Malcolm X's murder on February 21, 1965. and Dr. King's assassination on April 4, 1968. However, the violence did not stop there and escalated against other groups, such as the Black Panther Party. The police brutally suppressed the demonstrations after the King's murder in places such as Newark, New Jersey, and Watts, California.

Coinciding with the efforts to pass the 1965 Voting Rights Act by Democrats led by President Lyndon B. Johnson, Southern Whites abandoned the Democratic Party and flocked to the Republican Party. The newly transformed Republican Party began a strategy to continue to attract Whites from the Democratic Party. They automatically relied on the age-old technique of stoking racial division created in the heyday of slavery. Starting with President Nixon's election campaign in 1968, a more insidious effort was undertaken to exploit the pseudo-culture of white supremacy. As it became known, the Southern strategy was based on a system of intimidation and fear mongering that solidified the voters of European ancestry into a reliable voting block while simultaneously demoralizing the African American vote. The Southern Strategy was employed continuously up to the 2008 election cycle by Presidents Richard Nixon (1969–74), Ronald Reagan 1981–89, and George Herbert Walker Bush I (1989–1993). To a lesser extent, President Clinton (1993–2001) and George Bush II (2001–09) benefited. The Southern Strategy was finally defeated with Barack Obama's election in 2008, as 46% of Whites voted for the nation's first black President.

The specter of the black bogeyman has been employed continuously from its inception after emancipation in the U.S. President George H. W. Bush I, for instance, combined his efforts with Roger Ailes, the Republican campaign manager, to frame the 1988 election debate along racial lines. The famous Willie Horton ads[9] produced by Floyd Brown depicted an African American as the model for criminality, and the Democratic candidate Michael Dukakis was accused of planning to release murderers from jail. Roger Ailes became the President of The Fox News Channel and focused on promoting a Republican agenda to suppress African Americans and liberal politicians.

With the election of Barack Obama in 2008, the politics of the GOP has evolved beyond the Southern Strategy to a policy of Obstructionism. The GOP has framed Obama's efforts as Socialism, with the implicit meaning that the President plans to redistribute the nation's wealth to African Americans. Right-wing radio talk show Rush Limbaugh, who died in February 2021, declared the President's plans as reparations.

President Obama campaigned on a platform of change, particularly in the healthcare sector. His efforts to bring change encouraged a backlash from Republican Party opponents who began racially attacking the 44th president. From his election in 2008, Obama faced a wide range of racist attacks. Some circulated via e-mail, while others originated from wealthy opponents of healthcare reform lobbying for the pharmaceutical and health insurance industries.

The summer of 2009 saw Congress recess and debate the Healthcare Reform Bill at town hall meetings. The dog days of summer, from July through early September, were made hotter by widely publicized emotionally charged right-wing demonstrations at August Town Hall meetings held across the country. The protests spread to the 9-12 rally in Washington, D.C., to commemorate the September 11, 2001, attacks on the World Trade Center in New York City. The signage betrayed the common aim of the right-wing demonstrations to disavow anything with an Obama stamp on it and to assault the senses. The rude and abusive language in the signage was further punctuated by the presence of gun-toting extremists at rallies near the President, brandishing signs suggesting anarchy and Armageddon itself.

There were signs depicting the President as an African witch doctor with a bone through the nose and "The Joker," the evil character from the *Batman* movie. Some signs read "Bury ObamaCare, with Kennedy," referring to the death of Senator Ted Kennedy on August 25, 2009. The

---

9   As viewed at The Museum of the Moving Image, available at: www.livingroomcandidate.org/commercials/1988/revolving-door

lunacy portrayed was reminiscent of the work of artist Hieronymus Bosch (1450–1516), the Dutch painter of extreme religious fantasy who depicted scenes of Hell and the human condition in an exaggerated form. However, amid the chaos, there was a sudden realization that these demonstrators had no alternative solutions to the Democrat-sponsored healthcare bill. In the aftermath of the Washington DC march, the main argument of the right was to condemn Obama's perceived socialist healthcare policy and decry government spending. Their main objective was to maintain the status quo—to do nothing to their privately run healthcare.

The positions of the right-wing or conservative groups were contradictory and inexplicable. They appeared to simultaneously reject a perceived socialist platform while overwhelmingly supporting Medicare, which is also a government-administered healthcare program. The demonstrators displayed signs using the latest computer-generated graphics, output on large-format inkjets, and mounted and laminated—an expensive undertaking for any fiscally responsible citizen during the 2008 recession. Corporate backing was evident in the brightly colored buses that shuttled demonstrators between the town halls and healthcare meetings. Consequently, the demonstrators were dubbed Astroturf rather than grassroots due to their connections to the pharmaceutical and insurance industries and the corporate media. The term is a fitting description of the ongoing pseudo-culture operating without a moral compass.

The pseudo-culture endures despite efforts at reparative justice to amend destructive trends in society, such as persistent poverty and its ramifications. Efforts fall short in each Western country, and the pattern extends to the African continent, where nations are in extreme poverty despite their incredible natural resources. Like in the past, idealism cannot change hearts or amend avarice. However, the change in the human condition must begin with the heartfelt intention to do what is fair, according to Universal justice applicable to all. Humans ignore the laws applicable to all life at our peril, as in our arrogance and ignorance, and we fail to see the workings of the universal consciousness.

Index

Appendix

Trans-Atlantic Slave Trade – Estimates

	Spain/ Uruguay	Portugal / Brazil	Great Britain	Netherlands	U.S.A.	France	Denmark / Baltic	Totals
1501-1525	6363	7000	0	0	0	0	0	13363
1526-1550	25375	25387	0	0	0	0	0	50762
1551-1575	28167	31089	1685	0	0	66	0	61007
1576-1600	60056	90715	237	1365	0	0	0	152373
1601-1625	83496	267519	0	1829	0	0	0	352844
1626-1650	44313	201609	33695	31729	824	1827	1053	315050
1651-1675	12601	244793	122367	100526	0	7125	653	488065
1676-1700	5860	297272	272200	85847	3327	29484	25685	719675
1701-1725	0	474447	410597	73816	3277	120939	5833	1088909
1726-1750	0	536696	554042	83095	34004	259095	4793	1471725
1751-1775	4239	528693	832047	132330	84580	325918	17508	1925315
1776-1800	6415	673167	748612	40773	67443	433061	39199	2008670
1801-1825	168087	1160601	283959	2669	109545	135815	16316	1876992
1826-1850	400728	1299969	0	357	1850	68074	0	1770978
1851-1875	215824	9309	0	0	476	0	0	225609
Totals	1061524	5848266	3259441	554336	305326	1381404	111040	12521337

Source: www.slavevoyages.org/estimates/aGkJSUeO observation_date LES1252881600Q

U.S. Median Income in 2001 dollars (1947–2001)

Year	All families	White	Black
1947	3,031	3,157	1,614
1948	3,187	3,310	1,768
1949	3,107	3,232	1,650
1950	3,319	3,445	1,869
1951	3,709	3,859	2,032
1952	3,890	4,114	2,338
1953	4,242	4,398	2,466
1954	4,167	4,338	2,416
1955	4,418	4,613	2,544
1956	4,780	5,002	2,632
1957	4,966	5,168	2,763
1958	5,087	5,300	2,715
1959	5,417	5,643	2,915
1960	5,620	5,835	3,230
1961	5,735	5,981	3,191
1962	5,956	6,237	3,328
1963	6,249	6,548	3,465
1964	6,569	6,858	3,838
1965	6,957	7,251	3,993
1966	7,532	7,825	4,691
1967	7,933	8,234	4,875
1968	8,632	8,937	5,360
1969	9,433	9,794	5,999
1970	9,867	10,236	6,279
1971	10,285	10,672	6,440
1972	11,116	11,549	6,864
1973	12,051	12,595	7,269
1974	12,902	13,408	8,006
1975	13,719	14,268	8,779
1976	14,958	15,537	9,242
1977	16,009	16,740	9,563

(Continued)

U.S. Median Income in 2001 dollars (1947–2001) *(continued)*

Year	All families	White	Black
1978	17,640	18,368	10,879
1979	19,587	20,439	11,574
1980	21,023	21,904	12,674
1981	22,388	23,517	13,266
1982	23,433	24,603	13,598
1983	24,580	25,757	14,506
1984	26,433	27,686	15,431
1985	27,735	29,152	16,786
1986	29,458	30,809	17,604
1987	30,970	32,385	18,406
1988	32,191	33,915	19,329
1989	34,213	35,975	20,209
1990	35,353	36,915	21,423
1991	35,939	37,783	21,548
1992	36,573	38,670	21,103
1993	36,959	39,300	21,542
1994	38,782	40,884	24,698
1995	40,611	42,646	25,970
1996	42,300	44,756	26,522
1997	44,568	46,754	28,602
1998	46,737	49,023	29,404
1999	48,950	51,224	31,778
2000	50,890	53,256	34,192
2000	50,732	53,029	33,676
2001	51,407	54,067	33,598
Highest value	*51,407*	*54,067*	*34,192*
Lowest value	*3,031*	*3,157*	*1,614*

Source: Source: U.S. Bureau of the Census, Current Population Reports, P60-218

Black Median Income Decreasing Percentages in 2001 dollars, (1947–2001)

Year	All Families	White	Black	YOY Black Percentage Below White Incomes (1947–2001)
1947	3,031	3,157	1,614	
1948	3,187	3,310	1,768	-46.586%
1949	3,107	3,232	1,650	-48.948%
1950	3,319	3,445	1,869	-45.747%
1951	3,709	3,859	2,032	-47.344%
1952	3,890	4,114	2,338	-43.170%
1953	4,242	4,398	2,466	-43.929%
1954	4,167	4,338	2,416	-44.306%
1955	4,418	4,613	2,544	-44.852%
1956	4,780	5,002	2,632	-47.381%
1957	4,966	5,168	2,763	-46.536%
1958	5,087	5,300	2,715	-48.774%
1959	5,417	5,643	2,915	-48.343%
1960	5,620	5,835	3,230	-44.644%
1961	5,735	5,981	3,191	-46.648%
1962	5,956	6,237	3,328	-46.641%
1963	6,249	6,548	3,465	-47.083%
1964	6,569	6,858	3,838	-44.036%
1965	6,957	7,251	3,993	-44.932%
1966	7,532	7,825	4,691	-40.051%
1967	7,933	8,234	4,875	-40.794%
1968	8,632	8,937	5,360	-40.025%
1969	9,433	9,794	5,999	-38.748%
1970	9,867	10,236	6,279	-38.658%
1971	10,285	10,672	6,440	-39.655%
1972	11,116	11,549	6,864	-40.566%
1973	12,051	12,595	7,269	-42.287%
1974	12,902	13,408	8,006	-40.289%
1975	13,719	14,268	8,779	-38.471%
1976	14,958	15,537	9,242	-40.516%
1977	16,009	16,740	9,563	-42.873%

(Continued)

Black Median Income Decreasing Percentage in 2001 dollars, (1947–2001) *(continued)*

Year	All Families	White	Black	YOY Black Percentage Below White Incomes (1947–2001)
1978	17,640	18,368	10,879	-40.772%
1979	19,587	20,439	11,574	-43.373%
1980	21,023	21,904	12,674	-42.138%
1981	22,388	23,517	13,266	-43.590%
1982	23,433	24,603	13,598	-44.730%
1983	24,580	25,757	14,506	-43.681%
1984	26,433	27,686	15,431	-44.264%
1985	27,735	29,152	16,786	-42.419%
1986	29,458	30,809	17,604	-42.861%
1987	30,970	32,385	18,406	-43.165%
1988	32,191	33,915	19,329	-43.008%
1989	34,213	35,975	20,209	-43.825%
1990	35,353	36,915	21,423	-41.967%
1991	35,939	37,783	21,548	-42.969%
1992	36,573	38,670	21,103	-45.428%
1993	36,959	39,300	21,542	-45.186%
1994	38,782	40,884	24,698	-39.590%
1995	40,611	42,646	25,970	-39.103%
1996	42,300	44,756	26,522	-40.741%
1997	44,568	46,754	28,602	-38.824%
1998	46,737	49,023	29,404	-40.020%
1999	48,950	51,224	31,778	-37.963%
2000	50,890	53,256	34,192	-35.797%
2000	50,732	53,029	33,676	-36.495%
2001	51,407	54,067	33,598	-37.859%
				Average = - 42.775%
Highest value	*51,407*	*54,067*	*34,192*	
Lowest value	*3,031*	*3,157*	*1,614*	
Median	*13,311*	*13,838*	*8,393*	

Source: U.S. Bureau of the Census, Current Population Reports, P60-218 with
      YOY percentage decreases calculated by author.

Black & White Median Income vs. All Families income (5 Yr Mean)

Year	All Families	Abs / Delta	5-yr Mean	Variance	Ave / Var	Sigma Value 2	Year	White	Black	Chart SigHigh 2.0	SigLow 2.0	5-Yr Mean
1947	3,031.0	#REF!	#REF!	#REF!	#REF!	#REF!	1,947.0	3,157.0	1,614.0	#REF!	#REF!	#REF!
1948	3,187.0	#REF!	#REF!	#REF!	#REF!	#REF!	1,948.0	3,310.0	1,768.0	#REF!	#REF!	#REF!
1949	3,107.0	#REF!	#REF!	#REF!	#REF!	#REF!	1,949.0	3,232.0	1,650.0	#REF!	#REF!	#REF!
1950	3,319.0	#VALUE!	#REF!	#VALUE!	#REF!	#REF!	1,950.0	3,445.0	1,869.0	#REF!	#REF!	3,161.0
1951	3,709.0	678.0	#REF!	#REF!	#REF!	#REF!	1,951.0	3,859.0	2,032.0	#REF!	#REF!	3,270.6
1952	3,890.0	703.0	#REF!	#REF!	#REF!	#REF!	1,952.0	4,114.0	2,338.0	#REF!	#REF!	3,442.4
1953	4,242.0	1,135.0	#REF!	#REF!	#REF!	#REF!	1,953.0	4,398.0	2,466.0	#REF!	#REF!	3,653.4
1954	4,167.0	848.0	#VALUE!	#VALUE!	#VALUE!	#VALUE!	1,954.0	4,338.0	2,416.0	#VALUE!	#VALUE!	3,865.4
1955	4,418.0	709.0	814.6	11,151.4	#REF!	#REF!	1,955.0	4,613.0	2,544.0	#REF!	#REF!	4,085.2
1956	4,780.0	890.0	857.0	1,089.0	#REF!	#REF!	1,956.0	5,002.0	2,632.0	#REF!	#REF!	4,299.4
1957	4,966.0	724.0	861.2	18,823.8	#REF!	#REF!	1,957.0	5,168.0	2,763.0	#REF!	#REF!	4,514.6
1958	5,087.0	920.0	818.2	10,363.2	#VALUE!	#VALUE!	1,958.0	5,300.0	2,715.0	#VALUE!	#VALUE!	4,683.6
1959	5,417.0	999.0	848.4	22,680.4	12,821.6	226.5	1,959.0	5,643.0	2,915.0	5,160.1	4,707.1	4,933.6
1960	5,620.0	840.0	874.6	1,197.2	10,830.7	208.1	1,960.0	5,835.0	3,230.0	5,382.1	4,965.9	5,174.0
1961	5,735.0	769.0	850.4	6,626.0	11,938.1	218.5	1,961.0	5,981.0	3,191.0	5,583.5	5,146.5	5,365.0
1962	5,956.0	869.0	879.4	108.2	8,195.0	181.1	1,962.0	6,237.0	3,328.0	5,744.1	5,381.9	5,563.0
1963	6,249.0	832.0	861.8	888.0	6,299.9	158.7	1,963.0	6,548.0	3,465.0	5,954.1	5,636.7	5,795.4
1964	6,569.0	949.0	851.8	9,447.8	3,653.4	120.9	1,964.0	6,858.0	3,838.0	6,146.7	5,904.9	6,025.8
1965	6,957.0	1,222.0	928.2	86,318.4	20,677.7	287.6	1,965.0	7,251.0	3,993.0	6,580.8	6,005.6	6,293.2
1966	7,532.0	1,576.0	1,089.6	236,585.0	66,669.5	516.4	1,966.0	7,825.0	4,691.0	7,169.0	6,136.2	6,652.6
1967	7,933.0	1,684.0	1,252.6	186,106.0	103,869.0	644.6	1,967.0	8,234.0	4,875.0	7,692.6	6,403.4	7,048.0
1968	8,632.0	2,063.0	1,498.8	318,321.6	167,355.8	818.2	1,968.0	8,937.0	5,360.0	8,342.8	6,706.4	7,524.6
1969	9,433.0	2,476.0	1,804.2	451,315.2	255,729.2	1,011.4	1,969.0	9,794.0	5,999.0	9,108.8	7,086.0	8,097.4
1970	9,867.0	2,335.0	2,026.8	94,987.2	257,463.0	1,014.8	1,970.0	10,236.0	6,279.0	9,694.2	7,664.6	8,679.4
1971	10,285.0	2,352.0	2,182.0	28,900.0	215,926.0	929.4	1,971.0	10,672.0	6,440.0	10,159.4	8,300.6	9,230.0
1972	11,116.0	2,484.0	2,342.0	20,164.0	182,737.6	855.0	1,972.0	11,549.0	6,864.0	10,721.6	9,011.6	9,866.6

Year	All Families	Abs / Delta	5-yr Mean	Variance	Ave / Var	Sigma Value 2	Chart Year	White	Black	2.0 SigHigh	2.0 SigLow	5-Yr Mean
1973	12,051.0	2,618.0	2,453.0	27,225.0	124,518.3	705.7	1,973.0	12,595.0	7,269.0	11,256.1	9,844.7	10,550.4
1974	12,902.0	3,035.0	2,564.8	221,088.0	78,472.9	560.3	1,974.0	13,408.0	8,006.0	11,804.5	10,683.9	11,244.2
1975	13,719.0	3,434.0	2,784.6	421,720.4	143,819.5	758.5	1,975.0	14,268.0	8,779.0	12,773.1	11,256.1	12,014.6
1976	14,958.0	3,842.0	3,082.6	576,688.4	253,377.2	1,006.7	1,976.0	15,537.0	9,242.0	13,955.9	11,942.5	12,949.2
1977	16,009.0	3,958.0	3,377.4	337,096.4	316,763.6	1,125.6	1,977.0	16,740.0	9,563.0	15,053.4	12,802.2	13,927.8
1978	17,640.0	4,738.0	3,801.4	877,219.6	486,762.5	1,395.4	1,978.0	18,368.0	10,879.0	16,441.0	13,650.2	15,045.6
1979	19,587.0	5,868.0	4,368.0	2,250,000.0	892,544.9	1,889.5	1,979.0	20,439.0	11,574.0	18,272.1	14,493.1	16,382.6
1980	21,023.0	6,065.0	4,894.2	1,370,772.6	1,082,355.4	2,080.7	1,980.0	21,904.0	12,674.0	19,924.1	15,762.7	17,843.4
1981	22,388.0	6,379.0	5,401.6	955,310.8	1,158,079.9	2,152.3	1,981.0	23,517.0	13,266.0	21,481.7	17,177.1	19,329.4
1982	23,433.0	5,793.0	5,768.6	595.4	1,090,779.7	2,088.8	1,982.0	24,603.0	13,598.0	22,903.0	18,725.4	20,814.2
1983	24,580.0	4,993.0	5,819.6	683,267.6	1,051,989.3	2,051.3	1,983.0	25,757.0	14,506.0	24,253.5	20,150.9	22,202.2
1984	26,433.0	5,410.0	5,728.0	101,124.0	622,214.1	1,577.6	1,984.0	27,686.0	15,431.0	25,149.0	21,993.8	23,571.4
1985	27,735.0	5,347.0	5,584.4	56,358.8	359,331.3	1,198.9	1,985.0	29,152.0	16,786.0	26,112.7	23,714.9	24,913.8
1986	29,458.0	6,025.0	5,513.6	261,530.0	220,575.1	939.3	1,986.0	30,809.0	17,604.0	27,267.1	25,388.5	26,327.8
1987	30,970.0	6,390.0	5,633.0	573,049.0	335,065.9	1,157.7	1,987.0	32,385.0	18,406.0	28,992.9	26,677.5	27,835.2
1988	32,191.0	5,758.0	5,786.0	784.0	198,569.1	891.2	1,988.0	33,915.0	19,329.0	30,248.6	28,466.2	29,357.4
1989	34,213.0	6,478.0	5,999.6	228,866.6	224,117.7	946.8	1,989.0	35,975.0	20,209.0	31,860.2	29,966.6	30,913.4
1990	35,353.0	5,895.0	6,109.2	45,881.6	222,022.2	942.4	1,990.0	36,915.0	21,423.0	33,379.4	31,494.6	32,437.0
1991	35,939.0	4,969.0	5,898.0	863,041.0	342,324.4	1,170.2	1,991.0	37,783.0	21,548.0	34,903.4	32,563.0	33,733.2
1992	36,573.0	4,382.0	5,496.4	1,241,887.4	476,092.1	1,380.0	1,992.0	38,670.0	21,103.0	36,233.8	33,473.8	34,853.8
1993	36,959.0	2,746.0	4,894.0	4,613,904.0	1,398,716.1	2,365.3	1,993.0	39,300.0	21,542.0	38,172.7	33,442.1	35,807.4
1994	38,782.0	3,429.0	4,284.2	731,367.0	1,499,216.2	2,448.8	1,994.0	40,884.0	24,698.0	39,170.0	34,272.4	36,721.2

(continued)

Black & White Median Income vs. All Families income (5 Yr Mean)
(continued)

Year	All Families	Abs / Delta	5-yr Mean	Variance	Ave / Var	Sigma Value 2	Year	White	Black	Chart SigHigh 2.0	SigLow 2.0	5-Yr Mean
1995	40,611.0	4,672.0	4,039.6	399,929.8	1,570,025.8	2,506.0	1,995.0	42,646.0	25,970.0	40,278.8	35,266.8	37,772.8
1996	42,300.0	5,727.0	4,191.2	2,358,681.6	1,869,154.0	2,734.3	1996	44,756.0	26,522.0	41,779.3	36,310.7	39,045.0
1997	44,568.0	7,609.0	4,836.6	7,686,201.8	3,158,016.8	3,554.2	1997	46,754.0	28,602.0	44,198.2	37,089.8	40,644.0
1998	46,737.0	7,955.0	5,878.4	4,312,267.6	3,097,689.6	3,520.1	1998	49,023.0	29,404.0	46,119.7	39,079.5	42,599.6
1999	48,950.0	8,339.0	6,860.4	2,186,258.0	3,388,667.7	3,681.7	1999	51,224.0	31,778.0	48,314.9	40,951.5	44,633.2
2000	50,890.0	8,590.0	7,644.0	894,916.0	3,487,665.0	3,735.1	2,000.0	53,256.0	34,192.0	50,424.1	42,953.9	46,689.0
2001	51,407.0	6,839.0	7,866.4	1,055,550.8	3,227,038.8	3,592.8	2,001.0	54,067.0	33,598.0	52,103.2	44,917.6	48,510.4

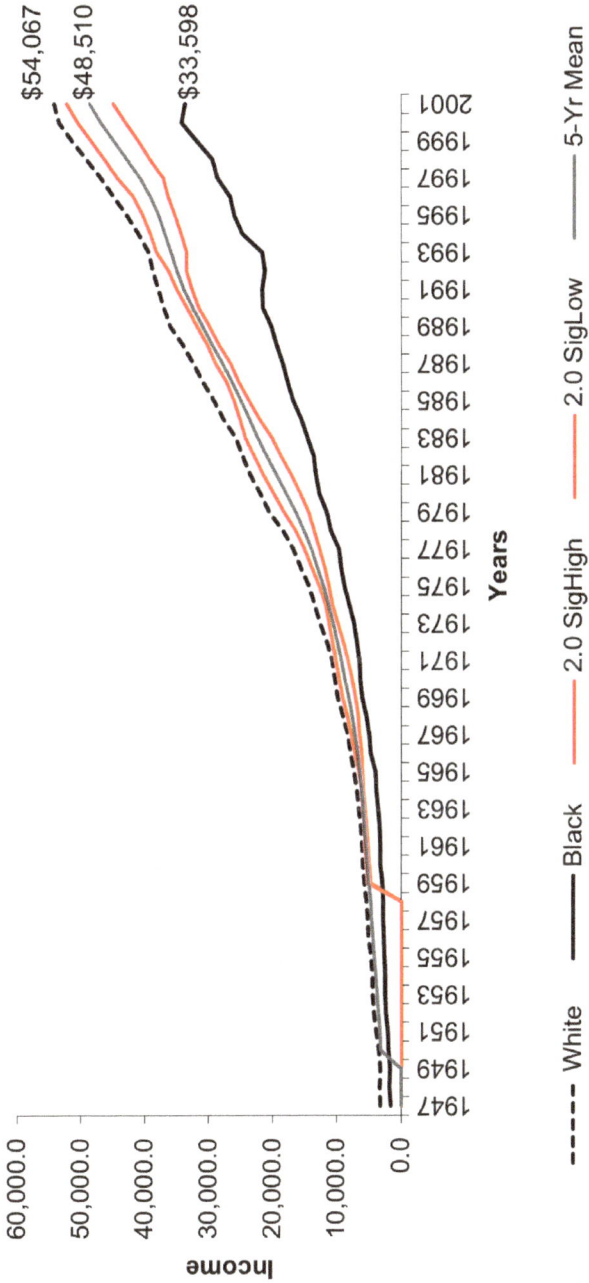

Black & White Median Income vs. All Families Income - (5-Yr mean)

www.ingramcontent.com/pod-product-compliance
Ingram Content Group UK Ltd.
Pitfield, Milton Keynes, MK11 3LW, UK
UKHW051023240225
455495UK00018B/270

9 798218 534233